1975

1976

1977

1978

1983

1984

1985

1986

1987

1993

1994

1995

1996

More Praise for
How to Succeed in Business Without Being White

"An excellent guide for personal success in today's business environment. While his strategies are aimed primarily at African Americans, his book will help anyone build a solid career."

—Robert E. Allen, chairman and CEO, AT&T

"Earl Graves has written a guidebook to Corporate America which is a 'must read' for those starting the journey."

—Carol Moseley-Braun, U.S. senator

"Anyone who believes American business today lacks sufficient integrity hasn't dealt with Earl Graves. And anyone who believes the struggle to become successful in business today isn't worth the effort hasn't read this book."

—Daniel Burke, CEO Emeritus, Capital Cities/ABC, Inc.

"Provocative. Underscores the most important, but often overlooked, tenet of the American Dream—that it is earned, not inherited."

—M. Anthony Burns, chairman, president and CEO,
Ryder Systems, Inc.

"A forthright guide to getting ahead with your dignity, integrity and optimism intact."

—Bill Campbell, mayor of Atlanta

"Each of us, young and old, asks ourselves at a significant life point if we are on our desired course and aimed in the right direction. This book says we are not on course—any of us—if we are not working to assist someone else along the way."

—Frank Carey, chairman and CEO, IBM (retired)

"Highly valuable for anyone—of any color—who cares about how issues of race impact our business and economic success as a nation."

—Kenneth I. Chenault, president and COO,
American Express Company

"The sheer weight of Earl's accumulated knowledge and the myriad of lives that he has influenced, as captured within these pages, gives a stunning sense of importance to this book. Well done!"

—Ron Compton, chairman, president and CEO, Aetna, Inc.

"A well-written, easy to read, instructive and inspiring how-to book. It is a prescription for success no matter what the task or tint of one's skin."

—Mario Cuomo, former governor of New York

"Graves makes it clear that no matter how high you rise in business, you must still stare down and conquer bigotry everyday. He also makes the case that for African Americans, now more than ever, it's worth it."

—David Dinkins, former mayor of New York

"If more people took Earl Graves's techniques and philosophies to heart, there would ultimately be more Earl Graveses in the world. That, to use an old marketing phrase, would be good for business— American business."

**—Robert J. Eaton, chairman and CEO,
Chrysler Corporation**

"For young people who have set their sights on a successful business career, here is a vivid how-to book about reaching your goals."

—Marian Wright Edelman, president, The Children's Defense Fund

"His career advice is superb, because it emphasizes a rational, well thought-out approach to the business world. I especially enjoyed his focus on the importance of follow-through, because in life, as in business, it's how you complete the task that often matters most."

**—George M. C. Fisher,
chairman and CEO, Eastman Kodak Company**

"Had not Motorola's vice presidents who are African American recently suffered such indignities as 'being roughed up by two policemen when stopping at a convenience store,' this book would not have hit home as pointedly as it did for me. Earl Graves comments candidly on racism in American business, but he also puts forth that certain important aspects of hope can and should be earned."

—Christopher B. Galvin, CEO, Motorola

"Earl speaks with conviction and rich experience, offering a no-nonsense approach and real-life solutions to an age-old question . . . how to make it in America."

—William H. Gray, president and CEO, UNCF

"Provides an illuminating inside look at what makes this man who he is and why his formula has worked for so many people."

—Gerald Greenwald, chairman and CEO, UAL Corporation

"In an age of often irrational rhetoric and excessive racial hostilities, Earl Graves has written a profoundly insightful book that advocates rational options and identifies available paths to make America the fair pluralistic nation that it should become."

—A. Leon Higgenbotham Jr., of counsel, Paul, Weiss, Rifkind, Wharton & Garrison; and former chief judge, U.S. Court of Appeals

"I knew Earl was a great salesman, an avowed capitalist, a family man of integrity and a leader in the constant battle for equal opportunity in this country. What I didn't realize was that he was such a powerful preacher. This book left me inspired and renewed. It will do the same for you."

—Jesse Lewis Jackson Sr., founder and president, National Rainbow Coalition

"Don't let the fact that this is a 'business book' keep you from sharing it with your children and other young people. The tenets Earl espouses here build more than wealth and individual success. They build character and self-esteem, they strengthen families, communities and the cities of our nation."

—Maynard H. Jackson, chairman and CEO, Jackson Securities; and chairman, Maynard Jackson Youth Foundation

"A powerhouse! Not to be missed."

—Robert L. Johnson, chairman and CEO, Black Entertainment Television

"The conventional wisdom is that the next five years will provide opportunities for entrepreneurs unparalleled in American history. In *How to Succeed in Business Without Being White*, Earl Graves not only talks straight, he hits the mark with laser precision. He continues to walk the talk."

—Quincy Jones, CEO, Quincy Jones Productions

"A provocative and practical book for those who are serious about doing well in business—and in life."

**—Michael H. Jordan, CEO,
Westinghouse Electric Corporation**

"Decisive. Introspective. Value-oriented. Packed with truthful insights that the average person overlooks, whether they are black or white."

**—David T. Kearns, chairman,
New American Schools Development Corporation**

"Loaded with tips for the enterprising individual to make it in business and life in America today."

**—Kent Kresa, chairman of the board, president and CEO,
Northrup Grumman Corporation**

"Earl Graves remains a towering role model for young black entrepreneurs who don't intend to compromise who they are in order to succeed in business. This book lays out the real deal for those who have the heart to compete in arenas where the competition never expected to have to deal with black businesspeople as equals."

—Spike Lee, president and CEO, 40 Acres & A Mule Productions

"A book for everyone who dreams big dreams. Earl Graves shows us how to succeed in America, despite the obstacles of racism and indifference."

**—Loida N. Lewis, chairman and CEO,
TLC Beatrice International Holdings**

"Tips on networking, job seeking and basic entrepreneurship make this an important resource for anyone interested in succeeding in the competitive world of American business."

**—J. W. Marriott Jr., chairman, president and CEO,
Marriott Corporation**

"Sound advice about how to handle a wide range of the things that come up in living life and making a career. These numerous practical lessons are bound to be useful for all of us."

**—John H. McArthur, dean emeritus,
Harvard Business School**

"So many in business today grab for all they can get, then scramble for even more. Earl Graves proves that you can remain driven and hungry in business without being selfish and single-minded. He generously shares his own success secrets in this book, and he genuinely seems to want readers to achieve all they aim for and then some."
—Hugh L. McColl Jr., chairman and CEO, NationsBank Corporation

"A free enterprise classic—how one man made it in America."
—Sanford N. McDonnell, chairman emeritus, McDonnell Douglas

"Whether you're not yet out of school, at mid-career struggling, or at the top wondering what more you can do to bring others along, Graves has been there. All of the topics he covers are critical, and with each of them, he hits the nail on the head, then hammers it home."
—Kweisi Mfume, president and CEO, NAACP

"Earl personifies the American Dream. One hopes that his role model will be what Americans of all colors focus on."
—Allen Questrom, chairman and CEO,
Federated Department Stores, Inc.

"Powerful truths about networking, business planning, personal development and ethics. What more could you ask for?"
—Jere B. Ratcliffe, chief scout executive, Boy Scouts of America

"Finally, we get more than a column's worth of this publisher's observations about what stands in our way and his strategies for overcoming those obstacles. You couldn't ask for a better source, or a more engaging one."
—Roy S. Roberts, vice president/general manager,
General Motors Corporation

"Of the dozens of offerings in bookstores purporting to provide the keys to success, few are written by authors who have surmounted obstacles—even when it meant stepping into harm's way—the way Earl Graves has for nearly all of his adult life. *How to Succeed in Business Without Being White* provides graphic proof that a man of profit can also be a man of principle, and that success can be achieved without selling out."
—Randall Robinson, executive director, TransAfrica Forum

"Earl Graves has constructed a ladder to success for minority entrepreneurs and all others who are trying to succeed in America. The ladder is built sturdy with his own experience and, with this book, he graciously lends a hand to others making the climb."

—Judith Rodin, president, University of Pennsylvania

"Just think: The compassionate wisdom of this business elder is yours for the mere price of a book!"

—Bernard Shaw, CNN

"Graves demonstrates that tenacity, business savvy and cooperation can break down the barriers that often stand in the way of minority entrepreneurs."

**—John F. Smith Jr., chairman, CEO and president,
General Motors Corporation**

"Anyone who knows Earl Graves has the sense that there's nothing he can't do. Almost universally, successful people share that trait. It's infectious. Read this book, and you'll get the bug."

**—Malcolm Stamper, vice chairman,
Boeing Corporation (retired)**

"This book tells young, black, aspiring entrepreneurs and corporate executives what they need to bring to the table and what's going to be offered—or not—regardless of what they bring to the table. Once you know that, you can deal with it accordingly. Graves certainly has, to stunning effect."

—H. Patrick Swygert, president, Howard University

"Filled with practical tools anyone at any level can use to become more successful in business."

—Susan L. Taylor, editor-in-chief, *Essence* magazine

"This is an important book. What one learns informs the thinking of people of all colors. Graves's book makes it clear that black Americans and white Americans run together—not as well as we'd like, perhaps, but we've picked up speed in the last few years. He explains why, despite our regular failures and falls, we must keep getting up. We must not drag on the chain."

—Steve Trachtenberg, president, George Washington University

"Earl Graves's book is must reading not just for African Americans, but for any manager who wants to understand the true power and potential of diversity."

—Daniel P. Tulley, chairman of the board, Merrill Lynch & Company

"A unique business book that combines straightforward advice on how to be successful with poignant personal reflections on the costs, rewards and responsibilities of being successful. This from a man who clearly loves American business, even though the sentiment is still not always reciprocated."

—Maxine Waters, U.S. congresswoman

"Earl sees capitalism for what it can do to release the potential of people and build communities. He cuts to the heart of the issue—how do we liberate more of our citizens with personal, economic power? The answer is in both what Earl has written . . . and how he has lived."

—Craig Weatherup, chairman and CEO, Pepsi-Cola Company

"No one in America has done more than Earl Graves to open business doors to young black men and women. His book, with its hard-hitting pragmatic advice, is must reading for young blacks and whites alike."

—John C. Whitehead, chairman and CEO, Goldman Sachs & Company (retired); and former Secretary of State

"Graves may sit on Fortune 500 company boards and ski in exotic locales, but he clearly hasn't lost his identification with the typical black striver who, like most Americans, simply wants to be successful and yearns for some support and helpful advice along the way. Here, he gives both in abundance."

—Lawrence Wilson, chairman and CEO, Rohm and Haas Company

"Earl speaks straight from his heart about the way he has lived his life and run his business affairs, admonishing readers that to be successful we need to bring our 'black experience' to the table."

—Andrew Young, former mayor of Atlanta

How to Succeed
in Business
Without Being White

How to Succeed in Business Without Being White

EARL G. GRAVES

 HarperBusiness

A Division of HarperCollins*Publishers*

HarperCollins books may be purchased for educational, business, or sales promotional use. For information please write: Special Markets Department, HarperCollins Publishers, Inc., 10 East 53rd Street, New York, NY 10022.

FIRST EDITION

Designed by Alma Hochhauser Orenstein

Library of Congress Cataloging-in-Publication Data

Graves, Earl G., 1935–
    How to succeed in business without being white : success strategies from America's premiere black entrepreneur / by Earl G. Graves — 1st ed.
      p. cm.
    Includes index.
    ISBN 0-88730-808-2
    1. Success in business. 2. Afro-American businesspeople.
    I. Title.
    HF5386.G675 1997
      650.1'089'96073—dc21   96-52510

97 98 99 00 01 ❖/RRD 10 9 8 7 6 5 4 3 2 1

*To my wife, Barbara, without whom this book
and all it represents would not have been possible.
And to Mom and Dad, who lit the way.*

CONTENTS

Photographs follow page 138.

When Earl Graves asked me to contribute the foreword for this book, I agreed without hesitation—for two reasons. First, I have known and respected Earl for more than 20 years, and I was sure his book would be good. Second, having known Earl for many years, I know him to be an extremely tenacious and persuasive person—a consummate salesman—and I thought it would be easier to agree quickly than to be persuaded later.

I first met Earl in 1973, when I was the head of American Airlines' marketing department and *Black Enterprise* was a fairly new magazine. As Earl points out in the book, businesses at that time—including American Airlines—had not fully recognized the buying power and emerging economic clout of the black community. Earl did a great job of convincing us that *Black Enterprise* represented a real opportunity for American to better position itself with an important, growing segment of the market.

Of course, we took some convincing, but Earl would not take no for an answer. He showed up early, late, and often, and assembled the analytical data required with skill and determination. In addition to admiring his tenacity, I came to respect the economic logic of his arguments. The key to Earl's success in convincing us to buy ads in *Black Enterprise* was that like any good salesman, he sold to our needs and not to his.

When I read the title of Earl's manuscript, *How to Succeed in Business Without Being White*, I thought it provocative, interesting and appropriate, because he is clearly an exemplary role model for any African American interested in a career in business. And he does share with us, as you would expect, some important insights on the unique challenges faced by African Americans in the business world.

But as I read on, I began to think Earl had made the title too long. Since much of this book's advice and wisdom would be useful to anyone wishing to either start a business or build a better career, I thought a better title would be simply, *How to Succeed in Business.*

Having finished the book and reflected on it, I concluded that because Earl has written about success in life, not just in business, and is clearly an expert on the subject, the best title might be an even shorter *How to Succeed.*

While I've always respected Earl's business sense, I also know that business is just one element of his life. The characteristics and behaviors that have propelled him to the forefront in business have also yielded a full and successful family life and a very broad civic involvement. These behaviors include pressing ahead, doing what's right and expecting those around you to do the same, giving back to the community and helping pave the way for those coming behind you. Many people speak about the virtues and rewards of such tenets; far fewer live them day to day. Earl does. And in this book, he shows how you can as well.

ROBERT L. CRANDALL
Chairman and CEO, American Airlines

ACKNOWLEDGMENTS

One of our top editors at *Black Enterprise*, and one of my top three daughters-in-law, Caroline V. Clarke, served the critical role of prodding my memory, focusing my attention and challenging me to dig deeper without digging myself into a hole. I forgive you for all of the harrassment, and I thank you, Caroline, with love.

I thank also my literary agent, Amanda "Binky" Urban, who believed in the value of this book from the beginning and only had to threaten or maim a few people to make it happen.

My writing collaborator, Wes Smith, helped me shape this book and, in the process, learned more about this country than he knew before. Thanks Wes.

My good friends Ossie Davis, James Comer, Sidney Liebowitz, Marilyn Duckworth and Carole Hall were generous with their sage advice and constantly cheered me on. This book and I both benefited greatly from their input.

And finally, for their encouragement and support, I thank Bob Crandall, my sons, the staff at *Black Enterprise*, the team at Harper-Collins and all of the others who have urged me on in this fulfilling project.

How to Succeed
in Business
Without Being White

CHAPTER 1

Opening Business

On December 4, 1991, less than two years after his release from 27 years' imprisonment, South African hero Nelson Mandela came to meet with many of the most powerful African American business and political leaders in the country at the corporate offices of *Black Enterprise* and Earl G. Graves Ltd. on Fifth Avenue in New York City.

In our executive boardroom, Mandela met with professional black men and women who have led the way in creating unprecedented wealth in this country. He met with leaders of government, founders of multimillion-dollar international corporations, investors, bankers, lawyers, industrialists, religious leaders, visionaries and entrepreneurs. All of them with skin as richly colored as his.

"We asked for this meeting because of our desire to learn the principles and strategies of economic empowerment for blacks in our country," Mandela said. "Until we have a very strong business class, it is going to be difficult for us to make real progress."

Mandela's powerful voice echoed themes near and dear to my heart and, I believe, to yours too:

- economic empowerment for African Americans and blacks around the world
- the creation of a strong business class with the ability to leverage its might for the good of the entire black community
- equal *opportunity* for blacks to achieve success at whatever it is that we want to do with our talents and initiative

In the pages that follow, I offer you the key to all of those things. No one, black or white, is going to guarantee you career success or financial security. You have to earn that yourself. But I offer the information here to shine a light on your path, as well as the encouraging advice of many African American professionals who have gone before you and succeeded in spite of the racist hatred and ignorance that continue to taint our society.

Economic power is the key to success in a capitalistic society. Business is the means to that power. African Americans can play this game and we can win at it. *You can succeed in business without being white.* We are doing it today in numbers greater than ever before, launching businesses as never before and leveraging a collective annual income that today exceeds $400 billion.

I am proud to say that hundreds of thousands of African Americans have been a part of this success story, and in this book I have chronicled many of those successes. In this book, too, I have provided you with what you need to know in order to join them in the next great movement in African American history—the historic march toward true freedom for black people around the world— economic freedom.

You and I may be at different stages in life. In different parts of the country. From varied backgrounds. But we are in this together, linked by our race, our history and our destiny. Rest assured, we will only improve the quality of our individual lives by working together for the collective success of all black people. Don't let anyone tell you differently.

Together, we have come a great distance already.

Since we began publishing *Black Enterprise* 26 years ago, the number of black-owned businesses in this country has grown from around 45,000 to more than 621,000. The number has jumped by 46 percent in just the last decade, outpacing the growth rate of *all* new businesses by 20 percent.

Sales, a crucial measure of success, have risen 63 percent in the last ten years for businesses owned by African Americans, according to the U.S. Census Bureau. The top 100 black businesses, tracked in *Black Enterprise* as the "B.E. 100s," now boast annual sales of more than $12 billion.

I mention this to make a point. The white-dominated business world needs to understand that we don't want charity. We want to do business. We don't want guaranteed success. We want the opportunity to earn it.

You may not be there yet. But believe me, the way has been paved. In some places, the paving stones have been torn up and replaced only to be torn up again, but the path is still marked. And the rewards are—as they always have been—still worth the struggle onward.

Within three years of his visit to our offices in New York, Nelson Mandela was elected president in the first democratic national election in South African history, and I was recruited to serve as a catalyst in bringing the first multinational business enterprise into the new South Africa—a $100 million Pepsi-Cola franchise of which black men and women are the primary owners and operators.

I did not have to look far for my partners in this multimillion-dollar enterprise. I merely plugged into The Network comprising this nation's leading African American entrepreneurs—many of whom are featured in this book. All of them have struggled and succeeded. Each of them understands the value of leveraging our collective economic strength to create more wealth, and with it a more powerful voice in every aspect of this country.

When I began soliciting partners for this landmark deal, one of my first telephone calls was to the great African American businessman Percy Sutton, whose empire includes the Apollo theater, Inner City Broadcasting and the World African Network. Also at the head of my list, the "Godfather" of the black music industry, Clarence Avant, chairman of Motown Records and a member of the board of directors of Polygram, who brought with him Shaquille O'Neal, Whitney Houston and Danny Glover, among others. I also invited famed defense lawyer Johnnie Cochran and a number of other investors from the swelling ranks of successful African American professionals.

Understand: I have no problem doing business with white people; I hear their money is green too. But this was an opportunity to make a statement proclaiming the growing strength and power of *black* entrepreneurship in the United States and around the world.

Over the years, we have fought our way forward, fallen back, picked up and marched on many times together. When *Black Enterprise* first appeared in 1970, there were only 3 black people among the 3,000 serving as directors on the boards of the Fortune 500 companies. They were Clifton Wharton at Equitable, Thomas Wood at Chase Manhattan Bank and Robert Weaver at Metropolitan Life Insurance.

Even before these pioneering black professionals came on the scene, a long tradition of black entrepreneurship had been established in this country. It began with the slaves who operated farms or mined salt on their own time to buy their freedom and the freedom of their families, and it evolved into major retail centers operated by black merchants and patronized by residents of thriving neighborhoods populated by working-class and professional African Americans.

Every year that I am in business, I have greater admiration and respect for these courageous and indomitable early black entrepreneurs, as well as those who came later: people such as Howard Naylor Fitzhugh, the dean of black business and the first African American Harvard MBA; Arthur G. Gaston Sr., founder of Booker T. Washington Insurance Company; Henry G. Parks Jr., founder of Parks Sausage Company; and of course John Johnson, publisher of *Ebony* and *Jet*; along with the many other unsung pioneers of black economic development.

In truth, it's probably impossible for me to understand how hard it was for those who came before me, although the concept of being black and in business was still considered to be almost seditious even when I was a student at Morgan State University in Baltimore from 1953 to 1957.

My classmates, and some professors too, were generally incredulous, even scandalized, when I told them my chosen course of study. "Why are you majoring in business?" they would ask, and with good reason. There were no corporations coming to recruit black students at that time, and there were no banks lining up to give us loans to start our businesses, nor was there a family business awaiting me back home.

Still, my response was blunt because I wanted to make it clear that I regarded my future as unlimited, regardless of how anyone else might have felt.

"I want to make a lot of money," I would respond. "And I want to create change."

Often that would provoke laughter. You see, back then there were a few wealthy black doctors, and every black neighborhood had its successful undertakers, retailers and restaurant owners, but the concept of a black businessman with his own corporation or with a high position within a corporation or with the power to "create change" was largely a foreign, even a laughable, one to blacks as well as whites. Business was the white man's game.

Well, basketball was once a white man's game too. We may not yet be dominant in the business world, but if you doubt that we are serious players I'll gladly sell you a subscription to *Black Enterprise* to enlighten you about the hundreds of thousands of African Americans who are serious businesspeople and tremendously successful. Or I'll take you on a guided tour of my alma mater, where the Earl G. Graves School of Business and Management was recently dedicated.

Today, in addition to *Black Enterprise*, the corporation that bears my name oversees B.E. Unlimited, the umbrella company for our annual conferences, special events and ancillary products and programs; the nation's largest minority-controlled Pepsi bottling franchise, Pepsi-Cola of Washington, D.C., L.P.; and Egoli Beverages, L.P., the Pepsi partnership for the South African franchise.

As a serious player in the game of business, I sit on the boards of Aetna Life and Casualty Company, American Airlines, Chrysler Corporation, Federated Department Stores, Inc. and Rohm & Haas Corporation. Had I suggested these possibilities to my Morgan classmates back in college, they would have howled.

Well, the fact is, I have succeeded in business without being white. So too can you.

Today nobody, black or white, is going to laugh at you, my friend, when you tell them you want to make a lot of money in the business world. I am here to tell you that it is entirely possible for you to make more money than you ever hoped for and to pursue whatever dreams you have for yourself and your loved ones.

I believe it is possible for you not only because thousands of us have already done it, but also because great numbers of us are dedicated to seeing you thrive. And you must believe it is possible, no matter where you are in your journey—semiretired from one career and entering another, rising through middle management, just starting a new company or, as I was in the '50s, still in school but yearning to get into business and make it to the top.

After nearly 30 years in business, I still identify with those who are struggling because, believe me, I am still in the midst of this fray. I know what my sons face every day in a world still dominated by white people who prefer to do business with those who look like them, belong to the same private clubs and share similar backgrounds.

This book and the information in it are proof of my commitment to African Americans in search of economic equality and the freedom it can bring.

You can succeed in business without being white. You can make a lot of money and do well by your family and community. And when you tell people you intend to succeed in business, no one will take it as a joke.

Black or white, when you've achieved your goals, the only joke will be on them.

CHAPTER 2

A Life's Mission Is Defined

Like most African Americans who aspire to business, I had few resources and far fewer black role models to inspire me when I decided to step into the white man's game. My parents were both the children of immigrants from the Caribbean island of Barbados. My father was a big man, 6 feet tall and 235 pounds. He had been orphaned in this country at 16 and was self-supporting from that age on, taking care of himself and a younger brother with his hard work and entrepreneurial instincts. He was a serious man, no non-sense and disciplined.

My father believed in keeping his nose—and mine—to the grindstone, and he believed in the power of ownership. Never rent, always own, he often admonished me. He expected me to train myself for the world, to go to school, get good grades, come home, study, clean the house and go back to school. Participating in sports or having fun generally was not on the screen for me as far as he was concerned.

I had two younger sisters, Sandra and Joan, and a younger brother, Robert, all of whom have done well and are close to me to this day. Our father treated us all with a very firm hand. I used to think he had surveillance cameras hidden in every corner of the house and on street corners too.

My father was much stricter than the parents of any of my friends. I didn't have much time to stop anyplace and hang out on the way home from school. He had most of our time structured. My mother was a much more benevolent presence and, in fact, a champion.

A diminutive, feisty woman of enormous energy and warmth, she was my harbor in the storm of my father's volatile temperament. She loved to have fun and was supportive of everything her children were involved in, from ice skating to Cub Scouts to school.

In one particularly vivid incident, she served as my champion in one of my first encounters with racism. I had gone to swim at the Central YMCA in downtown Brooklyn, only to be ordered to leave. It was, I discovered that day, the White YMCA. When I told my mother that I had been kicked out for SWB (swimming while black), she wasted no time at all in storming the Central Y and registering her righteous indignation.

In terms that left no question about her feelings on the topic, she inquired about the right of a public national organization to decide that a certain racial group could not swim in its pools. I was not surprised when the YMCA capitulated. And so my mother, and I in a lesser role, integrated the Central Brooklyn YMCA. The experience ultimately gave me such an appreciation for the joys of swimming that I later spent summers working at local beaches, and in college I was the most enthusiastic, if not the fastest, swimmer on the squad.

My mother was, at the very least, an equal partner to my father. She was president of the PTA at my public school, and during World War II she worked in a General Electric munitions plant. The plant hired black women but not black men, so my father was shut out of a job that paid a good deal more than he earned. This may have caused some of the tension that led to his being a strict disciplinarian with his children.

We lived in a brownstone on Macon Street in Bedford-Stuyvesant along with what seemed to me virtually every other West Indian in Brooklyn. It seemed to be required that when you immigrated to the United States from the Caribbean, you had to go by way of my neighborhood. My father rented out the upper levels of our brownstone to supplement his income. Our quarters were on the first floor and the parlor floor, but the parlor did double duty as my father's showroom.

In 1928 he had been among the few people, black or white, to graduate from Erasmus Hall High School (where I was honorary chairman of the 200th anniversary celebration not long ago), but the only job he could find was for the Overland Garment Company, at 265 West 37th Street in Manhattan, first as a clerk pushing racks of clothing through the garment district and later as an assistant distribution manager. Like most West Indians, however, he usually worked at least one other job as well. I remember that he would often work as a waiter or bartender at parties held by the owner of the garment company.

My father's most lucrative side job, however, was selling clothes on consignment out of our home. Overland would let him bring women's clothes home to sell wholesale to people in the neighborhood and to our tenants. A natural salesman, my father really seemed to come to life and enjoy himself most when he was working deals with the women who came into our house to shop.

If a winter coat was marked at $10 and a woman tried to get him down to $7, he would offer instead to sell her two coats at $9 each. A sharp dresser with a shoe shine that could blind you on a sunny day, he was a kibitzer of a different color. "Hey, you look good but you would look even better in this little dress!"

As a boy I watched and listened, and I think without realizing it I absorbed a great deal of business sense—as well as my penchant for doing deals—from this remote but intriguing figure in my life. I imitated my father's sales patter when I undertook my first job, selling boxed Christmas cards for my Uncle John.

I did well, but my territory was severely limited. My father had a rule that I could only sell to people living on our side of the block. I could not cross the street. I didn't ask why. To question my father's authority might have cost the undertaker a new set of teeth at my premature burial.

I learned salesmanship and hard work from him, and I learned discipline too. It was hard to appreciate it at the time, but his high demands and expectations made me both a striver and a doer. And while his stern, aloof manner prevented us from ever being close, it made me determined to be close to my own children, which I'm proud to say I am.

My father died of a heart attack at the age of 48 when I was a junior at Morgan State. By the time he passed, I had already made a name for myself as an entrepreneur in his image. I hadn't been on campus long when I realized that Homecoming Week was approaching and that there was a big market for flowers for all the ladies who would be attending. I have always liked flowers—and the ladies too—so it was a natural market for me. I went to two competing local florists and cut deals with both to sell flowers on campus, where these white merchants rarely ventured. For a percentage of the profits, they provided the flowers and I covered the campus.

I made a lot of money off those corsages and kept the business going until my senior year, when I learned an early lesson on the pitfalls of business. I had ordered and taken delivery of enough bouquets to serve every couple on campus when a student protest was announced. Homecoming was canceled and so was my flower business. My florist partners were not at all happy, but because my investment was relatively light I didn't go bust. It helped that I had also followed the West Indian tradition of what jargon-loving academics today might refer to as "multiple-task entrepreneurial self-employment."

There was a bulletin board for student jobs that hung in the dorm known as Banneker Hall, and I watched that board for fresh postings, ready to pounce on any opportunities. My secret weapon was a matron in charge of the dormitory, whose favor I curried so that she frequently told me about job listings before they even made the public domain.

I may have been the slowest man ever to have a place on the Morgan State track team, but when it came to running after money, I was an Olympian, then and now.

By the time I claimed my diploma, I had established a reputation as the hardest-working man on campus. I mowed lawns, waited tables, was a vendor at baseball games, worked security in a department store and sold soft drinks in the stands at Baltimore Memorial Stadium. (The white guys who called me "boy" got a little something extra in their cups.)

Perhaps influenced by my father's militaristic penchant for order, I had been drawn early on into the ROTC program at Morgan State. I liked the discipline and the structure it gave my life. After graduation in 1957, I entered the Army, where I attended Airborne and Ranger School and completed my career with the rank of Captain, as a member of the 19th Special Forces Group, the Green Berets.

Around that time, I made the smartest personal and business

move of my life by courting my future wife, Barbara, who for all her charms and talents was not cut out to be a military wife. We both knew that we wanted a more open field than a military base in which to run and raise our family.

After we married, I left the service and we moved into one floor of my mother's house in Brooklyn. I took a job selling real estate and we started our family. Both ventures went well. I'd been attracted to real estate after hearing a presentation by a real estate broker during a career seminar. He said he'd been making several thousand dollars profit on each house he sold, and after I did a little math, I decided I could probably outsell anybody in that game.

My timing was right. I set to work to make my fortune in real estate in Brooklyn when white flight was making it a ripe market for a black agent. My goal was to earn a salary of $20,000 a year so I could move my family into a house in a great neighborhood with good schools. I was motivated, and I was my father's son when it came to selling. I sold nine houses in my first three months on the job. I developed a sales philosophy of romancing my clients rather than trying to sell them. I courted clients on the telephone and over lunches and dinners. I got to know their every need and desire and how much they could afford to spend down to the last penny.

Selling real estate came easy to me, and I found myself looking for something else to help burn off all the energy I'd built up in the military. Initially I tried local politics, but my timing was off. I walked into the local Democratic headquarters at election time, and the sight of a well-dressed black man volunteering to sign up must have put off the local political leaders because I got the cold shoulder from them. So I did the typical thing for me: I wrote a letter to the chairman of the Democratic National Committee, volunteering to work at that level instead. He suggested I report to the New York State Democratic campaign headquarters, and I did.

In 1964 they put me to work as a volunteer on the Johnson-Humphrey presidential campaign, which encompassed Robert F. Kennedy's successful run for the U.S. Senate. The following December I was called upon to help when Kennedy decided to hold a series of Christmas parties for underprivileged children in the five boroughs that make up New York City. I offered to put together the party in my old neighborhood in Brooklyn. This was a big deal for the kids and for the neighborhood, and I was not about to blow it. I planned this party with all the precision of the war games that I had masterminded in the Army.

Fate played into my hands by setting me up as a genius compared to the competition. Every event in the other four boroughs that the senator and his group, which included his sister-in-law, the widowed Jackie Kennedy, had attended earlier in the day had proved a fiasco. They had been subjected to poor planning, driving mishaps and more. At one of the parties someone had stolen all the gifts intended for the kids.

Not on my turf, though. When Bobby and Jackie stepped out of their car in front of the National Guard's Thirteenth Regiment Armory in Brooklyn, they were greeted by comedian Soupy Sales posted at curbside. Providing musical support behind him was the local drum and bugle corps firing off round after round of "Jingle Bells."

When the Kennedy party entered the building, they were nearly blasted backward by a ringing "Hallelujah Chorus" from a full gospel choir assembled in the darkened interior. The lights came on to a packed house of neighborhood youngsters who let out a cheer that was heard all the way to Albany. It was at that point that Kennedy turned to the smiling young black man at his side, looked him in the eye and said, "This is really very good. Tell me your name again."

"Graves," I said. "Earl G. Graves, sir."

Over the next three years, I received an education in the use of power and money in this country. For the first time in my life, I was exposed to the white power elite and how it operated. In Robert Kennedy's case, at least, it operated like a well-tuned and highly efficient machine. I saw firsthand what sort of freedom could be had with wealth and power. I became even more determined to claim at least some of it.

I most likely would have stayed with Kennedy if he had succeeded in his bid for the White House. I was with him on June 5, 1968 in Los Angeles at the Hotel Ambassador, where we were celebrating his victory in the California primary. We rode down in the elevator together headed for an appearance in the hotel ballroom. We split up on the first floor because he had to make an entrance from the stage. He headed for a back entrance through the kitchen of the hotel while I went through a back door to come around to the front of the hotel and enter there.

As I approached the front of the hotel, one of Kennedy's press guys came up to me and said he thought he had heard shots inside the hotel. I told him he had been working too hard, that he had probably heard a firecracker or something. Just then a police squad car pulled up. From their manner I could tell something was wrong. "I'm with Kennedy," I told them. "Which way is the kitchen," one of the police officers said. I led them through the hotel, and when we stepped into the pantry of the kitchen, there was Kennedy on the floor with a black physician working on him. Rosey Grier, the gigantic former football star who had become Kennedy's friend, had already broken the hand of the assassin while taking the gun away from him.

I cannot tell you that Robert Kennedy and I had a close personal relationship. He was my employer; I was one of his staff. Like many other African Americans, however, I was deeply affected by his death because he was one of the few white leaders at the time who at least appeared to have a deep interest in furthering the cause of civil rights. The years I spent on his staff have had a lasting impact on me and on how I approach my businesses and my social responsibilities.

Of course, his death also meant I was out of a job at a time when I had three young sons, so along with grieving his loss I had to face my own loss of employment. Had Kennedy lived, I have no doubt that he would have gone on to become President of the United States. I had planned to follow him, and I had no Plan B.

Fortunately, Kennedy was respected through all tiers of society, and when he died his staff members were welcomed almost anywhere. Most of us were offered jobs in the corporate world. Some went to IBM or to the Equitable Insurance Company. I took advantage of an offer from the Ford Foundation, which offered Kennedy's staff members work-study grants to give us an opportunity to regroup. Contemplating a career as a consultant to black businesspeople, I accepted a grant to study entrepreneurship and economic development in my grandparents' native land, Barbados.

Truthfully, I spent most of my time pondering my future in those beautiful surroundings, but Barbados also provided me with a microcosm of the plight of blacks in America. This Caribbean country had a thriving economy, and the government was controlled by the black native leaders, but the economy was largely dominated by white outsiders. Without control of commerce, the Barbadians had no real control over their own lives. It was a lesson I took into my heart. I realized that true power lies not in government but in business. It was true then and it's true now, wherever you go.

When I returned to the United States from Barbados, I started a consulting business for black economic development, and through my Kennedy connections I was given a seat on an advisory board formed by Howard Samuels, director of the Small Business Administration. I told him I was contemplating publishing a newsletter for black entrepreneurs and corporate managers inspired by civil rights legislation. Samuels, among others, encouraged me to consider a magazine instead.

I talked with some people I knew in the advertising business because I wanted to be certain the magazine would pay for itself through advertising. My priority roles at that point were husband and father of three boys. After consulting with several people, I decided the advertising could be sold. Gradually the magazine took on a life of its own as the need became obvious.

The time had come. The heroic efforts of black civil rights leaders led to great strides being made for African Americans in the late 1960s. The Civil Rights Act of 1964 demanded that federally funded institutions admit blacks or lose their government subsidies. The Supreme Court's favorable ruling in *Brown* v. *Board of Education* had mandated equal opportunity for public education. With the federal government prepared to back up integration with military power if necessary, African Americans began pouring through the doors of higher education.

Although thousands of blacks had received outstanding educations at historically African American institutions, at that point more of them than ever before began entering other public and private colleges and universities. The Black Power movement had established that African Americans were no longer going to sit and wait to be noticed and perhaps served. They were demanding to sit down and join the party.

Black trade unionists, schoolteachers, librarians and professionals at Xerox, AT&T and other corporations were forming caucuses to press for their fair share of opportunities. There was still a rebellious and even revolutionary contingent that included the Black

Panthers, the separatists and the Black Liberationists, but there were also more conservative African Americans aggressively pushing for a more active role within the system. Many civil rights activists such as Julian Bond, Andrew Young and Charles Evers were running for public office to build black political power.

African Americans were also turning to the business world in search of economic power. In 1940, 65 percent of black men and women with jobs were working in agriculture or personal services. By 1974 only 15 percent of the black labor force worked in those menial jobs. The rest had entered the higher-paying industrial, technological and white-collar workplaces. Between 1960 and 1968, the median earning power of the black family rose by $1,800. The number of blacks living below the poverty level dropped from 11 million in 1959 to 8 million in 1968. Black poverty rates still declined more slowly than those for whites, but clearly African Americans were seizing newly won opportunities with enthusiasm.

Bolstered by the Civil Rights Act of 1964 and the power of the federal courts, a new, aggressive form of black power was emerging under the banner of the growing black professional class. In 1968 the Small Business Administration launched its redistricted-competition 8(a) set-asides program to aid minority businesspeople in pursuit of government contracts.

In 1969 President Richard M. Nixon signed Executive Order 11458, which directed the U.S. Secretary of Commerce to coordinate the federal government's efforts to promote minority enterprise. The order led to the establishment of programs that American business now accepts—sometimes grudgingly—as part of the business world. The Office of Minority Business Enterprise, now known as the Minority Business Development Agency, came into being, along with minority enterprise small-business investment companies, minority set-aside programs and other initiatives aimed at advancing black economic development.

Nixon's mandate brought to light an idea that was long overdue: black capitalism as the next stage of the civil rights movement.

In 1970, the first Minority Enterprise Small Business Corps was formed. That same year, two pioneering black entrepreneurs whom I had long admired as role models made history. Henry G. Parks Jr., founder and CEO of Parks Sausage Company (remember their slogan, "More Parks sausages, Mom—pleeease?"), became the first black CEO to take his business to the National Association of Securities Dealers Automated Quotation Exchange (NASDAQ), and Johnson Products Company, founded by George E. Johnson, became the first black company to have shares publicly traded on the American Stock Exchange.

These events further convinced me that the time was ripe for a magazine devoted to economic development in the African American community. Into this climate, *Black Enterprise* was born. The publication was committed to the task of educating, inspiring and uplifting its readers. My goal was to show them how to thrive professionally, economically and as proactive, empowered citizens.

Again, my timing proved sound. Over the next two decades, major programs and laws were put into place that created a myriad of unprecedented opportunities for African Americans as we sought to establish ourselves in the business world.

■ In 1971 Daniels and Bell became the first black-owned investment banking firm to be admitted to the 178-year-old New York Stock Exchange.

■ In 1972 the National Black MBA Association was founded to help African Americans enter the business world and progress in it.

■ In 1974 Atlanta Mayor Maynard Jackson established a minority business enterprise program that set a goal of 25 percent participation on all city contracts. The goal was raised to 35 percent by his successor, Mayor Andrew Young, 11 years later.

■ In 1978 the Federal Communications Commission issued a minority preference policy aimed at increasing the number of minority- —and specifically black-owned—radio and television stations. That same year, the Department of Housing and Urban Development began administering grants and federal funds to cities to finance low-interest loans for private investment in depressed neighborhoods. A decade later, the program was dismantled under the Reagan-Bush administration.

■ In 1980 U.S. Representative Parren J. Mitchell, a Democrat from Maryland, launched the Minority Business Enterprise Legal Defense and Education Fund in Washington, D.C.

■ In 1986 Congress passed Section 1207 of the Defense Authorization Act, with the help of Representatives John Conyers Jr. and Gus Savage. The legislation mandates that 5 percent of U.S.

defense contracts be set aside for small and disadvantaged businesses. That same year, a group of black corporate climbers started the Executive Leadership Council, an association of senior-level black executives in major corporations.

▪ In 1988 *Black Enterprise* published the first list of the top 25 African American corporate executives.

▪ In 1992 former chairman of the Democratic National Convention Ronald H. Brown was appointed U.S. Secretary of Commerce and began a major push for the development of African American business around the globe. That same year, New York City's Mayor David N. Dinkins implemented the city's first contracting policy calling for the awarding of contracts to enterprises owned by minorities and women even if their bids were 10 percent higher than the lowest bid. (Two years later, his successor, Mayor Rudolph Guiliani, struck down the policy.)

▪ In 1993 legislation was approved allocating $3.8 billion for the first federally funded empowerment zones.

▪ In 1995 Robert Holland became the first African American to be recruited as CEO and president of a major mainstream company, Ben and Jerry's Homemade, Inc. He returned the ice cream company to profitability in short order and resigned the position in 1996.

Using public policy as a tool to break down the barriers of racism and economic injustice has been key to the growth of black-owned business despite the tradition of discrimination that still thrives. At the same time, corporate America has been forced to diversify its employee ranks, and African Americans have worked inside the corporate cultures to mentor and develop executives for the benefit of both black professional managers and the corporations that have flourished because of their leadership and talents.

Nixon—who was not a champion of civil rights over the long haul—became the first president to articulate the idea of opening opportunities for black entrepreneurs. Today black economic empowerment is the primary weapon in our fight for true freedom and equality. We have made great progress.

My magazine and the black professional class have dreamed, fought, struggled and strived together over the past 25 years. Affirmative action programs helped African Americans squeeze into corporate America in the 1970s and 1980s. Downsizing over the last ten years has pushed far too many of us out, but it has also led to a return to our entrepreneurial roots, which over the long run may be far more energizing for our community as a whole.

Now, more than ever, African Americans are searching for entrepreneurial opportunities, even as more and more blacks fight their way through the iron ceiling in America's major corporations. In the pages that follow, you will find what you need to succeed, no matter which course you choose to take.

CHAPTER 3

Overcoming the Nuisance Factor

In my office suite overlooking Fifth Avenue in Manhattan stands a wooden podium holding a bound black leather book with the embossed title *The Beginning.* This book contains the cardboard presentation displays that I lugged around Manhattan while trying to convince skeptical white business executives that it would benefit their companies to purchase advertising in the very first issues of *Black Enterprise.*

Sometimes, when I expected a lot of resistance, I brought along backup.

In the summer of 1971, the vice president of marketing for Hertz Rent-A-Car Company received an odd request for a meeting with three black men, two of whom were legislators from Georgia. He agreed to meet with them, although he had no idea what it was about.

He was even more confused when he did a little checking on these men. One was State Representative Julian Bond, who had been a founding member of the Student Nonviolent Coordinating Committee (SNCC) and later made headlines when he had to go to the U.S. Supreme Court in 1965 to force the Georgia House of Representatives to allow him to take the office he had been elected to. Seems some of the sitting members of the House didn't want to allow an antiwar activist to join their club.

Another was John Lewis, who had been the leader of SNCC and was also an antiwar and civil rights activist. Then there was this third fellow. His name, Earl Graves, rang no bells.

On the day of the meeting, that Hertz executive met three black men in business suits in the lobby, and apparently deciding that we were not going to stage any type of sit-down demonstration, he allowed us into his inner sanctum.

Julian led off our presentation. He spoke briefly on why he felt it was vital that corporations such as Hertz be responsive to the minority market. John Lewis followed with his own version of the same theme.

Then my door-busters got out of my way so I could get down to business. I began with my explanation of "the *green* side of *black*." I reeled off statistics about the nation's emerging black middle class, then represented by 45,000 black businesspeople, 15,000 black dentists and doctors, 8,000 black lawyers, 25,500 black college students, 2,000 black ministers, 2,000 black elected officials and 1,000 black heads of trade associations, fraternal groups and other organizations.

I emphasized these points with my presentation boards, flip charts and other visual aids. Meanwhile, Julian and John sat quietly, looking faintly amused as I hit the Hertz man with figures on the number of Hertz cars rented each year by minorities—statistics he had never heard before.

Finally, I went for the gold. Looking the marketing boss in the eye, I demanded that he show his appreciation and awareness of his loyal African American customers by purchasing full-page color ads in several issues of *Black Enterprise* during the next several months. He didn't know what hit him. He said yes, and Julian, John and I got out of there before he could change his mind. Some 26 years later, Hertz is still a regular *Black Enterprise* advertiser.

In this chapter, I will offer my advice on how to use all of the resources and guile at your disposal to overcome what I consider to be the nuisance factor of race when trying to succeed in the business world. Sometimes my methods weren't exactly textbook, but then if there had been textbooks for blacks in business in those days, I probably wouldn't have seen the need for *Black Enterprise* magazine.

Black or white, tall, short or ·rectangular, every businessperson has personal and professional obstacles to overcome. For some it's a lack of education, for others, sexism or a financial crisis. Racism poses its own unique challenge. It is often enraging and, at best, highly frustrating to encounter it when you are simply trying to do your job, but it is not an insurmountable barrier. It may always be there, whether overtly or in more subtle forms, but to preserve my sanity, I have come to regard it as more of a nuisance than a major obstacle. I call racism "the 30 percent nuisance factor" because in my sales presentations then and now, the problem of race generally takes up 30 percent of my time.

I'm not alone in my belief that racism, while definitely a problem in trying to do business, can be dealt with if you use your wits and determination. A recent *Black Enterprise* poll found that while 24.2 percent of our readers felt that racism had held them back a great deal in their efforts to achieve their goals, 48.9 percent felt it was only somewhat of a factor and 26.1 percent felt it was not a factor at all.

But make no mistake: The problems of people starting out today are considerably tougher than mine were 26 years ago. For a time, racism was subdued. It did not disappear, certainly, but it receded. Now, however, it has arisen again. You can see it in the ashes of burned out churches and hear it in the voices of Texaco executives recorded by one of their own. Believe me, if this explicit racism still exists within one of the biggest brand name corporations in this country, it lives on in far, far too many others as well.

Back when I started in business, there was an awakening in white America inspired by the loud and angry and truly righteous demands for equality that had marked the civil rights movement. Racists were still in abundance, but our leaders had raised the consciousness of those who were willing to see how segregation and prejudice were denying this country its true greatness.

Laws protecting our civil rights had been hammered out, sometimes in blood. For the first time, the white establishment seemed to be recognizing that it was wiser and far more cost-efficient to provide opportunity to 12 percent of the population of this nation than to deny it. That worked to my advantage in the early days of *Black Enterprise* as it did for other African Americans seeking a foothold in business at the same time.

The challenges for black Americans seeking to succeed in business were formidable in 1970, but compared to the racial climate today, it was Brotherhood Week back then. We were pioneers in those days. Today we are warriors. The social, political and business environments today are far more hostile than they were 26 years ago. People now say things to me and my sons and our salespeople that they never would have dreamed of saying back then, because the conservative political climate today has created a backlash against black economic development and equal opportunity.

Have we progressed? Of course. But that progress has slowed dramatically in recent years. There are people in high office and seeking high office today who are eagerly turning the clock back to erase the accomplishments of the civil rights movement. They relish the chance to eradicate the laws and the organizations that have provided opportunities for African Americans—the very opportunities that have made this nation stronger and far more cohesive than it once was.

The liberating language of the 1970s—words such as *preferential* and *progressive*—today brings scorn and bitterness from the mouths of congressional and business leaders as well as talk radio demigods. Affirmative action, which greatly accelerated the growth of the black middle class and spurred economic development throughout this country, now is blamed for everything from the epidemic of corporate downsizing to the spread of gout among white country club members. The noble and inherently fair idea of providing opportunity for those to whom it had been denied is now strapped to the whipping post and regularly flayed by Republican conservatives. In the meantime, many of those in the Democratic Party, which stood with us through the civil rights movement, are ducking and running for cover, fearful of being wounded in the backlash.

Certainly, we African Americans must bear a good portion of the blame for our own vulnerability. We still are not leveraging our economic and political clout as aggressively as we must. We have to show the white business establishment that we are willing to match blows with every weapon at our disposal, whether it is our more than $400 billion dollars in income or our more than 12 million votes.

Because we have not marshaled our resources and taken the initiative, we are still scapegoated and marginalized. It happens in our neighborhoods. It happens in corporate boardrooms and sales conferences. But it begins on the floor of Congress. Every day, before we can sit at the table and get down to business, we must overcome or find a way to circumvent entrenched racism and racial ignorance. At *Black Enterprise*, my sales staff and I are not allowed the luxury of simply pitching the merits of our product. First we have to make a case for the legitimacy of our market. Sometimes we still have to assert our very right to be in this game.

I can't tell you how often my eldest son, Earl Jr., a graduate of Yale with an MBA from Harvard, has been interrupted during his sales presentations for our magazine and congratulated for being "so articulate." I doubt seriously that advertising salespeople for *Business Week* magazine are so patronized. I doubt that any of them have ever had to put to rest an advertiser's notion that *Business Week*'s readers don't purchase new cars or homes or computers or that they buy liquor by the half pint instead of the liter.

If my words seem weighted with anger and frustration, rest assured they are no less charged with pride and steadfast determination. I have been in this battle a long time and I have won far more than I have lost. *Black Enterprise* was profitable within its first ten issues. It is profitable today. But the racist refrains continue: *Why should we advertise with you? There aren't enough black people out there interested in our product. Are you really going to try to convince me that African Americans will invest in financial instruments? In stocks and bonds? In insurance? In luxury cars? In personal computers? Well, what you say makes sense, but we're still not interested. We don't want our product associated with African Americans.*

For all of his military prowess, General Colin Powell might have been taxed by our campaign to land our first advertising contract with a personal computer manufacturer. Getting major credit card companies to advertise was an adventure. Investment banking or stock brokerage firms? A trial by fire. Today the largest consumer-oriented brokerage firms may want to recruit black brokers featured in our magazine, but they balk at acknowledging that African Americans are consumers for their services—even though *Black Enterprise* has encouraged investing and reported on financial vehicles for decades.

Today corporate downsizing and restructuring have squeezed every company and every budget. It is more challenging for us to do business than it has ever been. When I launched *Black Enterprise*, I wasn't pitching an ad sale to General Motors at a time when they had just decided to get rid of hundreds of vice presidents. Banks were not merging all over the place. Today's business environment is tough for everybody, and with things changing so rapidly it is more difficult to establish relationships, particularly for African Americans, who generally don't belong to the same tennis and golf or yachting clubs as the majority of business executives. Some things change, but racism always rides with the black business-person, whether out front or hidden.

White Blindness

It was the spring of 1971. *Black Enterprise* was ten months old. I called a strategy meeting in the Bahamas to bring together the *Black Enterprise* advertising sales staff with several important clients, including Justin Gerstle, the senior vice president for media sales of Ted Bates Advertising Agency, which represented one of our major advertisers.

Although the magazine was already making money, this meeting was crucial to our growth and to our economic survival. We had to be able to sell ads to the major corporate clients represented by these advertising executives.

I will never forget how Gerstle, one of the most important men in the business, looked at us and bluntly said that the advertising community—the lifeblood of our magazine—did not have a clue about the emerging black middle-class market that was our target readership.

Gerstle and I were just getting to know each other. Over time we would become close friends, in spite of the fact that I used to tell him he was to the right of Genghis Khan. He was one of the most conservative white guys I'd ever met. But Gerstle and I were totally honest with each other. He cemented his reputation for candor at that meeting. Now deceased, he became a real friend.

From the moment he sat down, he told my staff in the bluntest terms possible that while he believed in *Black Enterprise* and its mission of self-determination, he felt it was going to be a tremendous challenge to sell advertising for a magazine aimed at the black community to corporations and advertising agencies dominated by white males.

"The white advertising community sees black people as drinking half pints of liquor and driving used cars," he told my staff.

Nearly a quarter-century later, as I was working on this book, I attended another meeting with a major advertising client whom I won't name, because I don't wish to embarrass him unfairly. He too was only being candid.

"In my business," he said, "black people are still considered *svartze*—niggers—and in order to do business with us, you are going to have to overcome that."

His words burned deeply. So much progress, and yet so little.

One of the key problems for African Americans in business is that we have great difficulty institutionalizing the value of our market. Because most whites have very little contact with or understanding of the black consumer market, they are generally blind to its value and diversity.

My sons Earl Jr. (known as Butch) and Johnny are still struggling to make contacts and build business relationships in companies like Apple and Microsoft, where I thought we had established ourselves and the value of our magazine a decade ago. But when there are changes in management or the corporate structure of these businesses, we have to start again from scratch. If it made sense 20 years ago to advertise in *Black Enterprise*, why do we have to reestablish the validity of the black consumer market on every sales call? Why do we have to keep helping white businesspeople see and understand the black consumer market?

It's because we are still invisible in their eyes. The Baby Boomer market doesn't have to prove itself constantly, because it is primarily white and the white consumer and the white businessperson live next door to each other. White businesspeople have a comfort level with that market, while the black middle class is generally foreign to them. That is why advertising aimed at the black consumer market is the first to get cut from corporate budgets when things get tight.

There are large corporations today—major consumer product makers—that we can't get into because they don't think blacks buy enough of their products. Their vision of the black community is generally limited to the inner city and to low-income housing. That's why when I have dinner parties with top-ranking black business executives such as Ken Chenault, president and COO of American Express, I generally include a few white CEOs or high-level white executives and their spouses. I want to expose them to a different side of the black community, a side they never see, growing up in their all-white suburban communities and going to predominately white institutions of higher education.

Just recently we held a book party for a black author at the *Black Enterprise* headquarters in Manhattan. The author's editor from a major New York publisher was there. This is a fellow who has edited other books written by African Americans. Most would consider him a worldly man. Yet after the book party, he told a mutual friend that he had never in his life seen so many beautiful, intelligent and well-dressed black people in one place. It was as if an entire culture existed right alongside his own world, and he had never seen it there. That is exactly the way it is for most whites.

When I have those dinner parties at our home or at the office, I generally also make sure that I have more black couples than white couples. I want the whites to have the "black" experience of being in the minority and feeling a little "invisible" themselves. I also want the white executives to understand that blacks in business are part of the main event rather than a side show. I want the whites to talk and eat with dozens of successful and intelligent and beautiful black people and perhaps understand what they have been missing.

It is important to note that while I believe that racism frequently impedes the process and cramps my style in business, I prefer to think that being black is, in fact, an advantage more than a disadvantage, primarily because we have to be better than average to make it. I know that, and you know it.

Being black means you take nothing for granted and leave no stone unturned. African Americans must use their wiles and employ every tool or weapon at their disposal to compete. There is no coasting.

Having said that, you can't go into a sales meeting or a job interview or any situation in the business world with a chip on your shoulder, or with the assumption that you are sitting face to face with someone who hates you because of the color of your skin. If you do, you will only damage yourself and be distracted from your purpose, which should always be to win. You have to give the person you are dealing with the benefit of the doubt until the doubt no longer exists.

Dealing with the Nuisance Factor of Race

1. Business first.

You won't make it if you go into every sales presentation or job interview feeling you have to convince people that African Americans are wonderful people. This is about business, not race, unless one side or the other forces race into the picture. If they force it, *you* have to decide whether it is worth your while to deal with it tactfully. You can do that, or you can look at it as an insult to your intelligence and professionalism and respond accordingly. That may be appropriate, depending on the situation, but it won't close the deal for you.

2. Don't deal with the subordinates if you can get to the chief executive.

This has been my philosophy since my first days in business because I've found that racism thrives mostly in the belly of business, in the lower tiers of management, and not so much in the head, at the top of the corporate structure where the deeper thinkers generally rule. Although it certainly is not guaranteed, in general those at the top are more aware of the need to at least appear to be committed to the black consumer market. The challenge, of course, is getting past the middlemen to the person who can make a decision.

Part of this involves doing your homework. I'm frequently appalled at the lack of preparation done by job applicants. They come into my office without having any depth of understanding about what I or my businesses are about. Believe me, when I make a call on another top-level executive, I know his wife's name, how many children he has, where they go to school and whether he prefers skiing to golf or tennis to mountain climbing. The CEO is the one with the answers, and he, or she, should always be your primary target.

I had to enact that philosophy early in the life of *Black Enterprise* when I encountered a stone wall in trying to reach the advertising buyer at Mercedes-Benz North America. Their man refused to even meet with me. He was arrogant, obviously racist and, worst of all, ignorant. His attitude was that there was no need to advertise in my magazine because its readers were not part of the Mercedes target market. Ironically, at the time there was a German luxury car parked in my garage at home.

After months of stonewalling from the marketing man at Mercedes North America, I decided to change my strategy. I targeted the chief at Mercedes-Benz, sending a letter to Dr. Joachim Zahn, the CEO of Daimler-Benz AG in Germany. I wrote that I would like to meet with him at the world headquarters of Daimler-Benz while en route to South Africa, where I had business to conduct with the renowned industrialist Anton Rupert, who had invited me to stay at his home. (It had not escaped my attention, mind you, that Rupert's son was one of Zahn's top aides.) I wrote that I wanted to discuss the African American market for his automobiles and the effectiveness of advertising in *Black Enterprise* as a means to reach that market.

Before I sent the letter, I made sure that several of my high-level contacts in the automotive industry dropped notes or telephoned their own high-level contacts at Daimler-Benz and passed the word that I was a serious player and that my magazine was indeed the prime advertising vehicle for reaching affluent African American business professionals, executives and entrepreneurs. I am certain also that Rupert's son was called upon to verify my meeting with his father and to check my business credentials with his father, who had a major interest in a company where I was then serving on the board of directors.

In addition, I went to Germany well armed with all sorts of impressive statistical data showing that wealthy blacks are extremely conscious of quality and that they are five times as likely to buy German luxury cars as wealthy whites. I even had a series of written testimonials with photographs of high-profile African Americans— most of them my friends—driving their Mercedes. But I needn't have bothered. The romance was already in full blossom.

One of the largest Mercedes stretch limousines I had ever seen awaited me at the Frankfurt airport, but to my surprise it did not deliver me to the local headquarters of Daimler-Benz. Instead I was taken to a little pub, which Dr. Zahn had rented so that he and I could talk privately in a relaxed setting. We must have seemed an unlikely pair of pub partners. I am 6 feet 2 inches tall, with muttonchop sideburns that are my trademark. He was much shorter, but powerfully built, and his trademark was much more imposing than mine—he had dueling scars on each cheek.

After our initial greetings, and a sampling of the German lager in my huge stein, I spoke pointedly. Mercedes-Benz of North America had a problem: Its executives failed to recognize the importance of the African American market for their automobiles.

"Mr. Graves, we don't have a problem," insisted Dr. Zahn.

"Yes, you do," I said. "I just told you that you have a problem."

"Mr. Graves, by the time you return to the U.S., there will be no problem," Zahn said.

Indeed, there was not a problem when I returned home, and there hasn't been one since. Mercedes-Benz of North America became a regular advertiser in my magazine, to our mutual benefit. But like most astute businessmen, Zahn came to our meeting with a dual agenda. After he had assured me that there would be no further problems with the North American division's marketing people, Zahn said, "You probably wonder why the problem was resolved so easily. Well, I need something from you."

I have to admit I wondered to myself, *What the hell could the CEO of Mercedes-Benz need from me?* Zahn quickly filled me in. He had learned of my itinerary for the South African trip, and after noting that I would be traveling in regions where Mercedes-Benz has considerable investments in auto assembly plants, he asked me to keep an eye open on his behalf as to the political climate and to fill him in upon my return. This, of course, was at a time before Mandela's release, when it was becoming increasingly clear that a revolution, whether violent or peaceful, was imminent. To his credit, Zahn told me that he felt "things must change" in the nation then torn by apartheid.

I was glad to be called upon by Zahn, and I did report back to him my assessment of the situation in South Africa. He must have been grateful because several years later I was approached about taking a seat on the board at Mercedes-Benz North America, an offer I could not pursue because I had already joined the board at Chrysler.

I have endeavored throughout my business career to focus on building personal relationships and then building business relationships. It has worked for me and it can work for you. Most people don't get private meetings with CEOs while in their first years of business, it is true. I had leverage because of my association with Kennedy. You will have to find your own leverage and put it to its best use. The network I have built has provided me over the years with incredible access to the highest levels of corporate America. I know that not everyone can do that, at least not all the time, but the mentality of using your wiles and every resource at your command to reach the person you need to reach to do what you need to do to grow your business—that mentality will get you through.

3. Sell to their needs, not from yours.

When I first started in the magazine business, people would say they were buying advertising in *Black Enterprise* because it was the right thing to do. It was demeaning, really, because they weren't buying it for the right reasons. There were times, also, when advertisers would say things to my employees like "I believe in you" or "I'm proud of you." Too often the person saying that was not smart enough to be carrying their shoes. I am more than 60 years old and white people are still telling me they are proud of me. That makes me nuts.

I want people to buy advertising in *Black Enterprise* because it makes sound business sense and drives up shareholder value for their company. And that is how you should sell your products. Not only should you sell them that way, you should believe in the value of your product. Otherwise the "smoke and mirrors" will catch up with you.

Take this advice to heart: You can never ask a white person to buy your product or service without giving him or her a solid economic reason for doing it. Forget that it's the right thing to do. In this day and age, doing the right thing doesn't mean a thing in the white business community. It has to make economic sense, and the person you are selling will have to have a reason to get the sale approved by his superiors.

4. Storm the castle.

You've seen it in the movies: The rebelling peasants storm the castle gate and get burning oil dumped on them. They put up ladders and get knocked into the moat. Finally they wise up and find a catapult or a secret passage, or they tip an indentured servant to open the service entrance. If the prize is inside, you have to get there any way you can.

Racism and racial ignorance are a nuisance, but they are not an excuse for failing or giving up. We hear it all the time when we interview businesspeople in our magazine, and it has probably been said inside our own offices more than once: We have a disadvantage because we aren't part of the white old boy network. It's true. It has always been true. But the answer is to build our own networks and to use them to get inside the castle.

I can't tell you how many late-night brainstorming sessions we have had at *Black Enterprise*, trying to find a way to get to the right people in some corporation that has put big stone walls and a moat around its advertising budget. White businesspeople play golf together in their exclusive country clubs. They meet in high-end supermarkets just outside their gated communities where they have cocktail parties and network to make business deals. Generally the only blacks present are the ones handing out cocktail napkins and valet parking the status cars.

Because they live, work and play together, white businesspeople generally aren't forced to use their ingenuity as much as we are. Most of them don't have to storm the castle—they're already inside eating a lamb's leg and swilling ale. But that can work to our advantage. If we don't let it make us bitter, it can make us better.

If I want to get to the CEO of a company and I can't do it by going in the front door, I'll sit down and examine the individual. What corporate or charitable boards does the CEO sit on? Whom do I know on those boards? What private clubs does he or she belong to? What church? Where do his or her children go to school? Whom do I know that might get me inside?

A man who was to become a lifelong friend, Tom Porter, did it for me years ago at IBM. Many others have helped over the years, just as I have helped scores of people through my contacts. Remember, if you want others to get you in, you have to be ready, willing and able to return the favor.

5. Never forget that business is personal.

I believe that the businessperson who builds the strongest relationships wins. I have worked to build a large network of business relationships with white as well as black people because we can help each other. Now this can be a challenge because, no matter what they say, most white people still don't have a high level of comfort around black people. I can sense it at parties, even on the elevator in the Manhattan office building where *Black Enterprise* is a major tenant. Racism rears its head at all levels.

Years ago, when I was trying to sell our house in Armonk, New York, where we lived in an otherwise all-white neighborhood, it didn't sell for almost a year, even though we had completely remodeled and landscaped it. One of my friends said, "You haven't sold it yet? Why don't you take down all the pictures of your family and then stay away from the open house so the white people won't know who lives there?" I did it. I took down all the family photos as well as the pictures of Martin Luther King. The house sold the next weekend for the full asking price. When we walked into the closing, the jaw of the white guy who'd bought it nearly hit the conference table.

In more recent times, *Black Enterprise* has purchased entire tables of seats at charity dinners, spending as much as $2,000 a plate, and been unable to fill the table with advertisers invited at our expense, because they haven't been able to round up enough white people to join them. Most whites can't handle the idea of sitting at a black table. It's crazy. I sit at white tables all the time. This skin color doesn't rub off, but you could never convince many white businesspeople of that. This year at a charity benefit at the Waldorf, some whites who were invited actually asked if there would be other white people present.

Other magazines host ski parties and golf outings for advertisers, tactics that are unlikely to work for us. We often have difficulty just getting clients to come to our Manhattan offices for meetings. It's not that we want to kidnap them, or even make a power play. We simply want the white people we do business with to see an elegant office complex with well-dressed and highly professional black people doing business at the highest levels. Is it an ego thing? Absolutely, but it's much more than that. It's a pride thing. It's a statement that we are in this game. We've had many of the highest-ranking business and political leaders in the world in our offices, and I have the photos on the wall to prove it.

But some white executives still balk at coming to us. They have their secretaries call to set up a telephone conference or a luncheon meeting at a restaurant. They don't say it, but the attitude is, "Why should I have to go see the blacks at their place?" It is contemptible.

And it is exactly the reason why we want them to come, so that we can change those hangups by developing personal relationships at a professional level. After all, I believe that one reason I'm invited to sit on so many corporate boards is that I have the ability to work and interact comfortably with white people.

Understand, when I encourage you to develop relationships, I don't mean just at the executive level. I believe in romancing staff people too. The higher people are in an organization, the tighter the grip of their secretaries or executive assistants on the executive pocket planner. When Robert Crandall, the president of American Airlines, tells you that his executive assistant really runs the company, he is being self-effacing to a point because Bob is a very smart, no-nonsense guy. But he is also telling you that her role is vital and that if you want to win favor with him, you will first have to win her approval.

I am not advising you to be insincere or to b.s. these staff people. That would be unwise, since they have survived and risen because of their sharp instincts. I'm saying take the time to learn their names and understand their personalities and let them know that you recognize their importance. Treat them cordially.

"Hello Mr. Graves, Mr. Galvin just left for the day."

"He did? It looks like he left you to do all the work again, didn't he? When I talk to him I'll tell him that I called and you were still working an hour after he'd gone home."

It may appear corny or insincere in this context, but brief conversations like that establish that you understand how hard these key people must work to keep ahead of their bosses. You are not simply brushing them off as functionaries or scenery, as many people do. When you make the extra effort without kowtowing or being overbearing, you establish yourself in their minds as someone who respects them, and the next time you call, your message may get put on top of the pile. Recently I sent a bouquet of flowers to a woman who works for the president of a major communications company because she had been helpful to me. The next time I wanted to reach her boss, you better believe I got through.

I make it a point to make a special effort several times a year to further cement business relationships with small gifts, notes or phone calls. On St. Patrick's Day each year, I send out bottles of Bailey's Irish Cream to several hundred people as a way of letting them know I value our relationship. On Valentine's Day, I send out mailings asking the recipients to *B.E.* our Valentine. Corny, maybe, but effective too.

6. Latch on to a guardian angel.

Every corporate culture has its own name for a person who looks out for you and helps you move up the ladder. Today most major corporations have African American mentoring groups that have come to be valued for the stability they bring. In some cases, the CEOs attend their meetings in order to stay in touch with the needs and concerns of minority employees.

Blacks need mentors every bit as much as, if not more than, their white competitors. Until many companies began throwing affirmative action out the window, it was easier for black employees to grab the attention of someone higher up. It may be more difficult today, but it's not impossible.

I met with a couple of executives from Pepsi-Cola recently, and I asked one of them how he'd risen to his position in the company. He said that he'd met the future CEO while giving him a marketing tour. They'd hit it off, and as the future CEO moved up the ladder, he'd brought this fellow with him. "At every step I did a good job, and as long as I was still doing a good job, he took me with him," the executive told me.

People like to work with those they are comfortable with. In a white-dominated business environment, that elementary bit of human nature can make it difficult for African Americans who don't have the ability to put whites at ease. Doing so in business often has more to do with preparation than with personality. It may sound trite, but there's no substitute for excellence, and there never will be.

Hard work, dedication, professionalism and integrity will win friends and influence people more over the long term than a back-slapping demeanor. I am on the national board of the Boy Scouts of America with the chairman of Bell South. We have a relationship, but if I didn't come to our Boy Scout meetings fully prepared and engaged, I would not be able to capitalize on that relationship in order to court Bell South's business. If you are going to leverage relationships out of self-interest, you had better have established that you are a player.

7. Do not sell your soul.

There is a notion among some that in order for blacks to be successful in business, they must assimilate into the white business culture. That is true only in very surface ways. When you are involved in a traditional business, you dress in that tradition, which is, for good or bad, rooted in the white culture. I have a wide assortment of business suits that my kids describe as ranging "from traditional to antiquity."

The truth is that some of those suits are too flashy to wear to many business meetings. I don't consider that selling out or being assimilationist. Nor do I consider developing skills in golf and skiing or becoming a leader in the Boy Scouts to be the actions of an assimilationist. Those are things I am truly interested in for a number of reasons, business being one of them.

I believe that the most successful blacks in the business world are those who do not forget for a minute who they are or where they came from. Bob Holland, who turned Ben & Jerry's around as the first African American CEO of a publicly held company, is fond of quoting *Bre'r Rabbit:* "No matter where you is or what you is, be what you is, 'cause if you is what you ain't, you isn't."

Another friend and business leader, John Johnson, founder and publisher of *Ebony* and *Jet* magazines, has a vacation home in Palm Springs, California, in a gated community where his neighbors are Bob Hope and Walter Annenberg, the founder of *TV Guide*. But I don't think anyone would accuse John Johnson of forgetting where he came from, or of selling out, or of trying to assimilate. John didn't buy a home in an exclusive community in California because he wanted to be with white people. He moved there because, as a multimillionaire, he can live wherever he wants to live and he wanted to live somewhere that was not as cold as Chicago in the winter. I respect him because he has never forgotten who he is, and he is comfortable wherever he lives. He is, and should be, a role model for all African Americans looking to succeed in the business world.

8. If you are selling the black consumer market, sell its buying power, not your social consciousness.

Modern Maturity doesn't pitch advertisers by telling them that if they market to senior citizens they will get extra points at the pearly gates. *Sports Illustrated for Kids* doesn't sell ads to candy bar companies because its sales staff convinces them of the redeeming social value of feeding the children. And when *Black Enterprise* makes a sales call, we don't want to talk to the community affairs representative, we want to talk business. Whatever your product or service, sell its business value, not its social value. Businesses don't take the Baby Boomer, senior citizen or Generation X market for granted. They would be foolish to take the African American market for granted.

But they do. Out of ignorance or lack of exposure, or simple bad business judgment, many white businesspeople have very narrow, often very warped, images of the black consumer market. I have been butting my head against that ignorance all of my life. But I have also been making a very good living by correcting those false impressions and closing deals based on the information I have been prepared to provide. In general, white advertising buyers don't want to hear about the black consumer market, but if you show them how buying space in *Black Enterprise* will be six times more effective than buying it in *TIME*, they tend to sit up and take notice. If you keep throwing snow at the wall, eventually some of it will stick.

If you are having trouble getting through during a sales pitch, don't get mad, get out the charts and the statistics. Make them understand that African Americans are the most brand-loyal, quality-conscious group of consumers on this planet. When we get good service, we show our appreciation by coming back. When we see that a company respects us as consumers, we respond in kind.

Several years ago, I was visiting with my mother before going out to a sales meeting with Jack Welch, the CEO of General Electric, and when I told her where I was going she said, "I always liked that man."

"But you have never met Jack Welch," I said.

"Oh no, not him, the other man from G.E., the man who took off his hat to me and called me Mrs. Graves when he came to fix the refrigerator in our old house," she said.

I was two years old when that refrigerator broke down and the repairman came. My mother had purchased G.E. products all her life because one of its white servicemen showed her proper respect more than 50 years ago. *That* is product loyalty. And that is typical of the black consumer. We respect those who respect us.

9. Get involved in your community.

When young people ask me how to get started in business, they often appear shocked when I tell them to first get involved in their community. Maybe they think I'm going to give them a job or a $100,000 start-up grant, or maybe they don't get the connection between being involved in the community and getting started in business.

There is a strong connection. One of the best pieces of advice I received early in my career came from a fellow infantry officer, a white guy named James Imhoff. Back when I was getting ready to leave the military, he suggested that I establish myself in my community by getting involved in politics, in the National Guard and in the Boy Scouts of America. I did all three immediately upon returning to Brooklyn, and I have been reaping the rewards ever since.

You may not get the opportunity to fully display your talents in a business setting early in your career, simply because of the realities of being low person on the totem pole. But chances are there are community and political organizations where you will be able to work side by side with top business leaders who are also volunteering their time. Along with providing you an otherwise rare opportunity to establish relationships with business leaders, volunteer work gives you the chance to showcase your talents. Robert Kennedy was never going to buy a house in Bed-Stuy, so he would never have known of my organizational skills if he hadn't walked into that Christmas party I put together in Brooklyn.

I wouldn't recommend joining just any community or political organization. You have to take some care in choosing one that interests you and is in line with your beliefs. I remember that very early on I took a seat on the Armonk Library Board because I had an interest in helping libraries and opening them up to everyone. The people on the board were dedicated, but after finding myself involved in long discussions on whether we should approve the purchase of large or small paper clips, I realized that I needed to be involved in a less parochial organization. I immediately began looking for a larger forum where my time wasn't spent on studying whether to purchase novels or nonfiction.

10. Work on developing a commanding presence.

You may be disappointed, but I am not going to be advising anyone to grow long sideburns in order to succeed in business. That's my trademark, for better or for worse, and it has worked for me. I won't guarantee that it will work for you. I will tell you, however, that it is important to establish a presence so that you and your business or your talents stand out. That includes an appearance that exudes confidence and class, no matter what your field of endeavor. It means appropriate business attire for your profession. In most corporate environments that means no earrings for men and no visible tattoos. If you want to be taken seriously, you have to show that you are serious about business, not just playing at it. Find another place to make your fashion statement.

11. Don't get frustrated because you can't hit it out of the park every time.

For at least ten years, my sales staff, my sons and I have been trying to sell advertising space to technology companies based in Silicon Valley. They don't seem to want to advertise to blacks. We have not given up, because we know the potential market, even if they don't. It's up to us to convince them that our product is right for them, and we will not stop trying until we do. Is it a challenge? Yes. Is it confounding? Absolutely. But we keep going back, stronger, not weaker, because we will not allow rejection to beat us down. It will only strengthen our resolve. To be successful, there is no other way.

CHAPTER 4

No-Nonsense Networking

In the spring of 1969, I began a campaign to get an advertising contract with what was then the nation's biggest computer maker—IBM. I had been trying for more than a year to get a piece of IBM's advertising budget, but I hadn't been able to squeeze a dime out of their middle-management marketing and advertising people. They couldn't get it into their heads that *Black Enterprise* was a serious business magazine and not some sort of minority charity looking for a handout.

In this case, I succeeded with the help of a well-placed insider, my friend Thomas Porter, who was then in corporate communications at IBM. Porter, whom I had known for several years, told me that the only way to approach IBM was at the top, because the lower-level executives were concerned only with protecting their jobs. They didn't want to change the status quo and advertise in black publications.

Porter went a step further than offering advice. He talked with his associates and convinced them that it would be in IBM's best interests to take a look at Earl Graves and his unique magazine. It took guts for my friend to grease the way for me to meet the CEO of IBM. The top man, Vincent Learson, was notoriously tough. In fact his nickname around IBM was "Attila the Hun." Learson had risen to the top of one of America's leading companies by setting sales records everywhere he was assigned, and he was not a guy who was easily charmed.

My meeting was penciled into Learson's appointment book for fifteen minutes, but the bet around Big Blue was that the black magazine publisher wouldn't last five. The vultures in pinstripes were actually circling outside the door waiting for me to come fleeing from his inner office.

The vultures had to eat crow. My meeting with Learson lasted nearly an hour. Learson was tough as a boss, but one-on-one he was a professional who knew how to listen and how to ask the right questions. I pitched him on *Black Enterprise* as a product that would open up new markets for his company and put IBM even farther ahead of the competition. I didn't ask him to make a business decision based on his social conscience, I asked him to make a business decision based on smart economics. We hit it off because I didn't try to impress him with anything other than the way my product fit his needs.

The naysayers were astonished when the door finally flew open and Learson and I emerged with our arms around each other, smiling like old war buddies. Seeing the looks on the faces of his shocked minions, Learson shot them a defiant smile, looked at me and announced, "We have just decided that we are the two best salesmen in the world!"

I didn't disagree with Learson. After all, I knew he was at least half right. I think you have to be a natural-born salesman to succeed in the business world, but more important, you have to have people like Tom Porter who believe in you and are willing to help you.

This is particularly true today for African Americans looking to succeed in business, where whites in particular, but also other racial and ethnic groups, have long understood how to make use of their networks to get ahead. Blacks, who perhaps developed a go-it-alone mentality after years of slavery and mistrust, have been slow to understand the value of networking. But in recent years, as more of us have entered the professional workforce, we have learned to work together for the benefit of each other and our community in general.

That said, I want to make the point that I was reluctant initially to even use the term *network* in this book because I think it is one of the most overused, abused and confused terms in business today. It does *not* involve pushing your business cards on anyone and everyone within reach. It does *not* involve confronting complete strangers and demanding that they carry out your agenda or contribute to your cause. It does *not* involve latching on to top-level VIPs and having your photograph taken with them so you can hang it on your office wall. Where does that kind of networking get anyone? Nowhere, because that is networking nonsense.

The Network

A few years ago, *Business Week* magazine wrote a six-page story titled "Inside the Black Business Network," complete with an elaborate color-coded diagram presented as a "Guide to Some Key Players." Since they wisely noted in the article that a certain New York publisher with unique sideburns was that network's "master communicator," I won't chide the competition for mistakenly including in our black business network a white Jewish guy from Chicago—the late Jerry Wexler.

In fact, I will let *Business Week*'s description stand as your introduction to my network:

> At its core, it is a cadre of entrepreneurs and smattering of high-ranking corporate executives who together make up the black business elite. But it envelops countless other African American businesspeople and heavy hitters in politics, social activism and religion. With much the same energy that characterized the civil rights struggle, this network is focused squarely on economic development. The eyes are still on the prize, but the prize these days is a slice of wealth and affluence.

This is a view of black America that is rarely provided in the majority-owned media. Though most whites have no idea that it exists, the black business network is an incredibly vital aspect of the African American community—and one of our best tools for competing in the white-dominated business world. It features our best and brightest business minds working together to increase the economic strength of black people in this country and around the world.

This network was not created by America's top black professionals standing in a room pressing business cards on each other and demanding favors. It was formed over a considerable amount of time. It was formed out of mutual trust and admiration. It was formed out of a mutual desire to help each other because relationships had been nurtured carefully and thoughtfully.

That is *no-nonsense networking*, and that is how I do business. It is how all of the people I respect do business. It is how you must learn to do business.

Cooperating for Mutual Benefit

Networking is a simple concept, yet it is often a difficult mind-set to establish in the highly competitive world of business. The pressures of competing as a minority, in particular, can instill a siege mentality in which narrow self-interest becomes a survival mechanism. Blacks in business sometimes feel that the only way to get ahead is to worry only about themselves and their interests. That is understandable to a degree, but inevitably it is self-defeating.

While African Americans tended in the past to think of business as a solitary endeavor, other racial and ethnic groups traditionally networked much more effectively. The Irish, the Jews, the Koreans and the Jamaicans have openly worked together within their communities to corner markets and build their collective wealth, to help each other rise from arriving immigrants to the middle class to the highest levels of this nation's business and economic community.

If black people do not leverage what we have, we are never going to be able to compete economically, politically or socially in this country or in the global market. After 12 years of Republican rule in the White House and now with a Congress dominated by Republican conservatives and Democrats scared to death to be labeled "liberal," the outside environment is not getting any friendlier. We have to be able to look within for strength and support.

One of my greatest concerns is that in this hostile business climate, many blacks who are in a position to help others are hunkering down and isolating themselves. I see a lot of younger blacks who are either not aware of their racial history or simply do not feel compelled to acknowledge that they have a responsibility to share their gifts. They feel they have somehow graduated from their blackness.

I am thinking in particular of one black executive whom we championed in the pages of *Black Enterprise* for many years. We trumpeted his successes and celebrated his rise up the ladder. We practically built a shrine to him and sponsored pilgrimages. But suddenly he refused to return phone calls when other African Americans called to network with him. He felt he had moved to a level where he no longer needed "the black thing." He has gone mainstream, he thinks. He is no longer a black businessman, he is a businessman who just happens to be black. He got his, go get yours and leave him alone.

It seems to me that while more African Americans than ever have attained a high level of professional and economic success, there are still far too few of us. We cannot afford to shun each other or to fight among ourselves for the crumbs. You may have become a top manager at Procter & Gamble, IBM or General Electric. You may have moved through the top levels of government service and landed a lucrative position in private business. You may sit on corporate boards and make regular calls to the White House. But you have not risen above your responsibility to your fellow African American men, women and children. You are still one of us, and if you don't know it, the cop who pulls you over for a DWB (driving while black) in a nice neighborhood will remind you.

None of us can afford to forget the rest of us. We have to be able to count on each other. Those of us in a position to help each other cannot afford only to be helping ourselves. Our competition is not from within. We have to realize that only by leveraging our collective strength can we achieve the only true equality—economic equality. The network is our primary leveraging tool. None of us can stand alone.

In truth, most blacks in business have come to embrace the concept of networking in recent years. I'd like to think that is at least in part because *Black Enterprise* has been touting the value of networking for decades. People running their own businesses need to network within their industry, with customers, suppliers, other local business owners, bankers and lawyers, their local politicians and with groups in their community. It is simple common sense that if you are in business, the more people you know, the more business you will attract and the better informed you will be to run your business.

Keep in mind at all times that networking is a two-way street. If you don't bring something to the table, if you aren't prepared to listen as well as be heard, then you've failed to grasp the concept. What makes networking work is that it sets up win-win situations in which all parties involved get to take something home. Networking is a sharing process. Until you understand that, you won't have much of a network.

Build Relationships Before You Tap the Network

One of the greatest problems with young people trying to network is that they don't grasp the concept that the most valuable form of networking cannot be done without investing in relationships. I can't tell you how many times I've been the victim of what amounts to drive-by networking, in which someone I've known for maybe ten minutes suddenly wants me to set him or her up in business, guarantee the bank loan and provide office space. Some want me to throw in a Chrysler too.

They get me on the phone or corner me at a party and drop to their knees swearing to name all their children after me if only I'll introduce them to a friendly banker. Often I have a hard time saying "Sorry, I can't help you." I do tell my staff that as a magazine that champions entrepreneurship, we have something of an obligation to help. So if someone calls or writes, we at least try to give them some sort of a hand or reference, maybe a telephone number to call or a business organization to try.

But at times people are so unsophisticated about networking that all you can do is walk away from them shaking your head. I used to buy some of my clothes from a father and son who own a custom shirt shop. They take good care of the shirts at this shop, sewing on buttons and changing collars if they become frayed. For a long time I was just another customer in this shop, but one day the owner's son saw me identified as a champion of entrepreneurs on television or in a magazine. The next thing I know, he's telling me about his idea for some sort of theme-restaurant franchise.

He asked for my advice, so I set up a meeting with him. Within minutes, I realized his idea was not something I was interested in and told him so. A few weeks later he was back on the phone asking for another meeting. Finally I explained to him that he could not count on me to help him with his business, nor could he count on me as a customer at his shirt shop anymore, because I couldn't go in there without being lobbied about another of his restaurant concepts. That is just not how real networking is done.

Networking Among Strangers

It is particularly important when you are first starting out in business, and even when you are still in school or still working for someone else, that you learn the basic rules of networking. Everyone has to start somewhere, and for many people that means your networking begins hopefully in college, where you join social and professional organizations that are crucial to building long-term relationships. Black fraternities and sororities serve mostly social purposes in college, but in your years after college you will find them invaluable networking sources.

When Tanya Savage was an undergraduate and president of the black students association at a predominately white women's college in Georgia, she made a point of attending conferences and seminars at her own school as well as others. The Pensacola, Florida, native found she had to face daily bouts with racism, classism and sexism from her professors and bemoaned the fact that at her college "there were no black professors. I was not exposed to any black leadership at all." So she wisely used these outside events as an outlet for her social and career networking.

Greek organizations and professional groups in college, whether it's the Black Engineering Students Association or the black student government, also offer you the opportunity to practice networking skills before you get out into the real world, where you can't afford to make a bad impression, at least not too often.

Here are some networking tips for beginners.

I. Relax.

Networking is like golf. If you try too hard, you'll never be loose enough to do it right. Networking is a social-first, business-second activity. If it were business first and social second, it would be called working, not networking. If you come up to me at a *Black Enterprise* seminar and immediately try to impress me with your grasp of South African economic development, I'll probably decide that you need to loosen your collar button a bit. The more comfortable you are, the more comfortable I will be with you. Now that definitely does not mean that you need to drink three glasses of wine before you approach me, so keep that in mind too. Sober but relaxed is just fine.

2. Listen at least half as much as you talk.

This goes back to my primary rule on networking, that it is supposed to be a mutually beneficial activity. If the other person is going to benefit, you have to allow him or her the chance to get in a few words. Don't just toss in your two cents and the name of your business and dash off to the next victim. You may miss out on an opportunity if you hit and run. Take your time. And don't interrupt. That's one of the most annoying habits of the uptight networker. Look the other person in the eye as you converse, and be attentive. You're part of a conversation, not giving a lecture or sales pitch. The time for that is on the follow-up phone call.

3. Find a common interest, and don't assume it is you.

The best way to get a networking relationship going is to establish early on that you and the other person have common interests and common goals. Don't try to create them if they aren't there, but at least look for commonalities by exploring what the other person is about before you begin tracing your own ancestry back to the Garden of Eden.

It is usually not difficult to find common ground, particularly when networking within black circles. We can usually get those six degrees of separation down to about three. In more diverse groups, it may be tougher, but you'll often be pleasantly surprised. Maybe you grew up in the same town, the same state, the same part of the country, the same size community. Maybe you went to the same college, or you know someone who was at the same college at the same time as your new acquaintance. If you can't find something in common in the first ten minutes of conversation, you had better move on because there is certainly no networking connection there. You might also want to check and see if maybe you have been trying to network with the statuary.

4. Do not strive to be impressive; instead, try to leave a positive impression.

These are not the same thing. Far too many networking neophytes come bearing their diplomas and wall plaques. A lot of people make the mistake, too, of trying to sound like an expert on topics they have no mastery of. Remember, you are swimming in unfamiliar waters and if you try to seem more than you are, you run the risk of encountering someone who may be all too willing to unmask you in public. Stick with what you know. If the conversation is over your head, wait until it comes back to your level. Better to seem quiet and thoughtful than foolhardy.

When Martin Luther King was assassinated, I flew to Atlanta to help with the funeral service. My specialty in the military and in Kennedy's office was logistical operations and events planning. I knew how to handle crowds, traffic, telephones and other technical systems. Shortly after I arrived, I found myself in a meeting of King's top aides and about 40 of the most powerful black leaders in the country. They were discussing whether the memorial service following the funeral should be held outdoors in the Quadrangle at Morehouse College.

Some at the meeting felt the Quadrangle was not big enough to accommodate the anticipated crowd of mourners. I had already gone out and surveyed it, and I knew the area was large enough to serve the intended purpose. In fact I had already arranged to have the area wired for telephone service and a public address system. I had been silent up until that point, but I felt I had something important to contribute, so I raised my hand and spoke out.

"The Quadrangle will handle the crowds," I said from my chair.

The Rev. Martin Luther King Sr., father of the slain leader, looked out and asked me to stand so that I could be seen. I felt the eyes of these men, many of whom were my heroes, upon me, assessing me. Daddy King, as he was known, was not going to easily accept the assessment of someone unknown to him.

"Who are you, young man?" he inquired.

A voice from the front of the room answered for me.

"That is Earl Graves. He works for Robert Kennedy," offered the Rev. Andrew Young, who would later become mayor of Atlanta and the U.S. Ambassador to the United Nations.

I gave my report, which was accepted and acted upon. The Quadrangle held the crowds and became part of history.

5. Make a graceful exit.

Once again, do not pump, dump and run. Networking is not a track and field event. There is, however, a reasonable time limit.

Stick around as long as you feel you have something to contribute, or someone to get to know better, and then gracefully say that you have enjoyed meeting and talking and that you had better move on. You may want to stick around one person or group of people if you become captivated for professional or other reasons, but try to keep in mind that if this is really a networking event, you should be trying to meet a wide variety of people. Believe me, there are few things that can move a career or a business along faster and more efficiently than networking friends in the right places.

6. Follow through.

I will resist the sports analogy this time, but keep in mind that it makes no sense to go to a networking event, make the initial contact with a potential networking ally and then never follow through with a telephone call or a note, or even an e-mail message. If you want to build on that first meeting, you have to act upon it. Do it in a proper and businesslike way, but do it. Otherwise, don't sit at home wondering why your business or career just doesn't seem to be going anywhere. There is *work* involved in networking, and if you are going to take your business or career to the next level, you have to put effort into building relationships over a long period of time, sometimes perhaps longer than you might think.

7. Practice networking etiquette.

Among the executives I deal with every day, there is an unwritten rule about referring someone to another networking source. The rule is this: If you truly want to help the person, you don't simply tell them to call a networking contact and use you as a reference, as in "Call Darwin Davis, senior vice president at Equitable, and tell him Earl Graves suggested you two talk."

I guarantee you that Davis, who is a serious networker, would not take that telephone call, because he understands that if I had really thought your call to him was vital, I would have made the introductory telephone call myself, asking him to take five minutes to talk with you. Once I had paved the way personally, he would be far more likely to take your call.

This may seem complicated, but it is part of the networking etiquette that you will have to master if you are going to be successful.

8. Acknowledge networking favors.

The most adept networkers, whether individuals or organizations, know how to convey appreciation for a networking favor. If someone has been helpful to you, let them know you appreciate it. At the very least send a thank-you note as quickly as possible. I've always been impressed with the folks at the National Urban League—they have been monsters at following up and expressing appreciation for any assistance I have ever provided them. And believe me, their skill at this makes me all the more willing to help them out next time they knock on my networking door.

9. Do not forget the personal touch.

Since networking is, at its most basic level, the building of mutually beneficial relationships, it is important to nurture those relationships beyond business. One way I practice this is by sending out elaborately staged family Christmas cards to all of my networking partners. The message is that I consider them an extension of my family and want them to feel that way too.

Networking to New Levels

When I first started publishing *Black Enterprise*, I'd often mention to potential clients that one of my role models was John Johnson, the pioneer publisher of *Ebony* and *Jet*. On several occasions I got feedback that some of Johnson's people were not speaking so favorably about *Black Enterprise*. Everywhere I went, people would ask me what I thought of *Ebony* and I'd say I thought it was a terrific magazine. Then they'd tell me Johnson's people had said my magazine should not be taken seriously.

It seemed that at first Johnson didn't much like the idea of another black publisher competing for advertising dollars in a market that was already tough enough. *Essence* had been launched around the same time as *Black Enterprise*, and it was in direct competition with Johnson's publications for advertising clients. Johnson had been the only black publisher on the block for a long time. He was not eager to relinquish any ground. Time after time I heard that his people were telling advertisers that there was no market for a magazine for black businesspeople.

Their words burned, but I didn't see any sense in taking on a man who was a hero to African Americans everywhere, including me. He had fought and struggled and opened many doors to get where he was, and I saw no sense in saying or doing anything that would tarnish his image.

For nearly ten years this went on. I laid low, but he kept coming. He can be a bare-knuckled businessman and he let me have a few licks, and not only with advertisers. Just about the time I'd find a good salesman or editor or art director, Johnson would wade in, wave a handful of money, and the next thing I'd know, their names would be on the masthead of one of his magazines.

There wasn't much I could do other than to stay on the high road, telling anyone who would listen that I thought John Johnson was one of the greatest African American entrepreneurs of our time. I went about my business, making friends and building my network with those who were interested in being a part of something greater than themselves. Our magazine grew because others saw the value in it and its message of black economic development.

Finally, after nearly a decade, Johnson called me on the telephone one day and said he wanted to come and see me in my office. I was stunned. A few days later, he walked in like my best friend for life and said that he had been doing his best to beat me back but that I had remained a gentleman. So he wanted to call a truce. In fact he suggested that there really was no direct competition between us and that it might work to our mutual benefit to make presentations together to clients who needed to better understand the value of the African American consumer market.

Since then, Johnson and I have become close friends, although we remain, in many respects, competitors. I count his magazine's ads regularly and I know he is checking mine, but we are both aware that the real competition is *Business Week*, *Fortune* and *Forbes*, which fight for the same advertising dollars we go after. Many times he and I have gone together into the den of some reluctant white corporate advertiser and convinced him of the value in advertising his product or service to the African American market.

On some occasions we have been joined by a third African American publisher, Ed Lewis of *Essence*. Certainly we each go on these calls to sell advertising for our individual magazines, but, more important, we go as successful black businesspeople to plant in the minds of white executives that there is money to be made in selling to people just like us—African American consumers.

When Keith T. Clinkscales launched a student magazine, *Urban Profile*, while enrolled in the Harvard business school, he wisely tapped into our network for advice. Bob Johnson of Black Entertainment Television, Ed Lewis and Eugene Jackson of the World African Network and I introduced him to potential investors, and we talked to him about the pros and cons of publishing for the black consumer market. Clinkscales built his magazine to a circulation of 50,000, sold it and later became chief operating officer for Quincy Jones's *Vibe*, where he is now recognized as one of the bright young stars in the publishing business.

That is leveraging our collective strength to build even more strength. That is working together for the mutual benefit of all parties. That is networking for economic empowerment in the black community.

Mandela Comes On-Line with the Network

When Nelson Mandela came to the meeting I described at the beginning of this book, he had more on his agenda than simply asking African American business leaders to invest in South Africa's economic future. He also met with us in order to formally join our network, and he began reaping the benefits immediately. At a reception in the executive boardroom, Mandela stopped in his tracks and for a moment stood marveling, not at the array of African American celebrities, dignitaries and religious, business and political leaders surrounding him, but at the large typeface of a prepared speech on a sheet of paper that I held in my hand.

"How did you get the type to be that big?" Mandela asked me.

He explained that he was intrigued at the size of the typeface because his eyesight had deteriorated during his imprisonment and he had difficulty reading the small type on his own speeches. I explained that my speeches were prepared on an Apple computer word processing program with special fonts for printing large-type texts. Mandela was not aware that personal computers could print in large type.

"Where can I get one of these Apples?" he asked.

The next day, I telephoned Kevin Sullivan, a senior vice president at Apple Computer's corporate headquarters in Cupertino, California. I told Sullivan of Mandela's interest in his product and stressed the opportunities for his company in a nation with more than 40 million potential consumers.

Within a few months, the African National Congress (ANC) headquarters in South Africa was nearly overrun with Apples. A delegation of Apple representatives presented Mandela, the president of the ANC, with his own personal PowerBook computer so that his speeches could be typed in large letters.

The story of how the black network worked on behalf of Mandela's South Africa is really a very minor one—many much more significant developments have been brought about by our network—but it illustrates the reach and speed with which significant connections can be made when African Americans in a position to help each other communicate and work together for the mutual benefit of all parties.

When conducted at that level, networking is a vehicle that helps drive black economic development in this country and around the world.

The *Business Week* article on the black business network featured several examples of our cooperative efforts to encourage and bolster black economic development. One involved the rescue of Motown Records, which a few years earlier had fallen on hard times after being purchased from its founder, Berry Gordy, a black music industry pioneer. Jheryl Busby, then the CEO of Motown Record Company and a 10 percent owner, was forced to sue partner MCA for failing to promote the label and its acts. He explained to *Business Week* that he came to the network for help because "When you're driven by fear, you reach for the familiar—[to those who] understand your story."

I brought together Busby and Robert Johnson of Black Entertainment Television along with several other members of the network and we helped create a strategy to leverage Motown's strengths and traditions. In the end, new markets and products were created for Motown, and it became so attractive that it was purchased by PolyGram NV for $325 million—five times what Busby and other investors had paid for it in 1988.

Networking the Big Deal

Networking is nothing less than developing relationships with people who can help you and who, in turn, you can help. It is nothing more or less than being willing to reach out when you need a hand or when someone else needs help. It is recognizing that our success as individuals is guaranteed only if we succeed as a community. It is all about leveraging contacts and personal relationships for our mutual and long-term benefit.

Probably the most celebrated example of the power of our black business network was the development of the deal that created the largest minority-owned business in the country. It began in 1986 when for the first time I met with Fred Joseph, who was then CEO of Drexel Burnham Lambert, the brokerage firm. I did not go into the meeting feeling particularly congenial toward him or his company or most of the rest of the financial services field. Drexel, and many others in their field, had been spurning our efforts to get them to advertise in *Black Enterprise*, and I was wound up to let them have it for being so ignorant about the huge market for investment vehicles among African American professionals.

Well, they said it couldn't be done, but Fred Joseph shut me up before I'd even warmed up my sales pitch. When he interrupted me, I was prepared to hear the usual lame excuses about blacks not being big investors in mutual funds or the stock market. I was well prepared to field that one. I had research data and statistical studies at the ready to shoot those misperceptions as soon as their ugly racist faces appeared. But Joseph, who I later found out had been a successful amateur boxer, was in no mood for a fight.

"I want to do it," he told me before I'd even suggested he do anything.

"Do what?" I said.

"I want to advertise in your magazine. In fact, I want to come see you in your office and do some other things with you," he said.

At that point I'd been in the publishing business for 15 years and had rarely had a client, particularly a white client, jump on board so quickly. It almost took all the fun out of it. I couldn't imagine what he was up to, but I got his name signed on the dotted line for a long-term advertising commitment and then agreed to meet him a few weeks later on my turf.

This is one unusual white guy, I thought as I walked out of his office. Joseph, a Harvard MBA who grew up in a blue-collar Boston neighborhood, proved to be full of surprises. When we met at my office, he floored me again with this little speech: "Most of our clientele looks too much like me, white and Jewish. I want to do business with black entrepreneurs. I think diversity in the market-place is the wave of the future, and I've been making it my business to find out who knows people. I'm told you're a major networker. I want you to help me. If you hear of someone thinking about buying a company and you think it's something I might be interested in, give me a call and I'll put somebody on it immediately."

At that time, Drexel Burnham was probably the biggest and most influential investment firm in the nation. It had become a vir-tual money machine, primarily because of its involvement in the incredibly lucrative but risky junk bond market. Later, junk bonds and alleged insider trading by key employees, including Michael Milken, would be the downfall of the company, but at that point it was Wall Street's best bet. So when a major player like Drexel CEO Fred Joseph asked to tap into my network, I plugged him in.

My first response was to tell my staff to alter arrangements for a breakfast being planned to honor executives of companies selected that year for the B.E. 100s top black-owned industrial and service sec-tor companies in America. The scheduled guest of honor was the head of the New York Stock Exchange; I added a second: Fred Joseph.

The breakfast was at the India Club on Wall Street. The invi-tees were all members of the largest black-owned companies in America, as well as many major banking and investment profession-als. The goal was networking at the highest level. And the result was to make headlines around the world. At that meeting, I intro-duced dozens of high-powered black business professionals to Joseph. One of them was financier Reginald Lewis, a brilliant, hard-nosed lawyer and financier who at the time was not widely known outside of our network.

Lewis was already a serious player in the venture capital and leveraged buyout games. Although it received little publicity in the white-owned media, his TLC Group limited partnership had pulled off a $22 million leveraged buyout of the New York–based McCall

Pattern Company in 1983. Lewis spent four years cutting costs and carefully nursing the troubled company back to financial health. In the summer of 1987, he sold it for $90 million, netting a $50 million profit.

Fred Joseph was duly impressed with that and with Reg Lewis, as we all were. I told him I'd dealt with Lewis early in his law career when he worked on a deal in which I purchased two radio stations. A year after I put the two men together at our breakfast meeting, Lewis was backed by Michael Milken and Drexel Burnham in his $985 million leveraged buyout of Beatrice International Food Company, an ice cream, snack and food distribution company with holdings in 31 countries. In making that deal, Lewis accomplished the largest leveraged buyout of overseas assets by an American company ever and created the largest black-owned business in the country. By 1992, before his death from brain cancer, Lewis's TLC Beatrice had revenues of $1.7 billion.

Lewis amassed a fortune estimated at $400 million, and before his death he contributed millions to philanthropic causes, including $1 million to Howard University and $3 million to Harvard Law School, where the Reginald F. Lewis International Law Center is the first Harvard building to be named for an African American. Think what that means to young people in our community.

That is my reward.

Networking and Playing

I'm always trying to cut a deal, whether it involves getting the guy in the health food store downstairs from my office to put extra carrots and celery in my veggie shake—for half the price—or calling on friends in high places to get IBM to let my employees use its private retreat for a weekend or persuading Percy Sutton, Danny Glover, Shaquille O'Neal, Johnnie Cochran and a whole array of other prominent African Americans to join me in a multimillion-dollar investment partnership with Pepsi to open a bottling company in South Africa.

But I derive the most fun from bringing together people in more relaxed social settings and having those gatherings spark real business deals. That is why I have long made it a practice to bring black businesspeople, and a few white ones too, together socially so that they can get to know each other and each other's businesses and maybe one day work together. Whites do it at their private clubs and private schools. We do it at our ski lodge in Vermont, our summer house at Sag Harbor and at our home in Westchester at our annual Super Bowl party.

At these gatherings it would not be unusual to see A. Barry Rand, an executive vice president of Xerox, talking with George Lewis, the treasurer of Phillip Morris. You might well find Maceo Sloan, chairman of Sloan Financial Group, talking with John Jacob, the former National Urban League president who is now executive vice president at Anheuser-Busch, and Ken Chenault, president and COO of American Express. Or you might find Maynard Jackson, the former mayor of Atlanta, talking about that city's successes with Darwin Davis, senior vice president at Equitable. These parties are generally also attended by my sons and their energetic young friends in business, who liven the party with their bold ambitions and innovative thinking.

The point is, I don't put together a bunch of stiffs. I want people who can move the needle on black economic development around the world. But they also understand the importance of socializing—as a way of building and enhancing business relationships. Blacks have long been excluded from such social events in the white-dominated business world, which is one reason that I began the *Black Enterprise* Golf & Tennis Challenge, cosponsored by the Pepsi-Cola Corporation, as a forum for African American businesspeople to network with each other and with selected white business representatives in a relaxed social setting.

If there is a dominant theme to this highly successful event, which is run by my son Johnny, it's not "Let's play." It's "Let's make a deal." Our Challenge has become your opportunity to network. Mannie Jackson, majority owner and CEO of Harlem Globetrotters International, says of his participation, "I met more decision makers at one time than I would run into in a year of trying to do it on my own."

Jackson wasn't just looking for a good tee time when he said that. At one Challenge event alone, he met with representatives from Pepsi, Apple Computers, Reebok and Chrysler, and each one of those meetings bore fruit. In fact, as a result of discussions initiated at the Challenge, Jackson signed a contract with Apple Computer that will have members of the Harlem Globetrotters touring historically black colleges.

Now going into its fourth year, the Golf & Tennis Challenge attracts nearly 1,500 people from the highest echelons of business over the Labor Day weekend. Unlike many other events we sponsor, the Golf & Tennis Challenge is devoted to serious play with perhaps some business on the side, rather than serious business with little time for play.

The golf tournament allows us to make some money while giving our sponsors, including some of their key white executives, greater exposure to the upscale black consumer market. It's a showcase for all that *Black Enterprise* represents, which includes our philosophy on leveraging our collective power for the general good of the black community. That's why the 1996 Challenge was moved from its planned site at La Quinta Resort and Club in La Quinta, California, to protest that state's attacks on affirmative action. It was not the first time the Challenge made its substantial clout felt on behalf of African Americans.

When word got out that not one golf or tennis manufacturer had seen fit to join the 27 corporate backers of the 1994 *B.E.* Challenge, several hundred participants wrote letters to the manufacturers, making it known how they felt about this arrogant disregard for the black consumer market. By the next year, Titleist and Ping, Penn Racquet Sports and Spaulding had signed on. Their awakening was a testament to the tenacity of our sales staff as well as to the leveraged power of those participants who conducted the letter-writing campaign.

Other Challenge sponsors who have shown a commitment to the African American market include Absolut Vodka, American Airlines, American Express, Anheuser-Busch, AT&T, Barbados Tourism Authority, Bell South, Black Entertainment Television, Chase Manhattan Bank, Chrysler Corporation, Clairol, Eastman Kodak, the Equitable, FedEx, Florida Division of Tourism, Frito-Lay, Lands' End, Motorola, PGA of America, Quad Graphics, Reebok, Ryder, Tiffany and Xerox.

Networking with Your Checkbooks

I list these sponsors because I want you to acknowledge their respect for the value of the black market. Recently I asked *Black Enterprise* readers to name the person whose decisions are most critical to the health of our economy. The correct answer was not the president of the United States, nor was it the Federal Reserve Board chairman. The answer was you, the consumer. You are the final arbiter of our economy. Every dollar you spend has the power to create opportunity—or leave it dormant and unfulfilled. As African Americans we have plenty of collective influence on this process—$400 billion and growing in annual income. How we choose to spend those dollars is the most important decision we can make on behalf of our economic empowerment. This is the foundation of the NAACP's call for African Americans to become disciplined consumers.

This is part of networking too—leveraging buying power where it can make the most difference for all African Americans. If Ping golf equipment manufacturers see that their sponsorship of the *B.E.* Challenge translates into increased sales, you can be sure they will come to value the African American market even more. If another sporting goods manufacturer realizes that it is losing sales to one of our sponsors, perhaps it will take the big hint.

By becoming an informed consumer, you can network in this manner too. Look at who advertises and who doesn't advertise in black-owned publications or on black-owned television and radio outlets. Ask for information about ownership structure and hiring practices by companies whose brand names you buy. Find out which companies and products have what I call reciprocal benefit premiums for African Americans. Those premiums would be a commitment to the black market such as hiring and promoting black employees, or corporate support of black groups such as the United Negro College Fund.

The bottom line is this: It should not take a visible public disgrace such as that of Texaco for us to clue in to who in corporate America is doing and saying what. We must maximize all of our resources, including our talents, our knowledge and experience, our relationships and especially our economic influence as consumers, to network together for the economic empowerment of all African Americans.

CHAPTER 5

Starting a Career

Several months ago, my personal assistant decided to return to college, so until I could hire someone new, a temporary worker was sent over by a temp service. Now I had some fears about using a temporary worker in such a critical position, but in this case I was delighted by the performance of this young woman, who immediately impressed me with her willingness to work long hours, her enthusiasm for every task I gave her and her eagerness to learn the skills necessary to do the job effectively. After a few days of observing her, I called off the job search.

In order to have a successful career today, you have to approach it as my assistant did—as an entrepreneur—even if you are working for someone else. Your career is your own private business. You have to market yourself and your abilities and knowledge just as you would a product or service.

You may be selling computer software for a manufacturer, but your real and most important product is yourself. There is probably nothing more daunting in your adult life than trying to decide on what you want to do to make a living and then starting a career. Even with unemployment and inflation dropping, the federal deficit falling and corporate profits rising in double digits, the general mood in the workplace is edgy as we near the end of this century. In general, business is doing well but people still aren't feeling good about it.

A poll showed that more than 100 million Americans are afraid their income won't be enough to pay the bills. U.S. family income has been stagnant since 1973. Census Bureau data shows median family income, after being adjusted for inflation, at $37,838 in 1973 and $38,782 in 1994—even though there was a 56 percent increase in the number of families with two working parents. Little wonder that one-third of all American workers fret that someone in the household will lose a job within a year, according to a poll by the Marist Institute of Public Opinion.

Who can blame them? Between 1989 and the end of 1995, the number of corporate employees who had been laid off reached 3 million. Another 170,000 jobs were cut in the first quarter of 1996—marking a 74 percent increase in downsizings over the first quarter of 1995. Top executives have had huge pay increases, but the average worker's salary has barely kept pace with inflation. Job cuts and the disparity between company profits and worker pay have all but wiped out the concept of company loyalty.

Downsizing, rightsizing, outsourcing and global competition: None of these terms was applicable to the business world when I started out, but they have come to dominate the pages of *Black Enterprise* and other business media in recent years, just as they are the dominant factors in determining how you approach your business career. Most economists, career counselors and futurists agree that these factors will continue to rule the business world for years to come. They predict a very modest economic growth rate of only 2.5 percent for the rest of the decade and into the 21st century. Thus financial and job insecurity will not be easing.

Even as I put this book together, major corporations began a new round of layoffs and firings. AT&T mailed buyout packages to several thousand of its managers. K-Mart closed seven stores after losses for 11 consecutive quarters. The merger of Chase Manhattan and Chemical banks caused an estimated 12,000 layoffs. Companies large and small are trimming the fat and, in some instances, cutting to the bone.

There are some indicators that the ten-year trend in downsizing may be leveling off to a degree, or at least that it is being offset because firms have eliminated obsolete jobs and are now hiring for new jobs created through restructuring. So the good news is that it's getting easier to find a job. The bad news is that it's also getting easier to lose a job. Companies are hiring at a faster clip, but many of the jobs are not considered long-term positions.

In the past, *Black Enterprise* has regularly recommended companies such as AT&T, Equitable, Gannett, General Motors, IBM and Xerox to our black readers because of their long-term commitments to affirmative action. But it is becoming increasingly difficult to find that commitment anywhere today, particularly for African Americans, who can no longer count on affirmative action or any real commitment to minority hiring.

Despite some employers (and politicians) wishing that we would just go away, our numbers continue to grow, our qualifications continue to become more undeniable, and our determination to compete and succeed in business intensifies as more of us realize that the business world offers economic independence—our greatest path to freedom.

At the same time, instability in the workforce and the increasing use of temporary employees has created what Labor Secretary Robert Reich called "the anxious class." African Americans certainly are among the leading members of this group. Affirmative action didn't force anyone to hire us, though it did create an environment that encouraged it. But when California, our largest state, moved to eliminate affirmative action programs in state universities, it opened the floor for a debate that altered that environment. It sent a message to employers that if they don't want to, they don't have to worry about hiring blacks anymore.

Washington-based economist Julianne Malveaux has noted that this new environment presents great challenges for African Americans in the business world. "If you hear that the unemployment rate is 5 percent for the general population, it's 10 percent for blacks; if it takes the average college grad two months to find a job, it takes four months for African Americans. We are always caught between optimism and despair. We have to believe there is hope or else we'll give up."

A recent Gallup Poll showed that many college seniors believe, perhaps too optimistically, that they will attain career success quickly. In the poll, most expected an annual salary of $98,000 by the year 2015. Nearly two-thirds expected their standard of living to be higher than that of their parents 20 years after graduation. I wish them luck. This is not your father's business climate. It probably is not even your oldest sister's.

Workplace 2000 promises to be a tumultuous place compared

to the business environment of the past. Employees of the future will have to be quick-change artists to succeed in the business world. Here are the primary factors that are expected to make this a unique and challenging business environment for everyone, but especially for African Americans.

■ **Short-Order working.** You may be working "on assignment" rather than "on the job." Hired guns rather than long-term employees will dominate in Workplace 2000. Economists say that a greatly increased percentage of the workforce will be working on a short-term contractual basis or as part of a "special team" approach to business. Some predict that workers may have several different employers at any given time. Already, temporary and full-time employment agencies have generated nearly 900,000 of the 4.1 million new jobs created over the last five years.

■ **Multiple-Careerists.** It used to be a truism that the average person had at least eight jobs in his or her career, particularly if they were of West Indian heritage like my father. But now people are expected to change not just jobs, but careers. Research suggests that people in Workplace 2000 will no longer follow one path in their careers. Instead, the average worker will most likely change paths three times over a career; for example, working as a manager, then consulting on management and, finally, teaching management.

■ **Thirty hours a week.** Shorter work weeks (not something I anticipate at my own company) will be the norm as technology increases productivity and the increased number of people in the workforce allows more time off. Some European employers have already shortened work weeks. In the United States, I imagine that many people will decide that the way to benefit from shorter work weeks is to hold a couple of jobs so they can work 60 hours a week instead of 40.

■ **Making nonprofits pay.** Futurists such as economist Jeremy Rifkin predict that the nonprofit sector will expand rapidly as government and corporations cut payrolls and pull back. Rifkin says that the nonprofit sector is already the seventh-largest industry in the nation and growing quickly.

■ **Flex-Time, flex-office, flex-worker.** Already some business managers run the show from home, holding meetings on the Internet and over cellular phones. People find and apply for jobs on-line and even earn advanced degrees without ever leaving home. Companies looking to cut costs are finding that reduced office space is one of the best ways to do it, and so the home office is becoming institutionalized.

Preparing Yourself to Play

So far I haven't provided you with a lot of encouraging news about career opportunities. The reality is that people embarking on business careers, or merely trying to stay in the game, are going to have to be highly competitive. That means you will need a strong background, good education and a dedication to lifelong learning. You will also need continuous computer training, flexibility, networking skills and the ability to market yourself as a commodity in a tight market. Might I suggest that you also develop a "take no prisoners" attitude. It's going to be highly competitive out there, folks.

People ask me all the time what I might have done differently to better prepare myself for a business and entrepreneurial career. The answer is, I would have gotten a law degree, as my son Johnny did. He graduated from Yale Law School and is licensed to practice in several states, yet other than the legal work he does for us on occasion his focus is on business development, new business enterprises and those entities you will read about further into the book.

Still, the law affects everything, and it has enriched his position as well as his perspective on business. I always need lawyers. Buying the Pepsi franchise made a couple of lawyers rich, on Pepsi's side and mine. Setting aside all the jokes about the world having too many lawyers, I see it as a great degree to have. Truth be known, though, I didn't even consider graduate school. Although I have numerous honorary degrees, it would have been nice to have an *Esquire* to finish off my signature. And in today's business environment it would have been a real benefit.

Your level of education will be a major determinant of your ability to compete. The U.S. Bureau of Labor reported several years ago that 14.3 percent of the black working population had four years of college or more, compared to 23.9 percent of the whites. The lower average level of education for blacks—especially in such fields as engineering and computers—explains why blacks, who make up 10 percent of the workforce, were only 6 percent of the executive and administrative ranks of American business at the time of the study in 1988.

The Bureau of Labor Statistics (BLS) projects that of the 25 million jobs created between 1990 and 2005, almost 94 percent will be service related in such fields as retail trade, education, business and health services. Over the next 15 years, computer and data processing services will be the nation's fastest-growing industry, increasing at a rate of 4.9 percent annually and rising to 1.2 million by the year 2000, according to the BLS.

Specifically, forecasters project executive and professional demand for an additional . . .

- 1.6 million teachers
- 598,000 general managers and top executives
- 416,000 computer analysts
- 400,000 engineers
- 340,000 accountants and auditors
- 313,000 engineering, science technicians and technologists
- 206,000 lawyers
- 193,000 financial managers
- 48,000 architects and surveyors

Today's business climate is competitive, bordering on combative, for African Americans. I've really been concerned in recent years with the number of young black people who graduate from good colleges but still cannot find jobs worthy of their level of education.

I have a friend whose daughter recently completed studies at the University of Pennsylvania. She was an honor student, but she is still unemployed. Part of her problem is that she is highly independent and does not want to rely on her father's connections. That makes no sense.

Everyone, black, white or otherwise, uses whatever is available to them to make it in this world. Do you think the sons and daughters of the Kennedy family don't use their family connections? Those family and social connections are *their* form of affirmative action. If we are going to be in this game, we can't be too proud to use the same strategies that our competitors have used for generations.

In the 21st-century marketplace, black men and women must

combine technical skills, management expertise and career flexibility to succeed. An overall 22 percent projected increase in the number of executive, managerial and administrative jobs by the year 2000 is largely attributed to the growing complexity of corporate activities, all of which increasingly depend on computer-generated statistics and telecommunications. The rate of growth for these top jobs is significantly less than the booming 66.4 percent rate of 1967 through 1988, but it remains one of the fastest-growing areas of the economy.

Carl R. Tinsley, an engineering graduate of Western Michigan University, represents the "new wave" of computer-literate managers. When I learned of him he just had been hired as operations manager for Chicago-based Best Foam Fabricators, Inc., which that year grossed $12.5 million and was number 74 on the *B. E. 100s* list. Before taking that job, he was a regional industrial and quality engineering manager for Great Northern Nekoosa Corporation, a paper products manufacturer based in Atlanta, but his job had been eliminated in a merger with Georgia-Pacific.

Tinsley had not panicked when his Nekoosa job was eliminated. He was on the hot track, with technical and managerial skills in statistical process control and total quality assurance. He also had a track record for reducing costs, making him even more appealing to cost-conscious employers. No surprise, then, that Tinsley received several job offers. "My opportunities came because of my background in meshing management with technical skills," Tinsley says. "If you can combine the two, the job market is definitely yours."

Getting into the Game

In many ways, finding a job is the first test of your ability to survive and thrive as a black person in the white-dominated business world. Do you have the energy and the commitment to go after the career and life that you want? Are you willing and able to use every resource, every contact, every possible approach to the problem of finding that first job? Here are 11 tips for job-hunting in Workplace 2000.

I. Don't wait for a job to find you.

No matter what your age or experience level, you have to be realistic and determined in selecting your career course these days. If you are a college student looking at your first job after graduation, you can't rely solely on a placement office setting you up. Nor is it any longer a given that the Fortune 500 will be hounding you with recruiters, no matter what school you attended or how high you ranked in your class. Go after what you want.

When I left the Army and made up my mind that I wanted to look for a job in real estate, I didn't know anyone in the business, so I got the Brooklyn yellow pages and walked around in my First Lieutenant paratrooper's uniform applying for jobs in real estate offices. The first guy who hired me said I looked like a 6-foot-tall Christmas tree. I may well have looked like Mr. Christmas, but I was also looking for my job and I got one.

Universities and colleges are reporting that campus recruiters for DuPont and Kodak are dwindling and in their place are recruiters for lower-paying retailers such as J.C. Penney and The Gap. It's also said that while the larger companies often came looking to fill a half-dozen job openings, the smaller ones have only one or two positions available. Your determination and ingenuity will be tested, and your success will be a measure of your ability to make it over the long term.

2. Think of your job search as a full-time job.

The old notion that success is a marathon, not a relay race, has never been more true. It can take 6 to 12 months just to find a job. It's a process that requires careful, strategic planning, which can be particularly difficult if you are a student trying to finish course work or a downsized worker in need of a job to pay the bills. Career placement services are definitely helpful. Studies show that students who use them get better jobs more quickly within their fields of study. It also helps to scan career files at the local library and to network with professionals in your chosen field. The earlier you get involved with professional organizations and human resource people in your areas of interest, the better. Leave no source untapped.

My mother was always finding me jobs during summers and college breaks through her network of friends. Mr. Louis Pennyfeather was the postmaster for one of the major postal stations in Brooklyn, and he was also our neighbor. When I came home from college one Christmas break, it became obvious that I needed to make some money in order to return after the break, so my parents said, "We'll talk to Mr. Pennyfeather." The next thing I knew, I was working on "the scheme," which sounded intriguing but meant standing in front of 50 boxes and sorting mail into them. I had to meet Mr. Pennyfeather at his house, and we would drive to a substation where I worked from 5 A.M. until 6 P.M. without any flaking off. Thanks to him, I earned enough money to pay for books, food and all of the above for the next semester. My point: Use all contacts that are available to you, whether they come from down the street or up the family tree.

Finding a firm where your skills will be appreciated requires a lot of research. Today's job market generally demands that workers going into an interview know a lot more about the company than may have been expected during the boom years. That is especially true for fresh college graduates looking at entry-level positions. A key area of research for African Americans is gauging the commitment, if any, that a company has to hiring, promoting and retaining people of color. A commitment to diversity can be measured by examining the company's hiring record, its promotion history, whether there are mentorship programs for blacks and whether there is a plan—and a budget—in place for increasing diversity.

3. Jump in with an internship.

Last year I took our summer interns at *Black Enteprise* to lunch to let them know that they had made an excellent contribution to the company during their tenure. There were seven of them. Each year we get nearly 110 applicants from colleges all over the country, although we always make sure to select one from Morgan State, my alma mater, and one from Brooklyn College, my wife's.

Once considered an opportunity just for students, internships are increasingly available to people who have already spent years, and even decades, in the workplace. The *National Directory of Internships* has reported an 8 percent increase in the number of companies offering midcareer internships over the last five years. Universities, job hotlines, and Forty Plus, a national organization that helps people over 40 find work, are good sources for internship opportunities. These internships are growing because companies that have downsized find them a good and inexpensive way to fill openings temporarily. Internships are available in a wide range of fields from health care to television production. Some pay a salary;

others offer college credit. They can last a month or even several years, and many offer flexible hours.

4. Don't be afraid to think small.

With larger companies downsizing and often placing priority on rehiring former employees at lower wages, it may be wise to look to smaller companies. While the wages may not be as good, or the prestige as high, smaller companies often provide you with the opportunity to take on more tasks and gain experience across a wider range so that you can later market yourself as a generalist with many skills. In the high-tech field, in particular, small companies have a habit of growing big fast, and if you get in early the opportunities can be incredible.

The real estate job I took right after leaving the military was with a very small company, but its size meant there was no opportunity for anyone to coast. I found myself thrown in with the sharks and I had to be on the alert at all times. You didn't go to the restroom if there was a chance of a customer walking in the door, because your co-workers would steal him or her away. I learned a lot about surviving in the business world in that little office.

5. Be flexible.

A lot of young people say that certain jobs aren't good enough for them, but Bob Beavers realized that any job is just a starting point. Beavers started as a hamburger cook and is now a senior vice president of the McDonald's Corporation. He was obviously hard-working, determined, open-minded and flexible.

I had no concept of being a publisher, or having a beverage distributor's business, when I started out. But I did know that I wanted to be in business, and when the time came I was confident in my ability to learn the publishing field and the beverage industry. I was also flexible.

Today you will have to have the same desire and self-confidence and more. Because of downsizing, young people just entering the workforce may well have to take a temporary or contract job to get into their chosen field, while more experienced people may do well to market themselves as consultants by using their proven skills to work independently. Be adaptable. Be open-minded. Be flexible.

6. Think of yourself as an entrepreneur, even if you are an employee.

Loyalty to your employer is commendable. Blind loyalty to your employer is dangerous. Layoff notices are far more prevalent than gold watches these days, so while keeping your nose to the grindstone, you have to keep your eyes open for opportunity and your mind ever alert for fresh information that will increase your value in the greater marketplace.

In addition, the entrepreneurial mind-set is increasingly valued by organizations that are reshaping themselves and the way they view their employees. Many have found that their past pursuit of profits has been at the expense of building relationships with customers. Now they are looking for employees with entrepreneurial leadership skills who can get close to customers and make decisions on how best to serve them and secure their business.

7. Develop specific skills for general application.

With such rapid shifts in technology today, it is probably best not to base your career goals on the growth of a particular industry. Instead, pursue a broader path such as sales, finance and data processing. People who want to rise in management should hone their skills in one or two of those areas and then be ready, willing and able to move from one industry to another if necessary.

The fastest-growing occupations appear to be in human services, computer engineering and science, systems analysis, special education, paralegal work and physical therapy. Each of these fields will need salespeople, finance experts and data processors. If you know a particular area and can apply that knowledge generally, your opportunities will be much greater than if you're locked into a narrow specialty.

In inner-city areas, knowing a second language such as Spanish can be a home run. If you can master Chinese or Japanese, you can pretty much pick and choose among career choices. At least half of the corporations I work with are looking at ways to develop more business with the Pacific Rim countries.

My friend Calvin Williams grew up in the early '50s with me and came out of Brooklyn College with a mastery of Chinese. I used to tease him about being a black guy who could speak Chinese. I said the only thing he was good for was ordering dinner in Chinatown. But Calvin had the last laugh. After college, he had his choice of a half-dozen job offers.

8. Stay on top of shifting market demand.

In a market that favors those who can apply their skills to whatever industry needs them, it seems wise to remain alert to opportunities and shifting demographics. That way you can stay one step ahead of either the corporate executioner or new demand.

For example, during much of my business career, there has been a scramble to reach the Baby Boom generation as it marched through the teenage years into college, young adulthood and parenting. Now the Baby Boomers are aging, which is creating a demand for skills in a wide range of areas related to their changing needs. The desire of Boomers to cut health care costs may well create a demand for assisted-care and long-term nursing facilities. With a decrease in the length of costly hospital stays, expect a tremendous demand for home health aides, physical therapists and assistants.

9. Be creative.

In Workplace 2000, periods of unemployment will be common, so workers will have to develop creative ways to find work and market themselves. It may be that to get the job you want, you'll have to take two or three less desirable jobs to maneuver your way into position. Very few people run on a straight and narrow career course. Most take many twists and turns and make the best of them. I was no exception.

My friend George Edwards, former president of the National Black Network, a radio information consortium, is now retired but had as varied and successful a career as nearly anyone I can think of. He started his career at British Airways while still in college, and within six months had worked his way through the reservations training program to become a supervisor and then the first black management trainee in the company's history. He was only 22 years old, and it was 1958, and it was such a major accomplishment for an African American in the white-dominated business world of that era that *Ebony* did a story calling him the first black marketing executive in the history of American aviation.

As Edwards himself jokes, you didn't have to do a whole lot

there for a while to accomplish a first as a black person in business. He became a celebrity, but it was for all the wrong reasons, even if he was doing the right things. Edwards remained at British Airways for seven years before joining the marketing team at Pepsi, where he was general sales manager of its New York bottling plant at the age of 29.

He went on to become director of marketing for one division of Pepsico, general manager of another and director of franchise development for its international division. Then he was a vice president of marketing at Heubelin in Hartford, Connecticut, which owned Kentucky Fried chicken, Smirnoff, Grey Poupon and many other great name brands. He was with Heubelin for five years before going to the National Black Network for twelve years.

Edwards often notes that he only filled out one job application in his life. The rest of his jobs found him. Of course, early on he established a reputation for doing great work, no matter what the job was. Your reputation, he says, is your most valuable job-hunting tool.

10. Dress appropriately.

When it comes to personal appearance, I take a firm stand and make no apologies to my employees or anyone else. I do not believe in dress-down days, hours, minutes or seconds. If you are going to be in this game called business, you have to wear the uniform. That uniform, for better or worse, is conservative dress.

My son Johnny ran head on into my rules on business dress when he came to my office for a meeting shortly after graduating from law school. He was impeccably turned out in a business suit, but he had a gold stud in one ear. He told me that he and a white friend had decided to get their ears pierced one day over lunch. I told him the white guy would be a CEO in ten years while Johnny was out chasing ambulances. I banned him from my office until his ear was unadorned.

African Americans are already saddled with offensive stereotypes and racist assumptions. We cannot afford to go to work looking as if we're merely stopping by the office on the way to a party. Classic, conservative clothing—with few exceptions—is the only way to dress in the business office. Impeccable grooming is a must. You don't need to set yourself apart by your appearance. You need to distinguish yourself by your performance.

11. Be early.

In the military I learned to be at meetings before they knew they wanted me there. I'll never forget the time, years later, when I let myself slide a bit and showed up late for a meeting with the chief executive officer at Tiffany. I was 15 minutes late, and he very politely told me that I had wasted his time and he did not appreciate it. He was right, and after he made his point, I decided I would never be late for another business appointment in my life.

Perhaps the most offensive and most tenacious racial stereotype is that of CPT, or "colored people's time." It may be true that in black culture punctuality is not a priority, but in the culture of business it is unprofessional to be late. If you aren't certain how to get to a meeting, scout it out the day before. If you can't do that, make sure you have a telephone number so that you can call if you get lost or if you are running late.

Where to Look for Work

Studies of trends in the nation's broad regional economies confirm the drift of jobs to the South and West. Following are some snapshots of regional employment trends to give you an idea of what is available in different parts of the country.

If I were just starting out, I would go south in a heartbeat. I really enjoy the quality of life there, where I think people still emphasize family values. Obviously there is the desire to do well there, but the pace of life allows for working with the Boy Scouts and contributing to the community, cutting the grass and getting to know your neighbor.

I have many friends in the South, including Roy and Rudolph Terry, owners of Terry Manufacturing, the B.E. 100s company that made the Dream Team uniforms for the Olympics. They also make more than half the uniforms worn by McDonald's employees. I envy their lifestyles because they seem to get so much done while still spending a lot of time with their families in Atlanta and Alabama.

■ **Northeast.** The major urban centers along the power corridor stretching from Washington, D.C. to Boston still contain the highest concentration of jobs in the financial services, accounting and legal industries. These fields have experienced increased demand for sophisticated computer software and data analysis, which can also help preserve the manufacturing base. Many big insurance companies are also headquartered in the region. For those with research skills, the growing pharmaceutical companies of northern New Jersey offer stable long-term employment.

▪ **Midwest.** Many of the same trends bedeviling the Northeast rustbelt states have also swept through cities such as Chicago, Cleveland and St. Louis, where service industries are replacing manufacturing. The explosive growth of telemarketing in states such as Nebraska offers opportunities. Sales of financial services products are projected to remain strong.

▪ **South.** As blacks reverse the direction of the post-World War I migration that filled northern cities with workers from Mississippi, Alabama, Georgia, Louisiana and Texas, sustained business growth is projected from the southern Atlantic seaboard to the Rio Grande. Many of the migrants are retirees, opening up opportunities in health care and the development of elder-care facilities. Population surges have also increased demand for food distribution, retail services and teachers.

▪ **West Coast.** As the country's fastest-growing and most ethnically diverse region, the Pacific coast states offer challenging opportunities for human resource professionals who might find their services less welcome in the declining cities of the Atlantic coast. The California population boom has created demand for architects, especially those experienced in designing habitats for the elderly. Silicon Valley, despite computer industry slumps, is still the place for engineering professionals in the high-tech field.

Searching for a Job On-Line

In the interest of full disclosure here, let me note that while I recently spent a half million dollars upgrading the computer system at *Black Enterprise*, I am still trying to figure out how to turn mine on. That said, take note: Anyone wanting to get going in business today, whether as an entrepreneur or working for someone else, had better get with it and get on-line.

In a recent reader survey, 91 percent of *Black Enterprise*'s subscribers said they use a computer at work, while nearly 84 percent have one at home. Interestingly, 43 percent said they spend one to five hours a week on-line; 29 percent spend six to ten hours a week on-line. And 83 percent asked the magazine to provide more information on the Internet.

Whether you surf the Internet or subscribe to America Online, BlackAmerica Online or other on-line services, you can find scores of job databases, résumé banks and job-matching services—200 or more by some accounts. In addition, computer stores are well stocked with job-search and résumé-writing software. On-line job-hunting is particularly appealing to some minorities because the Internet is color-blind. When you apply on-line for a job, your qualifications get first consideration, and generally race is not a factor in the early going.

The process of job hunting on-line can be time consuming, and if you haven't had extensive experience on-line there is a lot to learn. So on-line searching shouldn't be considered a substitute for the traditional methods of searching the wants ads, mailing out résumés and, most important, networking with people in your field of interest.

Although the Internet has been around for 15 years, employers have been slow to go on-line to search for job candidates, but the explosion of "home pages" has greatly increased the number using it. A recent poll of 435 human resource professionals by Lee Hecht Harrison found that 47 percent use the Internet to recruit and 31 percent use résumé banks. Among those recruiting on-line, naturally, are high-tech telecommunications companies, which are among the best growth industries for job seekers.

Danny Thomas, national employment manager of the business market division at MCI Telecommunications in Atlanta, and 16 other MCI recruiters across the country use Internet services like Job Bank USA and Online Career Center to find technical and sales support professionals. Low-tech companies also conduct electronic searches because they can seek people with specific qualifications.

Marianne Blanchard, human resources consultant at Abt Associates, a social policy research and management consulting firm in Cambridge, Massachusetts, looks for minority candidates on Net-Noir, LatinoNet and the *Ebony* Room on-line. (She notes that, in general, those who respond to her on-line inquiries are more qualified than those who answer newspaper ads.)

Greg Jensen of Caribou, Maine, hadn't taken job hunting on the Internet seriously until he plugged into Career Mosaic, a World Wide Web site, and found hundreds of computer industry job listings. In minutes, he had copied his résumé from Word for Windows, typed a short cover letter and e-mailed both to a company that had openings in interactive television. Jensen received a call the next day, and within a month he had moved from a $55,000-a-year job to an $80,000-a-year job with Tele-TV, an interactive television company formed by Bell Atlantic, Nynex and PacTel.

Job bank software provides access to hundreds of ads posted on electronic bulletin boards. Most services get their listings directly from employers, but some cull them from newspapers and other sources. As a result, the jobs listed may sometimes no longer be available by the time you see them, so before buying any job bank software, be sure its listings are updated regularly. Also, look for software that allows you to target jobs according to industry, geography, position, company and salary.

Job banks are also available on bulletin board services (BBSs), which often require a lot of work to search. There are helpful books on on-line job-hunting that provide lists of BBSs and their addresses. The best BBSs list various jobs and companies, but most usually target a select audience. BBSs can come and go quickly, so don't be discouraged if the telephone number given is disconnected. There are plenty more to try.

Résumé banks are another helpful on-line job-hunting tool. They allow you to market your qualifications 24 hours a day, seven days a week. The cost of posting your résumé in a database is usually less than $100. In some cases it might even be free if the database is run by large organizations looking for new hires. Your résumé can remain posted for a few months to a year. These banks also can have short life spans, so be sure to call before sending your résumé and enrollment fee.

A key to résumé databases is using catch phrases that employers type in to do their searches. If you're looking for an accounting job, use *accounting*, and if you would like to work for Price Waterhouse, use the firm's name. Usenet is a high-profile Internet "newsgroup" of job and career services and its "welcome" posting offers guidelines on how to post your résumé for each newsgroup. Many of the jobs are listed by employment agencies or recruiters.

Job-matching services are especially recommended because they act as a liaison between on-line candidates and employers. Many are free to the job seeker, while some charge a fee of $10 to $50. When a match is made, a good job-matching service will call and ask the applicant for a résumé, which will be given to the prospective employer. This safeguard is important to ensure that your résumé doesn't get delivered to your current employer, causing problems you probably don't need. You can also request to block out certain employers.

Be suspicious of any electronic service that doesn't provide an actual street address and customer service phone number. If that information is missing, it might not be legitimate.

Again, the Internet is only one tool for job-hunting. You have to decide what works best for you, but "electronic hiring" is certainly becoming a major part of the job-search field. If you make use of it, as well as networking, job hotlines and trade and specialty publications, you'll enhance your ability to find a job in a highly competitive environment.

Thinking Temporary Long-Term

Many young people leave college and enter the job market today with unreasonable expectations, and when confronted with cruel reality they panic. A better response to a tight job market, or to any challenge, is to face reality and work within it.

If someone shows spirit and eagerness to learn, most employers—like myself—will go out of their way to give him or her every opportunity to succeed.

Those who face the greatest challenges in the volatile job market of today are the oldest and youngest members of the workforce. Companies often feel that veteran employees are overpaid while newcomers lack the experience and expertise needed to compete.

One outgrowth of this is the rise in hiring of temporary workers during high- and low-workload cycles. In 1994 almost 25 percent of America's workforce were contingent workers—temps and independent contractors. From 1990 to 1995, temporary and full-time employment agencies were responsible for close to 900,000 of the 4.1 million new jobs created.

More and more people will be working on a short-term contractual basis in Workplace 2000. It is important that African Americans not neglect the trend because they consider temporary work to lack prestige. It used to be that most temporary employees were clerical or blue-collar workers, but the temporary market and perceptions of temporary work have changed. As more people move in and out of permanent positions, the stigma of temp work as a less desirable form of employment is diminishing. Temporary workers now run the gamut from administrative assistants to highly specialized technicians, accountants, engineers, lawyers and middle- and even senior-level managers. About 40 percent still are clerical, but there have been dramatic increases in the use of temporary workers, particularly in health care, where even doctors have joined the temporary service pool of talent.

One common misperception is that companies hire temporary workers as a way to save money on salaries and benefits. According to a Conference Board survey, only 12 percent of the firms contacted cited lower costs as a reason for using temp workers. Some say temp costs are higher because a company must pay the temp service a 25 to 30 percent markup fee for its referrals. In some instances, a company may pay even more for a temp than for a permanent employee because the temp may have skills that are needed immediately.

With the increasing competition for temporary workers, agencies are offering better benefits, including medical insurance, paid holidays, vacations and 401(k) plans, depending on length of service. Some provide dependent-care reimbursement accounts and tuition refunds, as well as tutorials and training to develop a strong workforce.

The National Association of Temporary and Staffing Services reports that there were more than 2 million temporary workers in 1995. Temp work, which can last from a few days to more than a year, now accounts for 1.8 percent of total U.S. employment. If you include independent contractors, America's contingent workforce tops 20 percent. In the past, temp work may have been less attractive because it meant a lack of job security and the inability to build long-term relationships with co-workers or bosses, but those problems are no longer unique to temporary work. Who has job security these days?

On the positive side, those who enjoy temp work say that it

offers flexibility, independence, competitive salaries and the chance to gain valuable experience. Temp work can also get you in the door so that you can showcase your talents and energy to win a permanent position.

It is important to select a temporary employment agency carefully, however, because not all have the best interests of workers in mind. I encourage you to look first to those owned and operated by African Americans. Not only will they have a greater understanding of your situation, but they may well work harder to get you where you want to go. Some temporary employment agencies have been known to send temps to jobs in which they have no interest or for which they have no training. Some don't have as big a client list as they may pretend to have. Here are five tips for choosing a temporary agency.

1. Find an agency that treats temps like individuals. Avoid clearinghouses that simply process people. Some agencies go out of their way to develop a team spirit, with employee-of-the-month awards, recognition for good attendance and company gatherings.

2. Choose an agency based on recommendations from people you respect. Then call for references. Try to speak with employees as well as representatives of companies that use the agency. Shop around.

3. Look for an agency offering benefits that fit your lifestyle. Many firms offer health and vacation benefits. Inquire about the required qualifications.

4. Locate an organization that shows concern about you as an employee. The firm should do troubleshooting for you and be an advocate or intermediary if you have any on-the-job problems.

5. If you have a choice of geographic location, choose an area where there is a demand for your skills so that employers will pay more.

Finding a career that challenges you and allows you to grow and expand your talents and your worth in the marketplace is critical. In the next chapter, I'm going to help you look at the opportunities that exist out there for African Americans as we enter the next century.

CHAPTER 6

Career Opportunities

In the course of running my businesses each day, I make scores of phone calls. I'm on the phone on the way into the office in Manhattan from our home in Westchester. I'm on the phone all day in the office. I'm on the phone on the way back home and often well into the night. I've been known to talk business on the telephone while at the beach, at the golf course, and even on ski lifts. At the end of each day, I sit back and ask myself, "Which calls did I make for fun and which calls did I make for business?"

The truth is, it is often difficult for me to know the difference because I take so much pleasure in what I do. I know it sounds trite, but it's true: I have a ball conducting business. I enjoy developing business relationships and then building social relationships from them. In fact, I can't think of too many of my long-term business relationships that are not just as much social ties. This is the subtle Graves way of delivering a message: I want you to work hard. I want you to fight for your right to compete on a level playing field with white people. I want you to make a lot of money so your kids and grandkids can have a good life. But I want you to have a good life too.

That means taking pleasure in your work and in your career. It may mean working for yourself rather than for someone else. It may mean a long and circuitous journey to get to a place in your career that is fulfilling and meaningful for you. Amid all the turmoil in the business world, there is opportunity out there, but first you have to decide what sort of work best suits your individual tastes, talents and desires.

Above all else, I urge you to pursue a career that is a passion and not just a paycheck. I know it may not always happen at the beginning, but if you are always working toward a career that involves doing something you truly love to do or something that you find fulfilling, it adds to the quality of your life.

People too often enter the workforce and after several years realize that they really don't have a passion for what they are doing. It's just a job. It is wise, though, to consider who you are and what you want before you plunge into the workforce. And when your vision shifts, try to shift your career to suit. I originally set out on a military career, but after a time I realized I wanted a less structured life for myself and my family. I decided to get out into the business world and find what I had a passion for. I have never regretted that decision, even though I still think I would have looked awfully good in the uniform of a four-star general.

Traditionally, the best employment opportunities for African Americans have been in public service—federal, state or local government jobs—because the private sector was largely closed to us. The first real breakthroughs were in local and federal government hiring during the Kennedy and Johnson administrations. Blacks poured into government jobs where the pay was competitive, the benefits were substantial and there was opportunity for advancement. But the Post Office is no longer regarded as the great provider for African Americans.

Uncle Sam Isn't the Boss He Used to Be

My late Aunt Olga worked for years for the New York State Department of Motor Vehicles (DMV). She found security there, though she didn't fit the usual sullen worker profile. I shouldn't say this, for fear of having my car listed as stolen, but it has always seemed to me that the DMV's real mission is to teach the driving public humility since anything you get from them requires standing in long lines and bowing to rudeness and inefficiency. Aunt Olga was the exception to the rule. She remained on the job there for more than 20 years and somehow retained her pleasant personality the entire time. She found a secure government job. But those days are long gone.

African Americans now make up 16.8 percent of the federal workforce. About one-third of them have clerical jobs, which are among the most vulnerable during layoffs because of lack of tenure. Under union rules, when a reduction in the workforce occurs, an employee with high seniority can avoid being laid off by retreating into a lower-grade employee's position. The practice, commonly known as "bumping," often results in the lower-level employee being out of a job. Instead of clerical help, many government workers now have personal computers, eliminating more jobs traditionally held by African Americans.

In response to calls for smaller, more efficient government, Congress and the White House passed the Work Force Restructuring Act of 1993, which is designed to reduce the federal workforce by 272,900 employees between 1993 and 1999. The cuts were hastened by the Republican takeover of the House and Senate in 1993. Buyouts have by and large gone to white male workers, but continued haggling over the federal budget does not bode well for government workers in general. Nor does the fact that both the Department of Commerce and the Department of Energy have been targeted for elimination by the Republican Congress.

Federal employment counselors have been warning that they expect downsizing to increase at an accelerated pace in years to come. While state and local government jobs increased slightly last year, the overall outlook is not promising. New York State Comptroller H. Carl McCall notes that since December 1994, New York City has cut about 11,000 government jobs. A stagnant economy and tax cuts have limited opportunities in New York State government. "If you look at the numbers, realism suggests that we shouldn't be steering people toward the public sector. We should be encouraging them toward private sector opportunities," he says.

Where the Jobs Are

The Council of Economic Advisors recorded 8.4 million new jobs in 1994 and 1995. Demographic and economic trends indicate three general areas of growth in the coming years.

▪ Outsourcing—independent companies that offer everything from management consulting to benefits administration, payroll, marketing, mailroom and transportation services to Fortune 500 companies.

- Computer technology, telecommunications, multimedia software and on-line entertainment. Computer systems analysts, software engineers, programmers and trainers are among the scores of openings in this rapidly developing field.
- Health care and other services for the aging Baby Boomers.

There are already reports of a shortage of medical expertise in health care for the aging. Physical therapists, transportation services for the elderly, home care and nursing homes are other related growth areas. The need for managers to run health care businesses has grown enormously with the demand for cost-efficient health care.

The other category most often cited by those who look ahead is knowledge workers, problem solvers who can apply their knowledge and training across a wide range of disciplines. Actuaries, accountants, career counselors, engineers and MBAs fit into this category, as do lawyers and human relations experts.

The undiminished demand for knowledge workers is part of the reason so many engineers, who fit into the technicians category, are pursuing graduate degrees to enhance their marketability. Take the hint. The greatest way to increase your own opportunities is to further your education, training and retraining with constant learning throughout your career.

Emerging Technology, Growing Opportunity

For blacks and others entering Workforce 2000, it appears that many of the greatest opportunities will be in computer and telecommunications technology. Labor Bureau forecasters say that technicians will represent one-fifth of the workforce by 2005 and the number of jobs in computer-related fields will grow by 90 percent.

No occupation will be unaffected by the technological revolution. Farmers are already carrying notebook computers aboard their tractors and combines to calculate the best use of fertilizers and weed killers and monitor the growth of crops. Journalists are filing stories from the most remote locations with portable computers and cellular phones. Illustrators "paint" on the computer keyboard. My grandchildren play games on CD-ROMs as naturally as we played stickball in the street.

Industrial designer David Rice, chairman of the Organization of Black Designers in Washington, D.C., offers this cautionary tale: "When I first started all I needed was a drafting table, a T-square and some basic drawing tools to go into business. Now if you are going to be competitive, you're looking at a minimum investment of $7,000 to $10,000 in computer equipment and training—be it on-the-job or formal."

Computers and sophisticated software have raised productivity and been responsible, in part, for some of the downsizing in corporate America. But new technologies are also creating opportunities in the job market. There is a growing rift in the job market. Whose side do you want to be on? Are you going to be one of those who embrace the technology and thrive? Or are you going to find yourself locked on the outside of this major market? At minimum, you need to have a basic mastery of computers, the Internet and word processing.

Low-Tech Jobs in High-Tech Fields

You don't have to be a computer whiz to work in high-tech, although a degree in computer science certainly doesn't hurt. Dyetra Hall, an associate technical writer at Lotus Development Corporation, has such a degree, but she says only a basic understanding of computers and technology is necessary for her work writing documentation for manuals and on-line help text for programs like Lotus Notes. "All you really need to be a technical writer are good writing skills and elementary knowledge of computer lingo, such as the difference between hardware and software," she notes.

Technology companies do more than create hardware or software. Many also provide training courses in various operational applications for their employees, opening the door for advancement from within. Outsourcing is also increasingly being embraced by high-tech companies, so there will be opportunities for individuals working as consultants or freelance experts. Among other varied high-tech job opportunities are . . .

■ On-line content developers. Journalists and other writing professionals as well as graphics designers will be needed to create and manage the growing number of Web sites and on-line publications.

■ Technical trainers. Technological advancements require trainers. Companies will need experts to train staffs on technology innovations.

■ Digital security. With information fast becoming the new form of commerce, more sophisticated means of securing digital assets will be necessary. For example, special encryption codes will be needed to secure on-line bank account information to inhibit digital thieves.

■ High-tech lawyers. The many new forms of business coming out of the high-tech field have created a new area of specialization for lawyers, who are called upon to make the case for legal freedoms, protections and limitations in this arena.

Telecommunications Is Calling

My nephew Walter Kydd is a great example of an African American who has built a career in high technology. Even as I write this, Walter is on a top-secret mission overseas for the U.S. Air Force where he is a specialist in high-tech electronics. An excellent student with a perfect grade point average, he says his technological know-how has added $30,000 a year to his military pay, and when he leaves the service, if he ever leaves, his opportunities will be virtually unlimited. Meanwhile, he enjoys the ultimate bonus: Walter is having a *very* good time working out of the Pentagon, so good that he turned down a promotion so that he could remain in the field.

Many of the best opportunities over the next several decades will undoubtedly be in the high-tech telecommunications industry, where firms will spend billions of dollars to develop new technologies and information-transmission systems to serve the information superhighway. Made up of several different components—telephone services (wired, wireless and cellular), broadcast (cable and satellite) and computers (hardware and software)—the telecommunications industry is exploding with the development of new technologies and applications every day.

Stampp Corbin provides a perfect example of how a savvy

entrepreneur can ride the telecommunications boom to riches. Corbin is the CEO of Resource One Computer Systems, a corporation that resells and distributes computer products. A former salesman for IBM and Honeywell, Corbin acquired a majority interest in Resource One in 1992 and engineered a turnaround that took the firm from $500,000 in losses on revenues of $12 million to 1993 revenues of $18.2 million and a profit margin that "he conceals with a grin."

Based in Columbus, Ohio, Resource One aggressively courts the regional Bell companies, pushing computer products and systems from top manufacturers such as Sun Microsystems, IBM and AST. Clients include Pacific Bell, Nynex, Bell South, Bell Atlantic and Ameritech.

For example, in 1995 Corbin's firm partnered with AT&T to establish a Technology Acquisition Center inside AT&T's Columbus Works manufacturing facility. The center provides equipment and support services for AT&T's laboratories, administration, testing facilities and production. "AT&T was looking at a better way to acquire computer technology, decrease the number of vendors they were using, control their costs and decrease nonconformity in their equipment. . . . So they basically outsourced that function to Resource One," says Corbin, whose firm has become indispensable for his telecommunications clients.

Serving the New Tele-Technology

Clearly you don't need to work for a big company to be successful in aligning with the telecommunications giants. Efficient companies with a strong understanding of new technologies, the financial resources to provide quality service, a solid track record of success with major prime contractors and responsiveness to client needs are vital assets. If small businesses devise strategies to serve the needs of companies developing the advances in technology, they'll be in a position to get rich twice—during the development stage and after the new technology has become popular.

Wireless and cellular services provide a good example of how opportunities are created within the telecommunications industry. By 1994 the cellular telephone industry already had more than 9 million service subscribers and accounted for more than $12 billion in revenues. Manufacturers of spin-off products such as pagers and beepers benefited greatly from this explosion.

As the telecommunications industry expands at a dramatic pace, the demand for products and services to aid that expansion increases with it. Those who look for opportunities at such companies, or by starting their own, will find plenty of them. Industry experts project that personal communications services and interactive video and data services will experience growth similar to that of the cellular phone industry. These new platforms provide the foundation for everything from sending wireless faxes to allowing people thousands of miles apart to play interactive video games.

My friend the black entrepreneur and financier Maceo Sloan, CEO of Sloan Financial Group in Durham, North Carolina, took advantage of the opportunities in this field when he led a group of investors in a successful bid for five personal communications services licenses that will provide national coverage. Under the name PCS Development Corporation, the group is expected to use its license to provide wireless communications that could link fax machines, pagers, portable computers and cellular phones. I am thrilled by Maceo's success (and I particularly admire his new corporate jet).

Plugging into the Cable Boom

The greatest opportunities for small businesses, however, are not in purchasing such licenses but in assisting in the development of such systems. There will be substantial need in cable television for employees and companies that provide software and programming and for those that lay wire and cable.

Bell Atlantic and AT&T Network Systems are building a full-service network to provide on-line shopping and on-demand movies that can be dialed up over telephone lines. They will need to partner with smaller companies to provide wiring, software and transmission equipment. In other words, AT&T will distribute subcontracts to firms to install wiring and setup boxes in homes, provide construction services for telephone lines and cable installation, supply mechanical hand tools and perform maintenance services. Both AT&T and Bell have agreed to goals of 15 percent participation by businesses owned by minorities or women.

Cable companies such as Time Warner Cable, TeleCable Corporation and Comcast are all upgrading cable lines to handle the increased load of telephone voice and data services. With cable's capacity increasing to 500 channels, there is expected to be a massive need for both game and video programming. The SEGA channel, once headed by the late African American CEO Stanley B. Thomas Jr., has responded to the demand for video games by offering up to 50 video games on cable systems using a pay-for-play format.

The need for computer hardware and software has exploded with the growth of the telecommunications industry, and computer companies will need high-tech workers to help them keep pace. Large companies such as Texas Instruments offer lucrative contract opportunities for computer sales and software providers, cable manufacturers and installers, electronic component suppliers and consultants to help develop new telecommunications technology. Texas Instruments minority sourcing engineer Anthony Brown says that they have a minority-owned consulting firm to help them find opportunities for minority suppliers.

Phyllis McCarley, manager of IBM's Minority- and Women-Owned Business Program in Somers, New York, says she is looking for companies that can do everything from supplying pagers and cellular phones to providing video teleconferencing services and moving complex phone systems from one location to another.

Science and Engineering

Despite setbacks for affirmative action, industry demand for black scientists and engineers is stronger than ever. Several programs such as the National Consortium for Graduate Degrees for Minorities in Engineering and Science (GEM) are working to enhance the preparedness of black students. GEM, which matches minority graduate students with industrial companies providing full scholarships and stipends, has grown from just 6 students at 3 universities in 1976 to 300 at 75 universities today. GEM alumni total more than 1,400 and the program, originally established for students seeking master's degrees, has been expanded to include doctorates in science and engineering.

Historically black colleges and universities have graduated about 15 percent of all African American undergraduate science and engineering majors, and they produce about 29 percent of the African American students who go on to complete PhDs in science and engineering.

No matter what career path you choose, you will have to be on top of computer technology to keep pace with the leaders in your field. At a time of rapid change in the job market, you must do all you can to be on top of the wave lest you get lost in its undertow.

Healthy Opportunities in Health Care

When I was working for Kennedy, one of my areas of expertise was health care. Today I am on the board of directors of Aetna, the largest health care company in the world. Through such affiliations, I have learned a great deal about the pressing need for good and accessible health care in this country. That need is growing greater as our population ages. According to a Swahili proverb, "Old age cannot be cured." People aged 85 and older are the fastest-growing segment of the population, and for many of them the extended life span will involve problems with chronic diseases and disabilities associated with the aging process.

Demographic and economic trends indicate a potential entrepreneurial and investment bonanza in the areas of retirement-related, medical and long-term care services for the elderly and their families. Companies will compete to meet the need for medical services to combat arthritis, osteoporosis, Alzheimer's and other afflictions that strike the elderly. There will also be a need for long-term care services to assist the elderly with limitations in the basic activities of daily living, from bathing to meal preparation, according to Alvin E. Headen Jr., professor of economics at North Carolina State University.

Most economists predict that there will be abundant opportunities in health care in the next several decades because of the aging Baby Boomers, but increasing competition, less autonomy and dwindling paychecks vex those generally considered to be near the top of this field—physicians. "Being a doctor is going to get worse before it gets better," warns Leonard Yaffe, a health care analyst at Montgomery Securities in San Francisco. "My concern is that we will make it so unattractive that the applicants will decline in quality and quantity by the time we do anything about it."

There is no doubt, however, that there is a great need for more black physicians. Although a record number of people applied to medical schools in 1995—more than 46,000—there was a 1.7 percent decline in the number of black applicants. Of the 3,595 blacks who applied to the nation's medical schools that year, nearly 40 percent were accepted. But that is not enough.

Still, young people considering a career as a physician need to be realistic in understanding what it takes and what the career options are once the medical degree is obtained. As managed health care transforms doctors into employees rather than autonomous health professionals, the trend has moved away from specialization toward general practice. Physicians are now forced to adapt their goals and expectations to deal with the changing nature of their profession. A medical degree is no longer a guarantee of independence, status or a large income. The average young doctor has debts of $100,000 upon graduating from medical school. In the past, incomes generally helped wipe that debt out quickly, but that is no longer a foregone conclusion.

African Americans will encounter prejudice in medical fields, as anywhere else. Black medical students and young doctors have to play by the rules and get top grades, because we generally don't have the benefit of fathers and grandfathers paving their way in the medical field. Opportunities for a medical education were not as available in the past as they are today.

Black Enterprise once did a cover story on the leading African American doctors in the country and featured Dr. LaSalle D. Leffall Jr., who is president of the American College of Surgeons and the Charles R. Drew professor of surgery at Howard University Hospital. As you get older, you will want to do as I have done and make friends with as many excellent physicians as possible. Dr. Leffall, who is among the best, notes that the opportunities are far greater today than when he was trying to get into medical school. Back then, he noted, African Americans had extremely limited choices, but today most medical schools actively recruit top black students.

"Overall, the opportunities are there, and black medical students can go anywhere they want. I could provide you a long list of people who have done very well, including Dr. Ben Carson who is chief of pediatric neurosurgery at Johns Hopkins Medical Center. That is big time, and he has an excellent reputation," says Leffall.

I second Dr. Leffall's opinion of Ben Carson, whom I have also had the pleasure of meeting and featuring in *Black Enterprise*. One of the pleasures of my life is to have met so many outstanding doctors who are African Americans. Dr. Leffall and Dr. Carson are two of the finest gentlemen in that profession. Another is Dr. Aaron Jackson, chief of urology at Howard University Hospital.

Although there may be greater opportunities to enter medical school, many medical school graduates today find that opportunities for independent medical practice are increasingly rare. Managed care by large health maintenance organizations (HMOs) has taken over. Managed care is designed to contain costs by managing a patient's account from proposed treatment to final payment. HMOs are made up of a network of hospitals, physicians and other health care providers who agree to offer services in return for certain guaranteed patient fees.

For many black physicians, racism and discrimination against their often poorer, sicker patient base can be a barrier to their participation in the HMOs that dominate modern medical coverage. The HMOs, which effectively rule medicine today, view poor blacks as high risks and not cost efficient. To counteract this, some black doctors have formed cooperative partnerships to handle African American patients forsaken by the HMOs. Others have abandoned their practices and moved into administrative positions with HMOs or other health-related businesses.

A physician who has a business background will be valued in a managed care system, maintains Dr. Charles Kennedy of Hayward, California, who left his practice, earned an MBA from Stanford and became a consultant on management and medical issues for hospitals, insurance agencies, pharmaceutical firms and academic institutions.

Even though the doctor's role is changing, there is an even greater need for African Americans who wish to use their gifts to serve one of the highest callings—helping others, particularly those from their own communities.

"The practice of medicine presents the African American physician with unique challenges and rewards," says Dr. Lanus Hall-Daniels, a resident in radiation oncology at Barnes-Jewish Hospital in St. Louis. "Because African Americans are disproportionately affected by numerous serious illnesses, the black physician can minister to a population both underserved and acutely in need. Black physicians have the opportunity to be especially sensitive to the cultural and socioeconomic factors that may impact upon a patient's well-being."

Dr. Hall-Daniels, who did her surgery residency at Howard University—and just happens to be the daughter of one of my great friends—says that when she meets with a black patient for the first time it is quite common for both of them to "heave a simultaneous sigh of relief—an acknowledgment of a shared history."

Personally, as a patient, I feel the same way, and I must note that patronizing black doctors is as important to our community as patronizing other black businesses and professionals. If you're looking for a world-class place to start, Howard University Hospital is marked by outstanding physicians and support services.

Health Care Entrepreneurs

Although the state of health care in this country is in flux, some fields, such as medical supplies and equipment sales, elderly care, temporary help and messenger services, have proved to be viable markets for businesses owned by minorities and women. The U.S. Department of Health and Human Services reports that health expenditures topped $600 billion last year. Medical equipment sales topped $52.7 billion in 1994, according to the Health Industry Manufacturers Association.

While HMOs have made life difficult for some black physicians, other black entrepreneurs have carved out a niche by serving the managed-care marketplace. Branches Medical in Lauderhill, Florida, sells medical supplies to hospitals, doctors and alternative care facilities. CEO Hamish Reed is seeking alliances with other black-owned small businesses to serve hospital conglomerates forming in his region.

Sprint Courier in Waukegan, Illinois, gets about 40 percent of its business from the medical services industry, particularly from huge medical laboratories and hospital conglomerates, according to vice president Ken Massey. Sprint transports blood samples to and from hospitals, doctors and blood banks. The company also transports feeding tubes for premature babies and home health care products. Its primary customer is Abbott Laboratories in Abbott Park, Illinois, a $9.2 billion business.

Courier services, by the way, are a not-so-well-kept secret in the entrepreneurial field. Speedy delivery can mean a quick return on your investment in this business. The average two-person operation grosses $200,000 in annual revenues, according to Bill Goodman, editor of the *Courier Times,* an industry newsletter. That's a healthy payoff for a business that can be run from your home with your own vehicle. Many messengers in larger cities such as New York and Los Angeles make their rounds on bicycles or on public transportation, which can be quicker than dealing with street traffic. They've also been known to use skateboards and roller skates.

Some courier services, such as Sprint, specialize in certain industries, but others have a more general client list. Ron Reid's Corporate Courier Services has more than 635 competing courier companies in New York, yet he has 600 firms on his client list including Con Edison, Philip Morris, UniWorld and McGraw-Hill. With 125 employees and 75 trucks guaranteeing same day or overnight service, Reid's company, which was launched in 1983, now has revenues approaching $3 million.

It is a highly competitive business that like any other can feel the pinch in a tight economy, but in general, courier companies have low overhead and can adjust. Most hire independent contractors who supply their own cars, and then split delivery fees 50–50 with their drivers, giving bonuses to proven veterans. Paying commissions makes bookkeeping easier—you don't have to deduct taxes—and the commissions are great motivators because the more drivers deliver, the more they earn.

A Sporting Chance

Although I enjoy watching sports, and I still play a few too, part of my enjoyment is diminished because I can't help but note that while a high percentage of the athletes in most major sports is black, the race of those in the front offices and broadcast booths is still overwhelmingly white. I have long championed the expansion of African American talent from the playing fields into the business offices of sports, and I am happy to note that we are aggressively moving into head coaching and top management positions in various aspects of the sports industry. Among the more notable is former NBA star Isiah Thomas III, who has a 10 percent stake in the $12.5 million

Toronto Raptors NBA expansion team and is taking an active role as vice president of basketball operations. And lesser known but no less important is the role attorney Johnnie Cochran is playing in this arena as well.

It has taken too long and the road still stretches before us. But many of the signs are encouraging. Job listings for sports-related careers appear to be plentiful, with league expansions and corporate investment in professional, semiprofessional and amateur sports. "I think sports is probably one of the hottest industries around. There are a lot of jobs coming to the forefront. There are opportunities that people are not aware of," says Larry Lundy, director of marketing for Disney's Wide World of Sports in Florida.

Far too many black youths pin all their hopes on athletic careers on the court or playing field without considering the more realistic option of applying their knowledge and interest in sports to related businesses such as special-events marketing, facilities management, sports agenting and equipment and clothing manufacturing and retailing. Of course, sports-related business is still in its infancy in many respects. But that should only heighten the attractiveness of getting in now. In 1980 the NBA licensing department had $100,000 in total revenue. In 1995 it took in more than $2 billion. The price tag was $15 million to be an Olympic sponsor in Barcelona in 1992. In 1996 the price tag for Atlanta was $40 million.

Naturally, the growth of sports-related business opportunities comes with the caveat that blacks who dominate in sport still have to struggle for respect in businesses built around sport. Sadly, the Marge Schott–Al Campanis attitude that blacks lack the mental capacity for business still lingers in some circles despite lip service about providing opportunities for minorities in sports.

For blacks to succeed in this white-dominated area of the business world, one strategy that appears to be working is early involvement in sports business operations, whether as a volunteer or lower-level worker or as an athlete. Arthur Triche, the first black public relations director for an NBA team, says he wouldn't be with the Atlanta Hawks today if he hadn't networked through volunteer work. He began as a volunteer ball boy at Tulane University while still in the eighth grade and four years later received a partial scholarship as a student manager for the basketball team. By his junior year he was on a full scholarship, jockeying duties as manager, sports information assistant, and editor of the school newspaper. He graduated from Tulane in 1983 with a BA in communications and stayed on as an assistant sports information director. He moved on to similar positions at Louisiana State University and the NFL Detroit Lions before getting the Hawks job in 1989.

Not one to rest on his laurels, Triche continues to network as a volunteer for the Olympic Games, Super Bowls, the Final Four, the NBA All-Star Games and the NBA Finals. His advice is to develop general skills in accounting, sales, marketing or other fields that can be applied to both sports administration and business rather than offering yourself based merely on an interest in sports.

Here are eight "hot" sports-related careers.

1. Athletic Director. Run athletic programs at colleges or secondary schools. Manage budgets and fund-raising efforts, hire and fire coaches, and oversee event scheduling, athletic facilities, scholarships and TV/radio broadcast rights. Salary range is from $25,000 to $140,000 at the Division I level.

Once a position generally given to former head coaches, which eliminated blacks, there is a trend to professionalize this position by hiring financial management and fund-raising experts, especially those with degrees in sports management or sports administration. In the 1993–94 academic year, the NCAA reported that there were 32 black athletic directors out of a total of 897. At the Division I level, African Americans held 13 of 296 positions. The numbers are better at the high school level, where in small school districts the athletic director may also coach and teach classes.

The NCAA maintains a list of accredited sports administration degree programs and has a job bank to help identify and link minority candidates with job openings and internships.

2. Sports Information Director. Provide information to the media and public about sports teams, leagues or conferences. Schedule television, radio and newspaper interviews for coaches and star athletes. Write news releases, media guides and playoff brochures. Coordinate news conferences and manage access to press boxes. Salaries range from $20,000 to $100,000.

Most SIDs today have a degree in journalism or communications and a strong interest in sports. Long hours and a lot of travel are required to be with teams and coaches.

3. Certified Athletic Trainer. Deal with health care problems of athletes, providing immediate, preventive and rehabilitative treatment. Salaries range from $23,000 to $95,000.

There are roughly 12,000 certified athletic trainers in the country working in hospitals and clinics, colleges, universities and high schools, according to Crayton L. Moss, director of the athletic training program at Bowling Green State University in Ohio. Many entered the profession by serving as student trainers or managers in their school's athletic programs. A bachelor's degree is required, with knowledge of anatomy, physiology, kinesiology, hygiene, nutrition, conditioning, taping, bracing, emergency procedures, prevention of injury, injury evaluation and rehabilitative procedures. Blacks represent less than 1 percent of all certified athletic trainers, while women now account for nearly 50 percent. No black college or university offers athletic training as a professional degree.

4. Front Office Executive. Act as chief executive, general manager and/or business manager for a professional sports team. Salary range is generally in the six figures.

In recent years, pro sports franchises have responded to pressure for more minorities in the front office. Former players have a big advantage, but professional business executives are being attracted by the salaries and benefits.

5. Personal Fitness Trainer. Create tailor-made exercise programs for those seeking individual attention and solid results. Fees range from $10 to $100 a session, and salaries generally run from $12,000 to $50,000 a year.

This is a booming business because many wealthy clients prefer one-on-one private training to crowded health clubs. Corporate executives and celebrities are among the best clients. There is no national certification program, although some colleges do offer programs. It pays to have experience in physical therapy, athletic training, physiology and anatomy.

6. Coach. Lead, teach and motivate athletes while dealing with administrators, parents and media. Good communication and administrative skills are important. Salary range from high school through professional can be $12,000 to several million a year, depending on what other duties are assigned.

There are more minorities in this profession than perhaps any other sports-related field, though again, not enough. Head coaching positions are still hard to come by for minorities. Even in basketball, where the most gains have been made at the college and professional levels, a black coach must have impeccable credentials and substantial experience to get the job. Cheryl Miller, the leading women's coach, gave up a broadcasting career to lead the University of Southern California women's team. Women's coaching salaries are often little more than half those of men at the same level.

The NFL has had only a handful of black head coaches in its 75-year history. At the end of the 1996 football season, there were nine head coaching positions open. Not one black candidate was seriously considered for any of these posts. Division I football and major league baseball are equally tough for black coaches to crack. Opportunities for minorities are more abundant at the junior high and high school levels, where teacher-coaches earn in a range of $19,000 to $85,000.

7. Marketing/Promotions. Market, promote and sell sporting events, programming, merchandise and positive images of athletes. Salaries range from $20,000 to more than $100,000.

This is a burgeoning field consisting largely of independent companies specializing in sports and event marketing of everything from tickets and advertising to luxury suites and merchandise. Marketing and promotions specialists need a solid business background as well as good communication, writing and sales skills.

George Washington University in Washington, D.C. has a Forum for Sport and Event Management and Marketing.

8. Sports Medicine. Medical specialist in prevention and treatment of sports-related injuries. Salaries range from $40,000 to $70,000 at entry level to over $100,000 with more experience.

This is a hot area of specialization for physicians and entire clinics. At one time sports medicine was largely limited to orthopedics, but it now encompasses nutritionists, psychologists, researchers, physical therapists, athletic medicine, athletic trainers and exercise physiologists.

A World of Opportunity

In many companies that I am familiar with, one of the swiftest ways to rise to the top is to take a tour of duty overseas. My longtime friend Robert Holland, the former CEO of Ben & Jerry's Ice Cream, had never been outside of his native Michigan until he enrolled in the mechanical engineering program at Union College in Schenectady, New York. "And if Greyhound hadn't known how to get there, I wouldn't have gone," he notes.

After working briefly for Mobil Oil while getting his master's degree at the City College of New York, Bob went to work for McKinsey & Company, management consultants, and in very short order he was offered the opportunity to head up a project in Amsterdam. He jumped at it, and not because it offered him a chance to see more of the world.

"My primary advice to people starting out in business and facing a major career decision is to always base the decision on whether or not you are making a move that will expand your opportunities down the road," Holland said. "There were people inside McKinsey who thought it was too early for me to go overseas, but I had a great two years and it really built my reputation within the company."

Not so long ago, doing business internationally was the exclusive domain of the largest and most aggressive multinational corporations. For African American enterprises, doing business outside the immediate neighborhood was impressive. Having a global presence was generally unthinkable, even for the most aggressive black entrepreneur.

I am here to tell you that has changed. In fact, I'm in South Africa to tell you that has changed. My participation in the South Africa Pepsi franchise is but one example of the move of African American entrepreneurs into the global market. More and more black-owned companies are expanding their businesses globally as countries from Eastern Europe to South Africa embrace capitalism as the key to their economic futures. Indeed, African American businesses ranging from B.E. 100 companies such as TLC International Holdings to black entrepreneurs in the import-export business are establishing themselves around the world. Black business owners and entrepreneurs realize that increasingly their greatest opportunities for expansion and growth lie in markets outside the United States. Going global is also a strategy for more and more African Americans in corporate positions who can expand their horizons by accepting international assignments.

Whether you own or work for a black-owned company or work

for a major corporation that is majority controlled, an overseas assignment can be liberating. Many African Americans say that international postings provided promotions they might not have gotten at home. Others find that many international assignments provide an escape from racism back home. They feel their performance overseas is more fairly judged.

A survey by the National Foreign Trade Council found that the number of American "expatriates" working overseas jumped by 30 percent in 1995. Of the 74 companies the trade council polled, 71 percent said they expect this growth to continue. While the vast majority of American expatriates are male, the number of women venturing overseas has increased rapidly in recent years.

Although an international assignment can be exciting, rewarding, even glamorous, it can also present a culture shock, as Belinda Miller, a native of Norfolk, Virginia, discovered. As director of human resources for Swissotel Beijing, she innocently offered advice to an employee, and the Chinese woman, who took Miller's advice as a rebuke, burst into tears. Miller quickly learned to use a more subtle Socratic approach. "The Mandarin word for *question* is the same as the word for *problem*. Knowing that helped me better understand that people who ask too many questions, or are too challenging, are viewed negatively," she says.

Martin F. Bennett of Bennett Associates, a cross-cultural and global management training firm in Chicago, notes that the successful expatriate is an open-minded, flexible individual willing to take risks. You must have the ability to adapt to different cultures. Even those who meet the criteria should acquire some form of cultural or language training before they enter a country. Some expatriates may expect America's strong work ethic to cross all borders. Often they encounter co-workers and employees who are much more relaxed and less focused on work, a trait that is more a reflection of their cultural setting than laziness.

Here are some things to consider before accepting or seeking an international assignment.

▪ While international assignments have great appeal for the young and single, people with children face greater adjustments and potential trauma. Family obligations are the primary reason many overseas assignments are refused.

• A move to an overseas post doesn't always mean an increase in salary, but it often proves beneficial to your finances because living expenses may be covered by your employer, cost-of-living stipends may be included, and leaves and trips back home may be paid for by the employer. Some employers also provide car and housing allowances as well as interpreters, housekeepers and drivers.

• Too many expatriate Americans cling to the emigrant community of fellow countrymen overseas rather than getting out into the country and learning about the culture. J. Eric Wright, an international employee of Citibank in Johannesburg, befriended two Soweto families and became a mentor for a 15-year-old boy who plans to attend college in the United States. By reaching out, he learned social mores that helped him do his job much better; for instance, the custom that young people do not look into the eyes of their elders, a custom Wright might have taken as a sign of disrespect had he not observed life outside his suburban African American neighborhood.

• Your return home can also be a culture shock. The expatriate experience often instills a greater sense of independence. In fact, 20 to 48 percent of expatriates leave their companies within the first year of returning from an international assignment, according to Bennett. Many returning workers feel that their newly acquired skills are not fully put to use back home.

• International experience can put you on the fast track, so you have to be prepared to greet and assess new opportunities at a quick clip.

Five Ways to Get on the International Track

1. Attend courses or conferences that focus on the international aspects of your field. Join professional organizations such as the National Black MBA Association or the Society of Human Resource Management.

2. Ask a colleague who has returned from abroad, or one currently on international assignment, to mentor you.

3. Rework your résumé to reflect your cultural experience. List the languages you speak and any international travel you have done.

Volunteer for those projects or assignments that will give you international insight or exposure.

4. Take courses in the language of the country you wish to venture to. If you're not sure of the country, then learn a language that piques your interest.

5. Consider pursuing a master's degree in international affairs, business or management. Your firm might even finance it. Just a few of the schools offering international curriculums include . . .

- American Graduate School of International Management, Glendale, Arizona
- Columbia University, New York City
- Cornell University, Ithaca, New York
- Florida State University, Tallahassee
- Georgetown University, Washington, D.C.
- Monterey Institute of International Studies, Monterey, California
- University of Southern California, Los Angeles

There are many other career opportunities and options out there, of course, and I'm not just trying to boost circulation by advising you to keep an eye on the latest edition of *Black Enterprise* for new trends and opportunities.

CHAPTER 7

Career Strategies

The standard advice for devising a career strategy used to go like this.

Step One: Get a college degree.
Step Two: Get a job with a solid employer.
Step Three: Produce results on the job.
Step Four: Pick up the gold watch at the retirement party and start cashing the retirement checks.

At least, that's how it went for the white folks. It wasn't quite that smooth for most blacks, in the old days, and it certainly is not today. Blacks have always had tough going in the business world, and maybe it's a good thing, in a sense, because we've learned not to expect anything to be handed to us. Throughout my life and still today, I have set goals and gone after them like a junkyard dog.

At 62 years old, I'm still making lists of what I need to do and how I need to get it done. If I pulled out my Wizard right now I could look at my seven goals for the year. (Number Four, by the way, is to write a best-seller. So tell your friends how much fun you are having right now.) Goals give you the opportunity to measure where you are and where you want to go. They have to be realistic goals that are achievable within a short time because you don't want to get discouraged by trying to do the impossible day in and day out. I know, because that is one of my problems. I'm always trying to win the war in a day. It comes from a lifetime of fighting for every inch of ground gained.

African Americans have always had to work twice as hard to get half as much, and we have also had to take risks in order to get ahead. In that sense, the times have caught up to us. This is the age of the risk taker. The best career strategies today still incorporate hard work. But it is a gambler's game—no place for the faint of heart or the unwise. If taking risks goes against your instincts, you need to upgrade your database.

Not taking risks is even more dangerous in a business environment in which . . .

- companies large and small are continually searching for ways to do more and make more at less cost.
- rapid advances in technology cause continual shifting in the job market and eliminate the need for people in one area while creating new opportunities in another.
- the greatest trends are in the hiring of contract and temporary workers at lower cost.
- increasingly it is the people who can apply and adapt a range of specific skills to general situations who are most valued.

There was a certain passivity in the way people approached their careers in the past. They felt that if they met certain criteria and worked up to expectations, they were safely locked in for life. Today's business climate demands that each and every person adopt an entrepreneurial attitude. Even if you're working for somebody else, you can no longer consider yourself a cog in the wheel. We're all wheels now, and at all times we have to be prepared to roll on to better opportunities.

Donald Lowery had spent nearly 14 years in journalism, but it took him only two weeks to decide that the grass and the money were greener in investment banking. A former newspaper reporter, Lowery was 35 years old when he left a position as director of public affairs and editorials at WHDH-TV in Boston for a far more lucrative position as an investment banker with Lazard Frères in Boston. "When I evaluated what I had achieved and what I could reasonably expect to achieve in television, I decided that the change would be good," he says.

Whether a career change is spurred by downsizing of your corporate job or a desire to pursue a more fulfilling or financially rewarding path, most black professionals at some point in their careers consider the risk of making a radical career shift. Management and career experts say that this risk is mostly a favorable one for people who take it relatively early in their careers, particularly if they are unmarried or without a family to support, as Lowery was at the time he made his jump. Employees over 40 with families, particularly those without some previous experience or at least some good contacts in the new field, should weigh the risks very carefully. It can be a very difficult move if you also have heavy financial obligations. To be worthwhile a career switch should provide a big jump up the ladder. That way, even if you fail, it shows that you were looking for growth in income and responsibility rather than simply a change of scenery.

To succeed as a black person in the white-dominated business world, you can take nothing for granted. Employers are evaluating employee work more ruthlessly than ever before, so you must constantly assess your skills and performance level. To survive in the corporate structure today, you have to continually develop and refine your skills to meet changing demand. Here is a checklist of sorts.

- Do you have a realistic game plan detailing where you want to be in the next six months to a year?
- Do you completely understand what your boss expects of you? Does your boss know what you need?
- Have you assessed where you stand from the company's point of view? Do you know the ins and outs of your company in addition to your role?
- Do you initiate projects or wait for them to be assigned to you?
- Do you display enthusiasm when working on assignments no matter how small they may be?
- Are you considered a leader by your superiors? Have you gone beyond your share of work on a particular project?
- Do you exhibit confidence about yourself and your capabilities? Can you accept criticism and learn from your mistakes?
- Have you made sure you are considered an asset in the company to those who count? How well have you managed the perceptions that others have of you?

- Do you fit your company's corporate image? Have you taken advantage of networking opportunities inside and outside the company?
- Have you acquired a mentor to help bring you along within the company? Do you have someone outside the company who can help you keep a perspective on your career and developments in your industry?

When I worked with Kennedy, I was always asking others how they thought I was doing within his organization. Sometimes I would have to make corrections and adjustments to my style in order to be more efficient within the demanding and hard-charging culture of his office. You must continuously monitor your status and your vulnerability in the constantly shifting work environment. You must always be on the lookout for ways to increase your value in the market while being alert to new opportunities.

Time and again, I hear from African Americans in the business world who have taken considerable risks to stay ahead of downsizing or stagnation in this fast-frame business environment. Rueben Stokes was 34 years old and national sales director for Allied Van Lines in Chicago. He had been promoted to that position over six more senior managers after only eight months with the company and had direct access to the president. He was only a step away from a vice president's spot. But in spite of his "golden" status, when a corporate recruiter called, Stokes did not turn him away. He knew that he had to remain open to opportunity. He had been fired at age 24 from his first full-time job, which taught him early on that he could be "iced" at any time.

He and other savvy African Americans have learned that the comfort zone can be the danger zone in these times when corporations have the attitude "if it ain't broke, break it." Stokes realized that those who get ahead are those who take well-calculated risks. Stokes's boss at Allied had told him to "be patient" for his opportunity there, but Stokes felt that as a black man he didn't have the luxury of being patient in the white-dominated business world, particularly with increasingly open hostility toward minority programs. So he listened to the recruiter, and while taking care not to burn his bridges at Allied, he made the leap to a much larger full-service transportation company, Ryder Systems, based in Miami.

His salary and benefits, as well as his responsibilities and visibility, increased in his new position of national sales director for Ryder Move Management, part of its consumer truck rental division. "If you don't take the risk, someone else will," Stokes warns. "They'll get ahead and you won't."

Taking risks does not always mean leaving your current job. Stokes took a risk by informing his bosses at Allied that he was entertaining the Ryder offer. They could have fired him on the spot. But he did it as a courtesy and, of course, to give them a chance to provide him with an even better opportunity at Allied. They chose not to do that and he moved on.

Through my oldest son and his wife, I have gotten to know their friend Glenda McNeal, a graduate of the Wharton School's MBA program. She experienced some anxiety when her employer, American Express Travel Related Services, went through a turbulent reengineering and cost-cutting period. She was on maternity leave when she learned that she would be coming back to an entirely different job. While analyzing her position, she lost sleep, sought advice, weighed her options, debated and second-guessed. In short, she calculated the risks. She decided to stay because she felt that opportunities within the company were still abundant for her. When she talked to me about her decision, she was vice president of the American Express Members of Distinction program, designed for its gold and platinum cardholders. "At this stage of my career, the risk was worth it because I am happy here," she said then.

Calculating Risks

Although these two case studies involved different circumstances and had different outcomes, the two risk-takers shared a common and thoughtful approach to calculating their risks. One decided that the risk of leaving his good job was worth it. The other decided that the risk of staying was worth it.

Each of them carefully weighed the options, consulted outsiders and pondered the possibilities. In general, they avoided some of the dangers of risk taking. Here are ten pitfalls to avoid.

1. Neglecting your homework

Whether deciding to stay, leave or move on, be sure to do your background work. If you are contemplating a move to a new company, check out its annual report and look up any articles about it by industry analysts. Talk to potential colleagues and get their assessment of the work environment. Find out if the company has already reengineered or downsized or whether it is contemplating such moves. Try to get the names of any employees who have left and find out why they did so.

I think you have to do your homework in everything, whether it involves researching the background of the doctor you are going to use or checking out your children's school or what professors are the best on campus. Anyone who doesn't make the effort required is asking for serious trouble down the road. Before I go into a meeting with someone I have never met, I know what church they go to, where they went to college and whether the kids were ever into scouting.

OK, I may be exaggerating, but part of my mission, and yours, is always to do the homework that is required because we want to be ready for opportunity when it presents itself. I can't stress enough that the spoils go to the person who is most prepared to leap when the opportunity appears, and that requires preparation, preparation, preparation.

2. Falling out of the loop

It is important to stay informed about the inner workings of your company. That doesn't mean you have to hang out around the water cooler, or the espresso machine, but it does mean networking within the company and not just within your own area of the company. Often those in other departments have information that could affect your career. Read industry newsletters and stock analysis to see what factors are impacting the decisions of your corporate chiefs. If you understand the influences on their thinking, you may be able to stay a step ahead.

I keep a pocket Wizard with me at all times so that I stay on top of all things. I have *Black Enterprise*'s sales charts in a file in the Wizard, and I monitor performance of our sales team that way. If I see that someone is not keeping pace with expectations, I am on top of it, and I make sure that the managers in charge are on top of it too.

3. Suffering from résumé malaise

In the modern business environment, you should always have an up-to-date résumé and the mentality that goes with it. Know what you bring to the table, and keep it on the table where you can display it on command.

4. Ignoring internal job postings

Even if you aren't really looking—and you always should be looking—it helps for you to make it known that you are open to opportunity. If you make regular inquiries to the personnel office, they'll know that you are looking to grow, and they may look to help you grow.

5. Keeping your head down

This is a mentality left over from the days when the IBM main-frame was the undisputed king of computers, Ford always had a better idea, and corporations valued longevity. A high profile may not guarantee that your head will be spared in the next downsizing, but the more people who see your abilities, the more opportunities you'll have.

6. Believing that you know all you need to know

Taking risks successfully is dependent on having the best and most recent information available. Being prepared for risks involves having the best and most up-to-date training available. If you aren't working on new skills and refining the old ones, you aren't prepar-ing yourself to take risks that can move you ahead of the pack and the executioner. Lifelong learning is essential.

7. Alienating your co-workers

These days, the situation may well be every man for himself and every woman for herself, but it is always foolish to make enemies. You can pursue your best interests without walking all over your co-workers and colleagues. In an ever-changing work environment, you never know who may be in a position to help you down the road. But you can trust that it won't be someone you have treated poorly. If you are in a small company such as mine, even the people who run the mailroom need to know that you are paying attention and that you are glad to have them working hard for you.

8. Dodging challenges

Inside every challenge is an opportunity. By seeking out challenges, you grow, even if you occasionally fail. If you've fallen into a routine, go to your boss and ask for new challenges or ask how you might improve your performance. Then follow through.

9. Lying

Sometimes it seems there is an epidemic of this in the business world. Every week seems to bring a new report of someone who has lied on a résumé or falsely portrayed credentials, or of a major financial institution brought to its knees because of an employee's deception. Maybe you won't get caught in a lie, but odds are you will, and the effects can be devastating in a market that doesn't need an excuse to send you packing. I have one rule for those who lie or steal: There is no second chance. If I find somebody lying through their teeth, they are gone. My rationale is simple: If someone lies to me once they will lie again.

10. Burning your bridges

If you decide to take a risk and move on to another department or another company, walk out with a smile on your face and your head held high. No one resents someone seeking greater opportunities, but few are willing to forgive someone who leaves in bitterness.

Asking for What You Want

All too often, African Americans who are openly ambitious are criticized by white co-workers and supervisors for being "too aggressive." Thus, too often we try to blend into the business world rather than make our mark on it. A common symptom of this is being afraid to risk going after what we want or need to move up the career ladder in the white-dominated business world.

Wanda Hackett of Seattle is a consultant on organizational effectiveness, who says she sees this lack of assertiveness frequently in black employees. African Americans need to carry a proactive mind-set into the workplace, she advises, but they need to be aware that there is a difference between style and mind-set. Perception, as they say, is everything. If someone complains about your aggressiveness in the workplace, you might:

1. Go to a variety of sources for honest feedback on how your style impacts people.
2. Ask for specific examples of the behavior that seems to be causing a problem.
3. Ask people to tell you what they think you could have done instead of what you did.
4. Find a role model, someone who is getting ahead the way you want to.
5. Consciously work on refining your style. And if anyone wonders what you are up to, lay the blame on that Graves guy at *Black Enterprise*.

Commanding Presence

Thanks to my military officer's training, I've never had a problem coming off as too meek. There aren't too many meek Green Berets out there. But far too many blacks tend to cower in the corner in the corporate environment. Rather than blending in, African Americans need to be more assertive on the job. This includes abandoning the temptation to be the strong, silent type, whether male or female. According to the National Institute of Business Management, concealing your challenges may also force you to hide your successes. Furthermore, toughing out work-related problems alone can compound the time it takes you to solve them.

After all, who is more admired, the CEO who keeps a handle on things without appearing to put forth any effort or the one who takes a company in turmoil and turns it around? My advice is to be open, let your supervisors know the problems you are dealing with and your successes in handling them, but:

- Be selective both in whom you talk to and what you talk about. Reach out to those in the best position to give good advice or assistance on the particular problem you're tackling.
- Send out progress reports. You don't want to beat people over the head, but keep them apprised of any significant movement toward a final solution.

- Always give credit where it's due. Share the spotlight with those who helped you, and they will be loyal and willing aides in the future.
- Remain professional and focused. It's wise to share your professional challenges—not personal gripes. Remember, your goal is to be perceived as a problem solver, not a whiner.

Assertiveness means standing up for yourself without stepping on others. You don't have to be pushy, but you can be insistent politely. Years of social conditioning have made it difficult for many African Americans and other minorities to be assertive, particularly in an environment dominated by whites. You can't change that conditioning overnight, but here are some tips I've put together from my own experiences and observations.

1. Have specific, attainable goals. If you want to be taken seriously on the job, break down each problem and set step-by-step goals that will enable you to assert control.

2. Speak up. Don't expect others to be mind readers. Make your points without apology. If you mean no, make certain that it is understood as not negotiable.

3. Control your emotions. If you lose your temper and start breaking windows, or burst into tears, you've lost the case and very likely done irreparable harm to your reputation. It may actually be helpful to raise your voice now and then to show you mean business, but always do it in a very controlled way so that you come off as forceful rather than volatile.

4. Nip little problems in the bud. You can't afford to let small problems fester until they become big ones. Deal with them swiftly now so they won't haunt you later.

5. Repeat yourself. Sometimes you have to deliver a message several times before people understand that you consider it to be a matter of importance.

6. Be willing to compromise. You can't always win, and sometimes you win by letting the other side come out on top. Pick your battles carefully so that you can go all out on the important ones.

It also pays to be assertive in your attitude toward your career, which means looking for jobs that offer growth opportunities as part of your strategy. A survey of 150 managers in some of the nation's largest companies revealed that—after skills and experience level—most managers place a premium on upward progression in reviewing the résumés of applicants. The survey, developed by Office Team, a national job placement firm, reports that 67 percent of those questioned believe increased responsibility demonstrates a job candidate's initiative and growth potential. After that, managers look for the caliber of previous employers and job stability.

Making a Move

If you find your working conditions intolerable or unsatisfying, you face the rather risky business of leaving a known situation for an unknown one. You have to be a risk taker to do that. Most people consider it, but few gather the courage or financial security to do it. Making positive, if nerve-racking, career moves does not have to be a daredevil feat if you employ careful, realistic strategies and determination.

Many African Americans in business never make it past the iron ceiling in their companies or corporations. When they hit it, feelings of isolation and stagnation set in, demoralizing them.

A study involving 500 black managers at many of the nation's largest corporations, by David A. Thomas of the Harvard Graduate School of Business Administration revealed that many black managers with great potential enter competitive, prestigious jobs only to become disenchanted after achieving a certain level of managerial responsibility. These feelings of disenchantment may arise if suggestions or ideas are ignored or if duties don't change even after promotions. At that point, many African Americans may be tempted to lower performance, and over time, low expectations become a self-fulfilling prophecy, Thomas explains. This creates a phenomenon he calls "de-skilling." To avoid getting caught in that trap, here are three tips to follow.

1. Find a diverse group of people within your organization with whom you are comfortable, and talk to them about matters of style and culture to restore your sense of belonging within the company.

2. Take part in multiracial organizations and events to ease your feelings of detachment and to increase your awareness of your role and the roles of those around you.

3. Engage in regular, proactive career planning and self-assessment to get past the sense of spinning your wheels. Actively look for opportunities to charge your batteries and give you a true measure of how you feel about your current position so that you can determine whether you are simply in a lull or need to break free.

Survivor's Angst

Another common problem among black employees in the corporate environment is the guilt and loneliness experienced by those of us who survive a downsizing. African Americans may be the last hired and first fired, but generally, for better or worse, companies don't fire every minority employee in the place. The good news may be that you still have a job. The bad news may be that you are even more in the minority than you were before.

When friends and co-workers are fired and you are left behind, feelings of anger, guilt, insecurity and loneliness are to be expected, but you can't let those feelings affect your behavior or dominate your activities. This is a time to rise up and review your career strategy rather than burying your face in the crying towel.

"People who have some idea of where they want to go in life and how they're going to get there will view this as another obstacle to somehow get around, get over or get through," says John Herring, president of J. H. Herring & Associates, management consultants in Oakland, California. "But people who don't have an established strategy with strong goals for their careers are emotionally vulnerable."

Herring notes that depression feeds on itself. If you are despondent and angry, you push people away, but if you explain to them why you are feeling low and ask for their understanding, they will be drawn to your more productive attitude. Pragmatically, it's critically important to shore up your outside support base and rebuild your internal one. You should also try to stay in touch with former colleagues. It may be difficult at first, but if you support them in tough times, they can motivate you too.

Coping with Career Stress

Everyone undergoes stress at work at one time or another, particularly in an era when companies are continually pushing employees to do more with less. It is impossible to avoid stress, but it is possible to deal with it in a healthy and productive manner.

African Americans face more stress than whites because whites in general, as the majority group in the workplace, are permitted a wider range of behavioral styles. Conformity is always an issue for blacks in business. Often blacks who rise to management positions have not been prepared as well as the dominant white males, who have the benefit of an extensive old boy network.

Black managers walk a tightrope. They worry more than their white counterparts about seeming threatening or too assertive, while their white bosses may criticize them for not being assertive enough. Black women have to cope with both racism and sexism to succeed. Breaking through the iron ceiling continues to be a major challenge for African American professionals, who often have to work twice as hard and stay in positions longer than white counterparts. As I've often said, blacks cannot afford the luxury of being average in anything they do in the business world. They must always be superior just to compete.

Here are a few general guidelines to help cope with stress in the workplace.

Before you react, seek to understand.

Every corporate culture is different. What works in one situation may not work in another. If you feel lost, angry and stressed out, you are not alone. Network with your co-workers, black and white, who are trustworthy. You may find that they share your frustrations and that it has more to do with the corporate culture than with anything you are doing. Your feelings may be entirely justified, and discovering that can alleviate a lot of stress. Most corporations and professions now have mentoring or support groups for African Americans. Seek them out.

Play to your strengths.

Nothing can be more stressful than being what athletes and coaches call "out of position." That occurs when you find yourself in a role that you are not best suited to fill. To avoid this, take a proactive approach and conduct regular assessments of your strengths and development needs in these seven areas: career, financial, spiritual, personal relationships, community, social involvement and health.

Ask yourself what kind of position best suits you. What kind of work environment is best for you? What career path would make you most happy? Career counseling can help you identify the type of work environment that will put the least amount of stress on you.

Strike a balance.

To reduce stress, you have to remove yourself from stressful situations. This means striking a balance in your life. If your work is stressful, you have to have activities outside the workplace to relieve that stress. When I need to relax, I am more inclined to do something strenuous like skiing in the winter or remodeling around the house.

Your work cannot be your entire life, unless you fancy a brief stay on this planet. Your career can help your self-esteem, your financial status and your sense of accomplishment, but you have to integrate other elements into your life and give a priority to supportive and empowering relationships, your spiritual needs and your physical and mental health.

Look for professional help.

If you can't successfully cope with stress on your own or with the help of co-workers or loved ones, go to those who are trained to help you. Stress can be overwhelming. It can be more than you can handle. It can be more than your friends can deal with. Many companies offer counseling or referral services through employee assistance programs. Often managers are reluctant to use them for fear that the information might not be kept confidential or might be used against them. For those who don't feel comfortable using company resources, there are outside therapists available. If you know you need help, getting it—whatever the potential risk—should be your first priority.

Reinventing Your Career

Disenchantment and alienation can affect anyone in the workplace, but African Americans are particularly vulnerable because they have to cope with all the problems of their co-workers as well as with ever-present racial prejudices. It is inevitable that there will be times in your career when you feel lost and drifting, but it is well within your power to recover by developing new strategies and, in effect, reinventing your career.

Joyce Roche had been a role model for countless African Americans in her career at Avon Products, where she appeared to have broken through the glass ceiling and beyond. A one-time *Black Enterprise* cover story subject in a piece about the nation's "40 Most Powerful Black Business Executives," she seemed an unlikely candidate for career gridlock.

But it can happen to anyone, at any level. At age 45, she was vice president of global marketing at the $4 billion company, when she resigned because her job hadn't presented her with the challenges and opportunities she'd once thought it would.

If you find yourself in a career crisis or spinning your wheels in a job that isn't taking you where you want to go, don't assume that you can't reconfigure your career strategy or that you don't have what it takes to break through. The decision to ditch a plum six-figure position in a major corporation grew out of Roche's realization that despite the great title and income, her job did not hold the level of autonomy or responsibility she had initially thought it would. That realization was a striking one because she had planned on working with Avon until retirement. Although she had some notable successes in her brief tenure as head of marketing in Avon's global expansion, conflicting visions within the organization had made for some tense and stressful times.

She began searching for a less stressful position, more suited to her personality. At first she looked for other positions within the Avon organization because of her successes there, but eventually it occurred to her that she might have to leave because "I didn't want to stay around until I got angry with Avon."

After 19 years with Avon, she resigned because she felt its leaders were not ready to make the difficult decisions required to make it a true global organization. She admits to being fearful at that point, but she immediately set up an office in her New York apartment and went about the business of finding a job.

It was a disorienting experience for this single woman who had not been out of a job since leaving Columbia University Business

School. "There would be periods for two or three weeks when the phone wouldn't ring and I'd say, oh my God, this is it. Everything that's going to happen has happened and you missed it," she recalls.

At first she found it awkward to network because she was uneasy with being out of work, but once she started talking with people, she says, it became a more natural process. She worked with career expert John Lucht to construct a five-page résumé, and she considered positions involving everything from telecommunications to toys before joining Carson Products Company.

Based in Savannah, Georgia, Carson's is a much smaller company than Avon, with $60 million in sales compared to Avon's $4 billion, but it too manufactures African American hair care products. Her new title there? Executive vice president of global marketing—similar to the one she'd had at Avon. But this time her job description was much more clearly defined. She also received a significant salary increase, and she has adapted well to the much less stressful climate of the serene southern town. Today she is president of Carson Products.

She is quite open when reflecting on how her reinvented career strategy affected her life. "Never in my career have I been able to answer the question Where do you want to be in five or ten years? If I had, I probably would have missed a lot of opportunities that came my way. Now I feel that I'm ready for the opportunities as they surface. I've learned a lot, and I'm definitely in a different place—literally and figuratively."

As Roche and many other African Americans in business have discovered, rising to the executive level does not guarantee either fulfillment or security. A landmark study conducted by executive recruiter Paul Ray Berndtson and Cornell University's Center for Advanced Human Resources Studies provides insight into how the nation's highly placed executives view their careers. It found that 75 percent of executives are actively job-hunting, that top executives generally are more dissatisfied with their jobs than lower-level employees, and that executives want to work less and enjoy more leisure and family time. Most put in about 56 hours a week and would like to cut that to 49.

If your career strategy is focused solely on moving into the executive suite, you might want to take time to ponder that strategy and decide whether you've given enough thought to the downside of being at or near the top.

If you have considered the drawbacks and still want to move up, as most people do, you may also want to take time to consider whether you are a logical candidate for promotion. Here is a checklist.

- Are your communication skills as strong as they could be? White people may be allowed to drop off into street dialect during business conferences. We cannot afford that.
- Have you supported colleagues, taken an interest in their projects and helped them achieve results?
- Have you shown a strong ability to confront and solve problems?
- Have you tended to management's priorities before tending to your own?
- Have you defined long-term objectives, and do you understand the role your current activities play in attaining them?
- Have you supported management by taking on work in difficult periods and offering good advice?
- Have you achieved a degree of political clout that reinforces the strengths outlined above?

If you answered no to any of the above, you are not a very strong candidate for a move up. It's time to get to work on improving your weak points if you want to make the climb up the ladder.

Bouncing Back from Setbacks

Dayna Wilkinson seemed to have a foolproof career strategy. She had an BA from Yale and an MBA from Harvard and was director of business development for Travel Related Services with American Express in New York. But after four years of following her winning strategy, Wilkinson's team was disbanded and she found herself out of a job. She responded not by dropping out but by bouncing back with a new strategy.

With the help of the Five O'Clock Club, a national organization for job hunters and career changers, she found a new job in only three months, before the benefits from her previous job ran out. She became vice president of global market development and sales support in the global securities services division of Chase Manhattan Bank in New York.

Wilkinson's experience serves as evidence that no career strategy is foolproof, but no setback is a total defeat.

Interested in interactive media, Wilkinson targeted Time Warner, AT&T, NYNEX and financial organizations. She met people in her targeted industries, worked with search firms, read and researched library databases and kept logs of her correspondence and contacts. She kept three notebooks with letters, contacts, classified ads and material from search firms.

The message is that job-hunting is a full-time job. "Job-hunting is a disciplined process," Wilkinson said. "Yet it's important to leave room for serendipity. You must be open to opportunities because you never know what's going to lead you to the job."

CHAPTER 8

The Key to Black Wealth Is Ownership

Since I did not grow up with a silver spoon in my mouth, my first exposure to the power of true wealth came during my three years as an administrative aide to Kennedy, who, of course, had grown up in what was then one of the wealthiest families in America, thanks to his tycoon father's investments in the stock market, real estate, Hollywood and nearly anything else that paid a good return.

It wasn't the limousines or any other displays of affluence that impressed me as much as Kennedy's casual attitude toward money and power. He wasn't flashy with either of them. There just was always the presumption that whatever he wanted, he could get. That was an attitude that most Americans have not seen a lot of—I certainly hadn't back in Bedford-Stuyvesant—but it was one I came to covet.

I had been on Kennedy's staff only about three months when we were gathered one day in his apartment in the United Nations building. There was a political discussion going on, and Kennedy turned and asked me to get the astronaut John Glenn on the telephone immediately. Glenn was just starting to use his fame as a springboard to a political career, but he was already a rising star in the Democratic Party. I went to the telephone and asked the operator back at our office to track down Glenn. In a few minutes, she reported that he was on a raft trip on the Colorado River. When I told my boss, he looked at me in exasperation and said, "Well Graves, he won't be on that raft all day, so when he gets off, I want to talk to him."

I got the message. When Kennedy asked you to do something, he expected it to be done. I can't remember if I had someone hang out of a tree and hand a phone to Glenn as he floated by, but you better believe Kennedy talked to the astronaut on a rubber raft that day. Later I learned the unofficial motto of his staff: "The unbelievable you do immediately, the impossible takes a little longer."

That was the way it was in an environment where great wealth translated into enormous power. When I look back on those years and think about all that I observed, one of the memories that always returns is the simple scene of Kennedy preparing to go out for the evening. Although he was not the dashing figure that his brother, President John F. Kennedy, had been, he wore the same expensive clothing, the uniform of the white elite. And yet what struck me was that I never saw him carry a wallet, money clip or cash. He'd stick a handkerchief, a comb and maybe a pencil in his pocket and he'd be out the door.

Obviously, this was not a guy who worried about getting the next paycheck in time to pay the rent or whether he was going to be able to pay his kids' tuition for college or where to get the money to pay for a serious illness. Like most people, I had never been exposed to that attitude before, and once I saw the freedom and power that kind of money brought, I was determined to go after it. Why shouldn't blacks willing to work and strive have the freedom money can buy?

Ownership Is the Key

Over the years, *Black Enterprise* has offered its readers hundreds of articles on career strategies, survival in corporate environments, job-hunting and a myriad of other topics related to employment. It is no secret, however, that our real mission is to encourage as many African Americans as possible to one day control their own fates by owning their own successful businesses. Ownership is where the true power and wealth lie. As my father told me, "Never rent, always own."

The importance of black business ownership cannot be overstated. Since the 1960s, economists tracking black economic status have concluded that there has been little progress toward achieving economic parity with whites. Instead, the latest Census Bureau data shows that the aggregate black income deficit in constant 1992 dollars grew from $102 billion in 1967 to $214 billion in 1992. The reason? According to David Swinton, a member of the *Black Enterprise* Board of Economists, there has never been a significant effort to equalize racial disparities in ownership.

In a free enterprise economy, economic forces flow from ownership of resources. Lack of ownership means a lack of control and power in the market. Those who own business control jobs, and that is power. They contribute more to the tax base, and that is power.

Those who work for others may have incomes, but in reality they have very little power over their own destinies. Clearly this is more true today than ever before. The impact of businesses owned by African Americans ripples throughout our neighborhoods and communities because black owners are more likely than other owners to recruit employees in low-income neighborhoods, just as they are more likely to hire black workers and to provide opportunities for them at all levels.

Black-owned companies do more than provide jobs. They provide training. I can't tell you how many bright and promising people my company has hired and developed over the years. I take a great deal of pride not only in those employees who have risen through the ranks and remained at *Black Enterprise* but also in those who have gone on to success in other businesses, including their own businesses. Many were stolen away from me by white businesses. One of our best advertising salesmen, Larry Hovell, became a successful Chrysler dealer. Derek Dingle went from editing our magazine to *Money* and then went on to establish his own publishing company.

Although it always hurts to lose good people, I acknowledge that part of my role as a black businessman is to develop talented and ambitious people and give them the tools they need to fly on their own. On the other hand, there are few things more rewarding than having talented people grow with your company. The current vice president and executive editor of *Black Enterprise*, Alfred Edmond, started out with us nearly a decade ago as an associate editor in the news section of the magazine.

Successful African American businesspeople provide an example that tells young people there are opportunities out there to rise above the streets and the gangs that lure, ensnare and ultimately destroy them. Black ownership of business brings hope, and it multiplies itself. It provides good entry-level jobs for unskilled workers and then gives them additional skills to move up to better jobs. Many of the larger black-owned businesses offer tuition loans and grants to their employees. Some even have public and private training programs, internships and apprenticeships.

Black-owned businesses alone cannot save the African American community, but they can have a deep and long-term impact on economic and social development. As long as we are working for others instead of employing them, we will not control our own destinies. We will not truly control our own lives until many, many more of us control the purse strings. Until we are titans of industries and the heads of multinational conglomerates, we will be much like a child with his nose pressed against the bake shop window that separates him from the goodies inside.

It is a simple fact of this capitalistic system that those who have the keys to the front door and the combination to the safe—whether they are white Irish Americans like the Kennedys or black African Americans like broadcasting entrepreneur Percy Sutton or entertainment phenomenon Oprah Winfrey—have the power to influence all other aspects of the society.

Black Business Ownership Is Thriving

How are blacks doing as far as owning our own businesses? Despite attempts by a conservative Congress to limit our opportunities, and in spite of the nuisances that plague us, black businesses are doing well. Existing black businesses continue to grow in an increasingly unfriendly environment, in which affirmative action programs and the Minority Business Development Agency have been under siege. The Census Bureau's Survey of Minority-Owned Business Enterprises found that the past several years have been good ones for starting black-owned businesses: Start-ups increased by 46 percent between 1987 and 1992.

Black Enterprise Board of Economists member Margaret C. Simms conducted her own survey examining the health of black-owned businesses. Looking at nearly 600 companies, she found that minority-owned firms generally are thriving. Over half of the minority companies responding reported that between 1992 and 1993 their gross sales had increased by more than 10 percent, with one-quarter reporting increases of 25 percent or more. On average, the firms she examined are 11 years old, and more than half were started with an investment of less than $25,000.

Georgia Institute of Technology professor Thomas Boston, another *Black Enterprise* Board of Economists member, noted that black ownership is increasing at the fastest rate in the finance, insurance and real estate industries. Wholesale, transportation, utilities and service industries are also strong growth areas for black entrepreneurs, he says.

Not surprisingly, our economists' findings confirm the fact that the benefits of black economic development are substantial. Simms found that more than half the minority firms she studied were located in the central city, and many were accessible to public transportation—key factors for black workers. Her survey also indicated that the black-owned firms recruit in low-income neighborhoods. While many of the firms in Simms's study were small, nearly 40 percent had more then 15 employees and 10 percent had a workforce in excess of 100.

Because of the way the Census Bureau gathers data, it is impossible to determine just how much increase there has been in new businesses owned by African Americans. But if you read the pages of *Black Enterprise* you can see the determined expressions of those blacks who are either being downsized out of corporate America or leaving on their own to start their businesses. They are tenacious, and they are willing to take risks to grab for the prize—true freedom through economic independence.

What It Takes to Be an African American Entrepreneur

Be warned, however, that entrepreneurship is not an easy road. What does it take to start your own business as a black entrepreneur?

1. A junkyard dog mentality

If you don't know what that means, you've never climbed a junkyard fence and encountered a guard dog trained to get a grip on you and not let go. True entrepreneurs don't let go. If one venture fails, they try another. If one product doesn't sell, they look for a better idea. If one company official isn't buying, they look for another who will. Like the junkyard dog, they hang on no matter how much they are shaken, cursed, beaten and kicked because they stay focused on the task at hand: making money.

2. A willingness to take a risky leap, but only after a good look

Successful entrepreneurs are not afraid to make leaps, but they look first. They don't have a death wish, but they are willing to take a risk to accomplish their goals. The really good ones take a risk only after they've established a Plan B and even a Plan C and Plan D to fall back on. They know what they are getting into and how they can get out.

3. A talent for focusing on solutions rather than problems

Entrepreneurs are usually natural leaders, and while the people around them are busy pointing at problems and pitfalls, entrepreneurs are usually engaged in finding solutions and bridges over the trouble spots. I have no patience with people who want to tell me what's wrong. I only want to hear from the person who first tells me the solution and then fills me in on the problem. I don't want to hear that your basement is flooded. I want to hear that you've found the phone number of the cleanup company. Then tell me why you're calling them.

4. A high level of energy

If you are doing business with me, chances are you can expect a call anywhere from six in the morning until, well, nearly six the next morning. And it might come while I'm on my exercise bike, in the car, riding a train or on an airplane. A real entrepreneur never rests.

If you're the kind of person who likes to go home on Friday night and hit the hammock or stay on the golf course for the entire weekend, you won't cut it as an entrepreneur. Entrepreneurs are always working, even on the golf course. True entrepreneurs play golf because it gives them at least four hours of concentrated time to sell something to their playing partners. They see social occasions as not so much an opportunity to relax as a time for increasing or deepening business relationships. Most entrepreneurs work longer hours and complain less about it than other businesspeople because they are working toward self-imposed goals. If you're a clock-watcher, this is probably not the life for you.

5. The drive to make money so that they can make more money

Other people might set a goal of making money so that they can buy a fancy house, send their kids to private schools, or pay off debts. Entrepreneurs will do those things, but most are driven to make money so that they can use it to make even more. They never say, "I've got enough money." They are capitalists to the bone, and the product is not as important as the return on investment. If there is an opportunity to make more, they'll generally pursue it.

6. A talent for starting companies, but not necessarily managing them

Like most entrepreneurs, I get my biggest kick out of finding and developing new companies and new products, though I no longer have a great deal of interest in micromanaging my businesses. I keep a close eye on my managers, mind you, but I prefer to focus on the long-range plans and new opportunities. That is typical of most entrepreneurs, and it is also a reason why many of them have problems running the businesses they have launched.

Many entrepreneurs mistake their talent for starting a business for the ability to keep it humming through all the cycles that businesses go through. Savvy entrepreneurs get their businesses up and running and then hire good people to keep them going.

7. Flexibility

The only thing that owning a soft drink bottling franchise and publishing a magazine have in common is that both are businesses that if run right will make money. Good entrepreneurs are flexible and adaptable. They can learn what they need to learn about an industry in order to make money in it. They leave the technical stuff to the hired experts. Entrepreneurs are focused on the profit potential, not the ingredients or chemical composition of the product.

8. An abundance of courage

Of all the qualities typically cited as crucial to the makeup of a successful entrepreneur, none is more taken for granted than pure courage. Countless would-be entrepreneurs armed with Ivy League MBAs, the latest management theories and fail-safe concepts fall by the wayside because they don't have the guts for it. On the other hand, many entrepreneurs armed only with dedication and intestinal fortitude thrive.

The CEOs of the top black-owned firms in this country have to combat a constantly shifting and often unforgiving economy, fierce competition and an array of hurdles created solely because the color of their skin colors society's perceptions of their competence.

It takes heart to build a business, especially if you are an African American. It took guts for Travers J. Bell, Jr. and Willie E. Daniels to launch the first black-owned investment banking firm admitted to the New York Stock Exchange back in 1971. It was a bold move for Edward G. Gardner to start Soft Sheen Products in 1964 with a handful of employees and only one product, and for John H. Johnson to borrow against his mother's furniture to start the first magazine aimed at a black audience.

Those pioneers had the courage to take the risks that were necessary because they understood the value of ownership—just like today's young and bold entrepreneurs, such as Robert L. Johnson, founder of Black Entertainment Television, Russell Simmons, the rap music entrepreneur and CEO of the $65 million Rush Communications, and Karl Kani, president of Karl Kani Infinity fashions.

A Dyed-in-the-Wool Entrepreneur

Kani, whose business had $59 million in sales in 1995 when it was named Company of the Year by *Black Enterprise*, is only 27 years old and a product not of the Ivy League but of Flatbush, Brooklyn. All he had going for him was moxie, a keen sense of style and an abundance of all the traits listed above. He has climbed to the top of the toughest industry out there. Its products may be clothing finery, but there is nothing delicate about the fashion business. In the early going, Kani has proved himself a survivor in a highly competitive and often cutthroat environment, but he will have to remain vigilant and fast on his feet to survive.

Like most of his friends in Flatbush, Kani, who was then known as Carl Williams, was into "freshly dipped" designer clothes, but rather than pay for those designed by others, he designed his own and had them sewn by a neighborhood tailor. His style caught on around Brooklyn, and while younger than most college students, he launched his own business, eventually moving it to Los Angeles where production costs were lower.

His business did not take off there until 1991, when he joined up with Carl Jones of Threads 4 Life and Cross Colours, marketing his Karl Kani line. His designs helped sales skyrocket from $15 million to $89 million in just one year. But by 1993, he felt Cross Colours was fading because of problems keeping up with its explosive growth. He negotiated the return of full ownership of his trademarked name and, in November of 1993, launched Karl Kani Infinity.

The line was successful from the start, but Kani's mettle was tested again when counterfeiters paid him the ultimate compliment and nearly put him under by flooding the market with their sincerest forms of felonious flattery. Not one to surrender, Kani countered by placing ads in L.A.'s media offering a reward for information leading to the arrest of those ripping off his designs. It was discovered that one of the counterfeiting rings was operating out of a warehouse not far from his own downtown L.A. design studio.

No sooner had that threat subsided when his market, young men's fashion, was suddenly targeted by a wave of companies large, small and in-between. Yet Karl Kani Infinity has succeeded so far with sales that have risen from $34 million in 1993 to $43 million in 1994 and $59 million in 1995. He has done it, in part, by bringing in experts to handle marketing, manufacturing and distribution, and he has been savvy in setting up licensing relationships that are more akin to partnerships so that he can keep a close eye on where and how his name brand products are sold.

Part of Kani's success to date can be attributed to his ability to keep finding fresh markets for his clothing and for his design expertise. After talking with several friends in the NBA about the fact that none of his merchandise fit them, he launched a special oversized line in Big & Tall stores around the country. Now that his core business of jeans and activewear appears to be doing well, he has plans to expand into footwear, women's wear, upscale men's couture and underwear. He has also expanded operations to include overseas manufacturing and distribution, with his shoe designs distributed in 14 countries.

"We want to be worldwide, that's the next level," Kani says. "You can't get bigger than that. After that, it'll have to be Space Kani."

I say more power to him and to that sort of entrepreneurial spirit. There are no guarantees that his business will continue to do so well in such a tough field of endeavor, but with his attitude, it will be hard to keep Kani down for long.

A Source for Outsourcing

Many of the people who will be starting their own businesses over the next decade will be coming out of corporations that have downsized them or sent them into early retirement with a buyout. The downsizing trends have ignited rapid growth in the hiring of outside consultants to fill in when needed in key corporate positions. If these trends continue, we may all be independent consultants one day. Consulting is a growing form of entrepreneurial business with low overhead and autonomy. But it can also be stressful and require a great deal of work.

"If you're going into a consulting business and are planning to build a firm, it's not for the weak of heart or those without physical stamina," says Greg Campbell, who with his wife, Alma Baker Campbell, left a corporate position and founded Baker Campbell Associates in Dallas. Over ten years they built their management consulting firm into a business with a staff of seven and billings approaching $1 million.

Along the way they learned that consulting work takes aggressive marketing and pricing strategies as well as the ability to handle a number of tasks at the same time. Sixty-hour work weeks are not uncommon for the Campbells.

Pricing is the most important aspect of consulting work. Many people fail to charge enough for their services when they start out, says Stan Berliner, president of Consultants' Network, a New York clearinghouse for consulting opportunities. There is a delicate balance between charging enough to reflect your experience, reputation, the market and the value of your services and scaring off potential clients.

Aspiring consultants need to determine what their competitors charge as well as what clients of all sizes generally are willing to pay. The American Association of Healthcare Consultants, one of many organizations for consultants, notes that most consultants are available 2,080 hours a year. Fees should take into account how much you want to make for a 40-hour week and what your overhead will be, they advise. It is essential to set consulting fees in a systematic way and include specific payment schedules in the contract. This provides you with payments throughout the course of the contract so that you can pay costs as you incur them.

Marketing your services is also vitally important. A low-cost way to do that is to write articles or serve as an information source frequently quoted in newspapers, magazines and trade journals related to your field of expertise. Speaking to special interest, professional and charitable organizations is another cost-efficient way of getting out the word about your product or service.

A long-term marketing strategy is vital, as well as an aggressive approach to opportunities as they appear. Pat Tobin, the former CBS Television media coordinator who launched Tobin & Associates public relations consulting firm, went after Japanese business clients in the United States immediately after she heard news reports that the Japanese Prime Minister had said disparaging things about African Americans. Determined to educate Japanese businessmen here, she targeted every Japanese-owned company in Southern California and landed a contract with Toyota Motor Sales U.S.A., which became her biggest client.

The Franchise Option to Ownership

Tobin's is a typical entrepreneurial attitude—the sky's the limit. Of course, not all would-be entrepreneurs have the resources to launch their own businesses. That's why I have long championed the opportunities offered by franchising, primarily as an entry-level entrepreneurial activity for African Americans. From Wally "Famous" Amos to Brady Keys, Jr., franchisor of All-Pro Fried Chicken in 1967, African Americans have been making advances and contributions to the franchise field for decades.

In 1970 *Black Enterprise*'s premier issue featured a report on blacks in franchising, and we have closely reported the franchise field—its opportunities and its pitfalls—ever since because it can be an important step toward economic independence and the building of wealth in our community.

When you choose the franchise option, you buy into a nameplate, a proven system and, with luck, a well-developed network of training and support. You can invest $1,000 or $1 million. You can buy or rent a location, or you can work out of your home office. Many African Americans have entered the entrepreneurial market by purchasing franchises and then upgrading to bigger franchises before starting their own businesses based on what they learned and how they profited.

Others, like myself, have established businesses of their own before ever considering making a go of franchising. My relationship with Pepsi-Cola began because I was the right guy in the right place at the right time. In 1990, Pepsi was making an effort to increase minority involvement because it made good business sense for them.

In Pepsi, I found a good company and a good deal. In me, they found an astute businessman. The deal has borne fruit for all concerned. Mine is a profitable business that was honored to be chosen Franchisee of the Year in 1994 and 1995, due in no small part to the vigilant efforts of my youngest son, Michael, who this year will become the vice president and general manager of our franchise.

A First-Class Franchise Opportunity

My franchise business began with a first-class ticket on an airline flight. Now a first-class seat will normally get you a few amenities such as more personal service, free drinks and an entrée that doesn't go down like a scouring pad, but I certainly never expected to be presented with a $60 million business deal on a flight from Washington, D.C. to New York City, especially not from the complete stranger sitting alongside me.

I've often been amused by the actions of white seatmates in the first-class section of airline flights. Generally they start by trying to determine whether I am an entertainer or an athlete, since many affluent whites assume that any African American who can afford first class must be one or the other. A few years ago, a white man turned to me on a flight and asked, "Aren't you a pro basketball player?"

"Good Lord, man, I'm 59 years old! What do you think?" I replied.

Usually I try to dispel those notions before takeoff so that I can get down to the more serious matter of determining whether there is any business to be done with whoever is sitting beside me. But on one particular flight to New York City in 1991, Tom Schadt beat me to the first question. After mutual introductions, he asked me what I did for a living. I didn't answer. I called for the flight attendant instead.

When I pushed the button, Schadt seemed to panic, wondering what he had said or how he had offended me. Noticing his discomfort, I told him that I was just calling for a magazine. When the flight attendant arrived, she handed me a copy of *Black Enterprise*, which I presented to Schadt. "This is what I do," I told him. Schadt, who had never seen our magazine, was intrigued. He spent the next hour carefully examining it, from editorial to advertising. When he completed his study, he turned to me and said, "You ought to be doing business with my company."

Schadt had already informed me that he was a senior executive for the Pepsi-Cola Company. I had noted, in return, that Pepsi was a frequent advertiser in my magazine. But advertising was not what Schadt had in mind. When he returned to his offices after the flight, he took my business card and a copy of *Black Enterprise* to his bosses. With an eye toward Coca-Cola's success with African American consumers, Pepsi-Cola had undertaken a campaign to increase minority representation among its franchise owners. I was to become a prime candidate.

Within a few weeks of meeting Schadt, I was invited to a luncheon meeting with Craig Weatherup, who was then CEO of Worldwide Beverages for the Pepsi-Cola Company of America. Initially, Pepsi had in mind selling me a midsized franchise, but I had eyes for bigger game. Eventually, after a great deal of networking and negotiating, I ended up with the Pepsi-Cola bottling franchise for Washington, D.C. and Prince George's County. That Pepsi franchise, like the franchise deal I put together in South Africa, has been lucrative, as such arrangements can be, but franchising is not for everyone.

The Good and Bad of Franchise Ownership

There are now more than 3,500 business franchisors with more than 550,000 outlets in 65 different industries nationwide. Franchises employ more than 8 million people, and their suppliers employ another 2.4 million. The total franchise market in this country is estimated to be a $975 billion business. Franchises offer everything from pretzel stores to lawn care, house maids, home improvement and gift baskets—nearly any type of business imaginable, and some you would never think of.

Not every franchise niche is a money machine. Much of the industry's double-digit growth has been in specific areas such as children's services; recreation, entertainment and travel; maintenance and cleaning services; retail food (not convenience stores); and construction and home improvement. Overall, the number of franchised businesses increases about 6 percent a year, according to the International Franchise Association in Washington, D.C. The association notes that a new franchise opens every six and a half minutes of each business day, drawing people from all walks of life—from corporate professionals to recent college grads to downsized workers and small business owners—into this form of entrepreneurship.

But is it for everyone? No, it is not. First, you need to consider whether your personality is suited to franchising because even if you have the traits that make for a good entrepreneur, this type of entrepreneurship has its own unique requirements and challenges, particularly for African Americans.

Franchisors are not social workers, they are businesspeople. Although many of them seem to revel in reciting their commitments to diversity, minority involvement and locating in minority neighborhoods and communities, in fact there is far more talk than action.

After more than a decade of glowing but hollow rhetoric about diversity initiatives, franchisors still are not making any great effort to recruit or retain minority entrepreneurs, according to Susan P. Kezios of Chicago, who is president of the American Franchisers Association and Women in Franchising. As of the fall of 1995, McDonald's Corporation had 9,796 franchises, and little more than 7 percent were black owned. Less than 3 percent of Subway's

10,646 franchise locations were black owned. Less than 2 percent of Wendy's 3,983 franchise restaurants were black owned.

It is a sad fact that the vast majority of franchises in this country don't have any African American owners. The perception seems to be that minorities don't have any money or any interest in franchising, so why should franchisors recruit them? This sounds all too familiar to me. It is the same attitude our salespeople frequently encounter when trying to sell advertising to white-dominated businesses.

A number of major franchisors have seen the light only after being dragged into court or threatened with discrimination litigation. Denny's Restaurants, Flagstar Companies, based in Spartanburg, South Carolina, is a prime example. It took a $46 million class-action lawsuit settlement to move the $1.5 billion chain into action. Denny's signed a fair share agreement with the NAACP as part of the settlement in two class-action suits. In the agreement, the chain promised to boost minority participation in ownership, management, marketing and purchasing.

On the flip side, there are some impressive African American success stories in the franchise field.

▪ The largest black-owned Burger King franchise is V&J Foods, Inc. in Milwaukee, operated by Valerie Daniels-Carter, who in 1994 negotiated a 17-store deal that raised the company's total to 32 outlets. The ten-year-old company grossed $30 million in 1994.

▪ Thompson Hospitality L.P. in Reston, Virginia, became one of the nation's largest black-owned franchises in 1992, when Warren M. Thompson acquired 31 Bob's Big Boy restaurants. His company had revenues of $29 million in 1994.

▪ In early 1995, Larry Lundy purchased 7 new Pizza Huts, bringing his total franchise properties to 41. His New Orleans company posted $23.4 million in revenues in 1994.

These black-owned megafranchises generate big revenues and employ hundreds of African Americans, but they are the exception rather than the rule in the franchise field. As part of the fight for a greater share of the franchise industry, minorities are calling for greater community involvement in pressuring franchisors to respect their market. Some financial institutions, such as Bankers Trust in

New York, have teamed up with community development corporations to put more franchise outlets in urban areas and recruit minorities to run them.

Nontraditional Franchising Opportunities

A trend that seems to be conducive to increased minority involvement is the movement of franchises into "nontraditional" settings. Once restricted to main thoroughfares and shopping malls, franchises are now being located increasingly on military bases, college and even high school campuses, in supermarkets, hospitals, airports, zoos, theme parks, concert arenas, sports stadiums and other areas.

This arrangement benefits minorities because it allows for lower start-up costs. Hannibal Myers, director of national special unit development for Wendy's International says that a nontraditional fast-food restaurant can cost around $250,000 compared with $1 million for a typical traditional franchise on Main Street, U.S.A.

Not surprisingly, McDonald's pioneered this trend. In 1994 black entrepreneur John Tillman opened a high-tech, higher education McDonald's in Texas. The restaurant, which has Macintosh and IBM computers, laser printers, copy machines and a fax, sits between the campuses of the University of Houston and Texas Southern University.

Location, location, location is especially important in the fast food franchise business, and nontraditional franchising opens doors in some heavily trafficked areas. Kenneth James and his family of African American franchisers opened their Wendy's in 1992 at Houston International Airport's Continental Airlines terminal, where foot traffic exceeds more than 40,000 passengers each day. James says that his sales revenues put his unit among the chain's top 3 percent worldwide.

Wendy's is expanding rapidly in this area as a way to bring more minorities into the fold, and so are many other franchisors, including America's Favorite Chicken Company, parent of Popeye's Famous Fried Chicken and Biscuits and Churchs. This $590 million chain based in Atlanta has joined forces with Kroger to open 15 to 20 Churchs in its supermarkets throughout Ohio. Former Arby's franchisee George Shanklin will spearhead the project and own the new outlets. At last check, only a meager 52 of Churchs' 941 outlets were owned by blacks.

As an African American entrepreneur experienced in the franchise field, Shanklin insists that many so-called diversity initiatives by franchisors are nothing more than smoke and mirrors, because the white corporate officers have failed to acknowledge that it makes sense to bring members of their consumer base into the family as owners too. He credits America's Favorite Chicken with committing to greater minority inclusion.

Buying into Franchising

The primary appeal of franchising in the past was that it was in general a less risky, less costly way to own your own business. The average cost of buying into a franchise today, however, is nearly $150,000, with the start-up cost of a McDonald's restaurant at about $500,000. A Burger King is close behind at about $400,000. There are still opportunities, however, for those whose pockets do not run so deep. For example, the janitorial service franchise Coverall North American can be purchased for around $1,000.

There are several independent programs designed to develop and finance franchise start-ups. One is the Banker's Trust Neighborhood Franchise Project, a joint venture with the Local Initiatives Support Corporation, a nonprofit organization that provides financial and technical support to 1,300 community development corporations around the country. These corporations are nonprofit organizations controlled by local residents. Traditionally used in developing affordable housing, they are now used for economic development, such as aiding franchise businesses that benefit inner-city neighborhoods.

But a franchise that has low start-up costs comes with no guarantees of growth potential. There are pitfalls, including inflated sales estimates, unfair contracts, the failure of franchisors to obey federal disclosure laws and the opening of competing franchises near existing outlets. Black franchise owners have also complained in recent years that franchisors only give them units in high-risk, low-return neighborhoods and that franchisors practice "sharecropping" by demanding more controls of black owners.

Here is some information that *Black Enterprise* has gathered over the years:

1. Franchise buyers need to know exactly what they are buying into.

Under federal law, each franchise is required to give you access to its Uniform Franchise Offering Circular (UFOC), which offers information about the company's finances as well as details of the franchise agreement. You need to know, for example, whether the franchise fee includes training, on-site support and advertising.

The most useful information is on the back of the pamphlet, where it discloses whether the franchisor or any of its executive officers have been convicted of felonies involving fraud, franchise law violations or unfair or deceptive practices. The UFOC also indicates if any key individuals have been found liable in a civil action involving the franchise relationship. It should also list current and former franchisees. You can call to check on their feelings about their relationships with the franchisors.

2. Franchises do not encourage independent thinking.

The desire to control and profit from your own business may make buying a franchise appealing, but it takes more than an entrepreneurial bent to be successful. As I noted earlier, most entrepreneurs are independent spirits who get more out of starting a business than running it. If that describes you, franchising may be the wrong way to go. Franchise owners are often required to follow strict guidelines laid down by the franchisor, which owns the trademark and concept. Those guidelines often predetermine how the business will be run, which can be good, but they can also restrict your own approach to marketing and delivering your service or goods.

3. You will need a solid business plan.

The guidelines provided by the franchisor do not eliminate the need for a good business plan. In fact this is the first vital step to owning and operating a successful franchise. To evaluate a franchise offering properly, you should ask the franchisor for a detailed list of all estimated start-up costs and working capital requirements. Find out how many units a franchisor has and how many have closed shop. According to the International Franchise Association, the primary reason franchises fail is that capital dries up.

4. Bad contracts make for bad partners.

No matter how inviting a franchisor's marketing material might be, never sign an agreement until an attorney has reviewed the contract thoroughly. It should spell out the rights and obligations of both the franchisor and the franchisee.

5. Franchise ownership is not a part-time job.

Do not make the mistake of many new franchise owners, who underestimate the time that must be devoted to the business. If you are looking for a straight nine-to-five job, you are not a candidate to be either an entrepreneur or a franchise owner.

You are responsible for the 24-hour-a-day maintenance of your business. You have to meet deadlines and quotas. You must stay abreast of the market. Most franchisors provide training workshops for new franchisees. Attendance at seminars and annual meetings will help you in operating, managing and marketing the business. Keep in mind, however, that as the owner, you can't afford to sit back and give direction. You may well find yourself on the frying line, cleaning the restrooms and sweeping up the parking lot at night.

6. Business training is important.

If you don't have a lot of it, you might consider partnering with franchisors that have well-established and extensive training programs, such as McDonald's or American Leak Detection. Business neophytes should look at franchises specializing in one product (such as pretzels) or service rather than one with a wide range of products and services such as a convenience store. Far too often, franchisors do not carry out promises of extensive training, guidance and market support. This is the most common complaint among franchise owners.

7. Equity is important.

Do not borrow all of the start-up fees. Conservative owners advise that operators should have enough money in reserve to last at least three years without profits.

8. Beware of uncontrolled growth in a franchisor.

Black entrepreneur Charles E. Peppers quit his job in database management at Illinois Bell to open an American Speedy Printing Center in Chicago's Loop. He discovered that the rapidly growing franchise had "a suburban mentality" while trying to expand into the city. They knew nothing about city codes so their floor plan was rejected. He received little marketing support and only one week of on-site assistance. Just as he was breaking even, his franchisor filed for Chapter 11.

9. Get expert advice.

Franchising does provide opportunities for African American entrepreneurs, but you should go into it, as I did, with your eyes wide open and all systems on alert. You need a specific and well-thought-out game plan, smart legal and accounting help and a finely tuned b.s. detector to get in and stay in for the long haul.

10. Know what it takes to get out.

Tough termination provisions in your franchise contract can bind you for life, calling for everything from deidentification from the franchisor to strict noncompetition clauses. Worse, some franchise agreements allow termination only if initiated by the franchisor, meaning that franchise owners could be stuck with a business even when they want out.

Additional Information

For additional information on franchise ownership, here are a few resources.

- International Franchise Association (IFA), 1350 New York Avenue, NW, Suite 900, Washington, D.C. 20005–4709.
- The American Franchisee Association and Women in Franchising, Inc. (WIF), 53 West Jackson Boulevard, Suite 205, Chicago, IL 60604.
- American Association of Franchises and Dealers (AAFD), 1420 Kettner Boulevard, Suite 415, San Diego, CA 92101.
- National Black McDonald's Operators Association, P.O. Box 8204, Los Angeles, CA 90008.

My parents, Winifred Sealy
and Earl Godwyn Graves,
on their wedding day.

Loaded up and
ready to go in
my pre-sideburn
paratrooping
days.

On the track
team at
Morgan State.

The best decision I ever made—business,
personal or otherwise—was to marry
Barbara Eliza Kydd in July 1960 (that's
my mom on the right).

Strategizing with Robert F. Kennedy on the family plane, the *Caroline*. We were on the campaign trail to upstate New York.

Escorting Coretta Scott King into a memorial mass for Robert Kennedy at St. Patrick's Cathedral in New York.

With John Lewis and Julian Bond on the steps of the Capitol, circa 1971. We were in Washington to drum up government advertising for this great new publication, *Black Enterprise*.

The original *Black Enterprise* Board of Advisers (*rear row, from left*): me, John Lewis, William R. Hudgins, Julian Bond, Thomas A. Johnson, Henry G. Parks Jr; (*seated, from left*) Edward Brooke, Shirley Chisholm, Charles Evers.

Addressing President Jimmy Carter and B.E. 100s CEOs, including B.E. Entrepreneur of the Century, the late A. G. Gaston (*third from right*), on the occasion of our 1978 visit to the White House.

My three sons (*from left*), Johnny, Michael, and "Butch," or Earl Jr., are outstanding businessmen. More important, they are terrific people.

A day to remember: Nelson Mandela and several black business leaders, including David Dinkins, then mayor of New York, gather in *Black Enterprise*'s executive boardroom in 1991.

Greeting President George Bush at a Camp David meeting of the New American School Development Corporation in 1991.

At a Boy Scouts awards ceremony in the White House with President and Mrs. Ronald Reagan.

Vice President Al Gore on a visit to Pepsi-Cola of Washington, D.C., L.P.

YOUR CHOICE IN D.C.

FROM YOUR TEAM IN D.C.

Earl H. Graves

EARL G. GRAVES, *Franchise Owner*, Pepsi-Cola of Washington, D.C., and the team that brings you Pepsi.

With the Pepsi team in D.C. That's my son Michael next to me.

A landmark picture during a landmark year: I'm flanked by Johnson Publications CEO John H. Johnson and Essence Communications CEO Ed Lewis at the Plaza Hotel in early 1995, the anniversary year of each of our publications. *Ebony* celebrated its 50th; *Black Enterprise* and *Essence* each marked 25.

Greeting President Bill Clinton in the Oval Office, as good ol' Abe looks on.

You have no idea how long it took to get my five grandchildren to face in one direction (*seated, left to right*): Erika, Veronica, Theodore, and Kristin. That's Earl III grinning in the front.

Yes, that's me. On the links, on the phone, on Labor Day.

The late secretary of commerce Ron Brown and me, chatting in his office. He was a true friend and the greatest commerce secretary this country has ever had.

To Earl
With appreciation and best wishes to a true friend
Ron Brown

CHAPTER 9

Planning for Business Success

Before we get rolling on this important chapter, I have to make a confession. When I began *Black Enterprise*, I was a man without a business plan. But consider me a true convert, because if there is one way to learn the value of a business plan, it is to try and start a business without one. I quickly learned that it is essential to have a well-defined, carefully thought out, strategy for getting the business started as well as for courting investors and gauging your progress. In my other businesses, particularly my Pepsi franchise, I have spent long hours developing business plans. I have also discovered that if there is a common thread among successful African American–owned businesses, it's that they have a plan that brings together the goals, the strategies and the resources of their companies.

At Earl Graves Ltd., we receive at least five solicitations each week from African American entrepreneurs seeking either our financial support or advice in their business ventures. Of those five, we generally reject four out of hand because they lack a cohesive and coherent business plan that lays out not only the concept but solid marketing and cash flow analysis.

One recent solicitation came in the form of a hand-written letter that was little more than a recounting of a dream this person had for the salvation of African Americans with some sort of an entertainment company. It was clear that this person had no experience, no capital, no articulated plan and simply no clue as to what was involved in starting a business.

Sadly, the majority of the business plans I do receive are half-baked documents that say, "Here is my idea. It would create jobs and be a huge success, but I don't have any money so please send me some and God bless you." Obviously, we have yet to respond to such a plea by sending a check. Nor do we tend to be sympathetic to those that essentially say, "I'm black. You're black. Please send money." And sometimes they don't even say *please*.

Your business plan is a reflection of how serious, how committed and how prepared you are to get in the game of business, and if it is not a well-prepared, carefully researched document, you won't get in my door or any other. There are too many other people out there who take the time to do it right, so why should a bank, an investor or a partner take a poorly prepared business plan seriously?

Your business plan should be your road map to success. It should be so thoughtfully done that with only slight alterations it can carry you through the first six months of your business, and even beyond. A solid business plan defines your business concept, lures investors, helps launch new products and services, evaluates the competition and controls risks. In short, it is the Holy Grail for any successful business. It is particularly important for African American entrepreneurs to have a strong business plan because of the obstacles we face in obtaining financing.

A carefully crafted business plan helped Gilda and Amir Salmon land a $30,000 small business loan to expand their hair care salon in Patterson, New Jersey. Their meticulously prepared plan convinced the Bergen Commercial Bank in nearby Paramus, New Jersey, and the Patterson Economic Development Corporation that the Salmons were worth a risk. "The business plan is the first thing bankers ask to see," says Amir Salmon, president of Gilda & Amir's Salon, Inc. "They want to know how much of your money is invested in the business and what you have to offer as collateral. For us, it was $5,000 in savings and our house."

In addition to scrutinizing the Salmons' financial projections, the bank took a hard look at the management section of the business plan. The bank was impressed that between them the Salmons had more than 15 years of experience in the hair care business. The business's conservative financial projections, strong management experience and a solid customer base outlined in the plan made it clear that the salon could compete in downtown Patterson, where mom-and-pop shops were suffering at the expense of mini-malls.

Thanks to the long-term financial projections in the plan, the bank loaned the Salmons an additional $5,000 over and above the Patterson Economic Development Corporation's $25,000 ceiling. It was a smart bet by the bank because the Salmons' business has more than exceeded expectations: 1996 profits were more than double the previous year's.

Getting the Numbers Right

Although your enthusiasm and reputation may be enough to convince family and friends to invest in your business, they won't hold much sway with bankers and other types of outside investors. When you are black and the banker is white, no amount of charm is going to convince them to open up the vault for you. They want the facts: an objective, in-depth analysis of the business—warts and all. If your numbers are no good, a business plan, no matter how perfectly prepared, won't fool anyone. Bankers are primarily interested in your company's fixed assets, including the building and equipment as well as other collateral you stake to the proposition. The bank, of course, wants to be assured that you are capable of repaying the loan at the going interest rate. It may require that you give them a deed to the house, the car and your first-born child.

Venture capitalists reviewing your plan, on the other hand, will want even more—a stake in your business in the form of a cut of your equity and its profits. Venture capitalists usually want to earn a 30 to 35 percent risk-adjusted annual return on their investment. They want to get back six times their money in three to five years. It sounds like a lot to surrender, but without the cash you may not be able to step up to the plate. Venture capitalists want to know not only what they are getting into but how to get out of the investment. So your business plan should provide an exit strategy that includes timetables plus projected returns.

Tell the Story of Your Business

A business plan should tell your company's story. An ideal length is about 25 pages—certainly no more than 50 pages. Spare your readers any puffery. Sophisticated investors will see right through the smokescreen. Expect to spend at least six months preparing the document. No two business plans are exactly alike—some can be overly long, running in excess of 100 pages. At least one business plan—Southwest Airline's—was scratched out on the back of a cocktail napkin by its irrepressible founder, Herb Kelleher. Bankers and investors sizing up your company will usually prefer something more formal.

No matter which route you choose, your plan should contain the following basic elements:

1. The Executive Summary

One of the most important tasks of this section is to convince readers that they should want to read the business plan in its entirety. The plan should convey the passion you have for your business. As the name suggests, this section should explain the company's objectives, history, management and financials in a two- to three-page nutshell. This section may be all that some people read, so make every word count.

A description of your product, market, customers and suppliers is important. Also explain what sets your company's goods or services apart from the competition. If your company anticipates turning a profit in three years, provide evidence of how that will be accomplished. If you're requesting money, state exactly how much is needed and for what purpose. Potential returns on investment also need to be addressed in this section.

2. Market Analysis

This section should elaborate on who your customers are and what attracts them to your business. Describe the demographics of your target audience, industry trends and what the future may hold. List all of your known competitors and their advantages and disadvantages compared to your business.

Trade associations are valuable resources for collecting market intelligence. Most groups are eager to provide information about their industries. The *Encyclopedia of Associations* lists their addresses and phone numbers. Other good resources include the *Thomas Register of Manufacturers* and the *Rand McNally Commercial Atlas and Commercial Guide*. The World Wide Web is another valuable source of marketing information.

Experts who review business plans say that many of them fail to address marketing issues adequately. The plans lack in-depth marketing analysis. Because a marketing plan is such a critical element of a business plan, I will discuss it separately later in the chapter.

3. Management Summary

This section needs to explain who will run the company. Investors are often more concerned about the management of the company than the product or service it offers. It's best to assume that potential investors know nothing about you and the people you have enlisted to run the company.

Biographies of yourself and your managers should note relevant skills, prior experience, degrees and certifications. You don't need to put in there that you had chickenpox when you were seven years old, but you must be thorough. You should explain each person's role and financial stake in the company. An organization chart is recommended for companies that have more than five managers.

4. Financial Analysis

Recap your company's financial growth projections for at least three and as many as five years. Explain how the money will be generated to operate the business.

If your company is already in business, you'll need to provide a balance sheet, which indicates the status of the company's assets, liabilities and equity ownership. Existing companies should also include a profit-and-loss statement. The so-called P & L, or income, statement reflects the results of operations by comparing total revenues against all operating costs—expenses such as supplies, salaries, insurance and other overhead.

Both existing and start-up companies should provide cash-flow forecasts that track the movements of income and expenditures. With a firm grasp of the company's cash flow pattern, it's easier to determine how much money or credit will be necessary to operate the company.

Both start-up and existing companies require a break-even analysis, which shows how long it will take a business to turn a profit. The break-even point is reached when sales revenues equal total cost.

A Sample Plan

To illustrate how a business plan can be constructed, I've put together a hypothetical one based on my own experiences and also on the teaching experiences of Sid H. Credle, Ph.D., director of academic programs at Florida A&M University's School of Business & Industry, who has appeared at our Entrepreneur's Conference.

Credle, who reviewed numerous small business proposals while he was president of a New York consulting firm specializing in business planning, has used the hypothetical start-up of a computer training school in Tallahassee, Florida. Called Tallahassee Computer Training Company, it proposed to train secretaries and administrators from the state of Florida and specifically from the city of Tallahassee, Florida State University and Florida A&M.

One of the primary reasons the business plan was drafted was to raise equity financing for the start-up.

1. Executive Summary. This very important section outlined the plan's key sections, including the industry description, industry analysis, target market and financials.

2. Company Description. This section explained how the company would operate in downtown Tallahassee with 10 to 15 computers. Instruction would be offered in four or five major software applications such as word processing and database management.

3. Industry Analysis. Research indicated that 3,000 personal computers were operated by the city, with 2,000 more at Florida A&M and 4,000 at Florida State. An additional 12,000 PCs were operated by businesses, including legal and medical practices. Those 21,000 workstations were each manned by a person potentially interested in learning five new software applications, for a total of 110,000 potential classes. This was the target market. The section also included demographic information and trends on the growth of PC usage in the community and the nation.

4. Competition. Here it was explained that the founders of Tallahassee Computer Training Company had checked the yellow pages and found eight computer training outfits in the community. It was discovered on further investigation that several were fly-by-night operations. More serious competition would be offered by several training centers operated by local technical schools.

Based on the analysis of the competition, the company estimated that it could snare about 20 percent of the market of people wanting to learn new software applications. It backed up that projection by noting that its new, well-designed downtown facility featured all new computers, the instructors would be well trained and present a professional image, the software manufacturers had authorized the company to train on their programs, the company had an impressive board of directors, and it offered a job placement service.

5. Market Plan and Sales Strategy. In this section the company outlined its media buying plan and explained how company representatives would visit decision makers at the major institutions it targeted to sell them on the company.

6. Operations. Here the company described its training facility and the types of computers it would have, as well as other machinery, raw materials and overhead used to operate the business. It is also noted that the classes would be taught by certified outside contractors who would offer classes during three periods each day: 10 A.M. to noon, 1 P.M. to 3 P.M. and 5 P.M. to 7 P.M.

7. Management and Organization. Because this section is so carefully scrutinized by investors, lengthy biographies of the principals were presented. In my experience, a business plan is viewed more positively if the investors or lenders know members of the company's management team.

8. Long-Term Development. In this section, Tallahassee Computer detailed its plan to expand into Jacksonville and Atlanta. Longer-range plans called for the company to launch franchise operations outside of the Southeast because a competitive analysis found that there were no recognizable national computer training companies. The section also indicated potential areas of weakness, to give the plan more credibility with skeptical investors.

9. Financials. A monthly cash-flow statement for the first year and a three-year cash-flow projection prepared by an accountant, a business consultant, an attorney and a banker were presented in this section. An income statement based on a three-year plan and a monthly one-year plan was presented. Also included was a break-even analysis. According to the break-even analysis, Tallahassee Computer, if operating at full capacity, would be in the black by the 25th week of operation.

10. Appendix. Included here was supporting evidence such as pie charts, graphs and other statistical analysis.

Preparing Your Business Plan

I recommend that you go through this exercise yourself. The blood, sweat and tears are well worth it because the exercise forces the entrepreneur to consider every possible angle in developing the plan. There are a number of books and software programs that can help an entrepreneur write a business plan. They can be used to provide a framework.

No matter how you draw up your business plan, remember that neatness counts. It should look as professional as possible. With the advances in desktop publishing and laser printing, there's no reason a small company's plan can't look as impressive as something spit out by a Fortune 500 company. Spend the extra nickel to buy a high-quality paper stock or add a second color, possibly four colors. The document should include a cover, a table of contents, headers and footers. Tabs can be used to help readers find their way quickly through the material.

It goes without saying that spelling and grammar should meet the most exacting standards. Graphs and charts must not only be attractive but packed with information to support your case. Carefully proofread the document for errors, and then hand it off to someone else to catch the mistakes you may have missed. Even the smallest error might raise questions in an investor's mind about how well you and your company will handle larger issues—including their money—if you're careless about the little things.

It's tough work, but stay with it. Hammering out a winning business plan is a good preparation for the trials and tribulations of actually running a business. The only difference is that it's probably 100 times tougher to run a business than it is write the plan that will serve as its foundation.

Presenting Your Business Plan

Over the years I have had dozens of people pitch me on their business plans and I can spot the ones who won't make it. How? They are the ones who almost collapse on the floor and weep if I question any aspect of their presentations. They are the people who don't really believe in what they are doing. They lack real commitment.

If Chase Manhattan had not loaned me the money to start *Black Enterprise*, I was fully prepared to go across the street to another bank, or to someone higher at Chase. A business plan has to be sold like any product or service. You can have a masterpiece of a business plan, but if you don't present it in a professional manner to your bankers or investors, you might as well have written it in the sand.

The secret to selling a business plan is the same as for marketing any other product: You have to have a passion for what you are doing, and your pitch for the plan must reflect your enthusiasm and commitment. Because investors and lenders are deluged with business plans, there must be something that sets your plan apart from the rest.

Not only should a business plan display some passion, but it should be pragmatic. Sugar-coated scenarios are quickly rejected. A best-case, worst-case and most likely–case should be presented to investors, lenders or potential business partners.

It's also important to customize or at least tweak your plan so that it's tailored to a particular audience. A plan directed at bankers may not sound as appealing to a potential member of the board or a potential key employee of your future company. Certain sections of the business plan, such as the financials or the marketing plan, can be pulled out for a quick presentation to someone considering becoming involved with the company.

In putting together a business plan, entrepreneurs should develop a strategic framework in which they determine where they are today and where they want to be tomorrow. Here are several other pointers for successfully developing and presenting a business plan.

1. Identify the good guys and the bad guys. Who can help you? Who might hurt you? By making a list of your competitors and anticipating any potential objections, the entrepreneur is less likely to be blind-sided in either the development or presentation phase.

2. Understand the needs and concerns of those you are pitching. Get to know the culture of the top executives and financial people you are going to be selling to, as well as other targets for your pitch.

3. Maintain your plan's confidentiality. Because wonderful ideas presented in business plans can be stolen by an unscrupulous lender or investor, it's recommended that your attorney draft a confidentiality agreement. Anyone who resists signing forfeits the opportunity to review the plan. The confidentiality question should be handled discreetly. Be honest with people. Tell them why you believe it's important that they consider signing the agreement.

Keeping Your Plan Up to Date

It is important to review your business plan frequently—at least once a year, perhaps every quarter—because it should serve as your day-to-day guide. Your market may change, and although you may make adjustments, you should review your plan to take account of possible long-range developments. This also provides the opportunity to check your budget against actual performance and to take a critical, objective view of your business.

Harry Davis and his partners are constantly updating their company's business plan and believe the exercise is one reason for the success of the New York–based television and multimedia production house. For example, the company's founders spent about three months in 1992 devising a business plan that was used to raise about $20,000 in a private placement stock offering to produce two short films. Later that year the company, known at the time as Real-to-Reel Pictures Entertainment, Inc., sold 40 shares of its stock to 12 people to raise an additional $100,000. The money financed a 30-minute television pilot called "Street Games," which featured interviews with star athletes, their families and childhood neighbors of the athletes. The company's five-year business plan smartly included a market study of the target audience for "Street Games," but the final projections for production costs proved to be more than the company anticipated.

Recognizing that changes needed to be made for the company to survive, Real-to-Reel restructured itself from a film production house into one that would concentrate on nonlinear television and multimedia pre- and postproduction. Known today as the Reel Deal, it produces film, television and music video projects. It also does licensing and merchandising under the name A Raw Art Vibe. Reel Deal modified its business plan to reflect all the changes that took place at the company. The revised business plan addressed such changes as staffing levels, new equipment purchases and plans to rent out the company's studios to generate additional revenue.

Don Sutton, founder and president of the San Francisco–based furniture company Just Chairs, found that the discipline of writing a business plan for his existing $3 million business opened his eyes to some opportunities he was missing. The original purpose of the business plan was to raise $1 million through a private placement stock offering to help expand his company, founded in 1985. He had been operating his company for years without a business plan for expansion.

Sutton hired an accountant to crunch the numbers and a writer to produce the copy for the new business plan. But he relied too heavily on them, allowing the writer to direct the content and the accountant to develop the ratios for the financial projections. The business plan was too long, and the accountant's numbers didn't pan out. The document was of little value to potential new investors.

The silver lining in the exercise was that it made Sutton realize his company had been sitting on excess inventory. The company had been targeting corporate customers and the high end of the home office business. To reduce inventory, Just Chairs opened a clearance outlet, offering discontinued products at discounted prices. The company can now compete with such office supply superstores as Office Depot and Office Max without hurting Just Chair's core business. The new store is the company's highest-volume outlet.

The beauty of writing a business plan in the later stages of a company's life cycle, as Sutton can attest, is that it can reveal short-comings or missed opportunities. Updating the marketing component of your business plan can be just as helpful in making sure that your company stays on track. Inattention to a company's marketing objectives and strategies is one of the leading killers of young companies. The mortality rate of new companies in the United States, unfortunately, is quite high. Two of every three new businesses fail within five years.

Making Adjustments in the Marketing Plan

As all hard-charging entrepreneurs already know, a marketing strategy is a key ingredient of a business plan—especially in the company's early stages. To be effective, a marketing plan can't gather dust on a shelf but must be a living document providing the fuel and direction to drive a company forward. The marketing component of your business plan will help you keep track of customers, the competition, distribution, pricing and market share.

A marketing plan should not be written in stone, but rather should be continually examined and refined to meet the latest market conditions. A good marketing plan establishes a demand for your product or service and can forecast your business's potential for growth. Developing a marketing blueprint calls for identifying a niche, summarizing objectives, preparing a strategy and tracking results.

One entrepreneur who readjusted his company's marketing strategy as it grew is Reginald L. Dunham, founder of Los Angeles–based DataPrompt, Inc. The company's initial marketing strategy was to recycle laser printer and copy machine cartridges, remanufacturing them and selling them back to major corporations. But because so many other companies began doing the same thing, Dunham concluded that a midcourse correction was in order.

DataPrompt rewrote its marketing plan and repositioned itself as an environmental consulting firm. The company's employees used desktop publishing to produce newsletters, brochures, product releases and catalogs to covey its modified mission to its target audience. The reconfiguring paid off handsomely for DataPrompt, whose revenues top $1 million and are climbing. The company has landed such blue-chip clients as Warner Brothers, Honda and Walt Disney.

Ebony Marketing Research, Inc., a market research firm based in the Bronx, New York, updated its marketing plan to capture government business. Originally the company did market analysis for Fortune 500 companies targeting ethnic markets. The company's new strategy calls for identifying government agencies that could use *Ebony*'s services. Bruce Kirkland, vice president of the firm, says that *Ebony* uses direct mail followed up by personal sales calls to generate new government business.

"Marketing is everything," he says. "You have to have a good product or service, but if it's not marketed correctly, forget it." Longer range, the company plans to target international markets.

When entrepreneurs map out a marketing plan, they must think in terms of the 5 Ps. They are . . .

1. **P**roduct. This includes the product's design and development, branding and packaging. Beyond that, entrepreneurs must determine what their product or service offers that their competitors do not. Another important consideration is to whom the product will be sold.

2. **P**rice. A pricing strategy allows you to price your offerings based on market information collected. It also establishes the level of profitability for your company. Much psychology goes into properly pricing a product or service. A premium product that is discount priced may not sell, because people won't perceive its true value. The price of a product or service also needs to be consistent with the company's image and concept.

3. **P**lace. This component includes the channels of distribution to be used in moving the product from the manufacturer to the buyer. Entrepreneurs should determine whether the product should be sold though retail outlets or via such direct channels as infomercials or telemarketing. Entrepreneurs should be mindful that certain channels are more appropriate for certain products. Products that might best be sold through mass marketing won't necessarily sell through networking channels.

4. **P**romotion. Also known as marketing communications, some of the best-known tools in this category are advertising and public relations. Direct marketing and grass-roots or event marketing are growing increasingly popular. A marketer doesn't need a $10 million ad budget to succeed. A clear understanding of how to integrate all the marketing communications tools can help smaller companies get the most bang for their buck.

5. **P**rofit. Young companies need to be savvy about managing their cash and should aggressively manage their accounts receivable. If the 5 Ps are well orchestrated, a company should end up in the black.

Analyzing Your Market

One of the first steps to establishing a winning marketing plan is do a complete audit of your market. Describe the past and potential growth of the market and identify current and future trends. Learn as much as possible about your customers by studying demographics—the statistical characteristics of people, which includes both economic and psychological variables.

Using demographic information, identify your target customers: their per capita income, age, sex, geographic locations and attitudes. Supporting data from trade associations, surveys and government statistics should be included. Also describe the market size in dollar terms, and provide an analysis of your expected or current market share.

You should establish short- and long-term goals, including increased unit sales, greater market share, better profits and entry into new markets, both foreign and domestic. If your goals are stronger sales and profits, it's again important to include best-case, worst-case and most likely–case scenarios.

It might be uncomfortable, but make a list of possible challenges or barriers that will inhibit your best efforts. The stumbling blocks might include cash-flow problems, quality control problems, a new tax law, competitive threats or personnel deficiencies. Anyone passionate about their mission will find a way to overcome the impediments to success.

The next task is to create a marketing budget. Experts say the best marketing budgets are divided into two areas: a fixed monthly amount to meet ongoing marketing expenses, and a contingency budget to handle unexpected marketing needs. It's impossible to predict when a new market might present itself, an old competitor might retire or a new competitor might roar onto the scene.

In this age of relationship marketing, the importance of your company's customer base can't be underestimated. Before you can begin to improve your marketing techniques, you must first have an intimate knowledge of the people buying your services or products. Marketing consultants or marketing professors at local colleges can help you gather information, although they will charge a fee. A consultant or professor can help you design a survey for your company that could provide valuable insights into your customers and prospective customers.

Checking Out the Competition

Just as sports teams send scouts to check out the competition, entrepreneurs should learn as much as possible about their opponents in the marketplace. I'm not suggesting anything of a cloak and dagger nature to thwart a competitor. Simply learn who they are, what they do and how they sell. Investigate their strengths and weaknesses. Determine what makes your product or service unique in the marketplace. If yours is merely a me-too product, your business may not be long for the world.

For entrepreneurs competing in fast-paced, high-growth markets, it's the future competition that poses the greatest threat. Sharp operators go where the money is, so it's hard to keep a hot market to yourself. Experts recommend keeping a file on each competitor in which to gather newspaper or trade journal articles, the company's marketing materials, news releases, catalogs and other documents available to the public. A publicly held competitor's filings with the Securities and Exchange Commission and other public agencies are also fair game. The information will help you learn about the competitors' new products, new markets, pricing and distribution strategies and sales techniques.

To ensure the success of your marketing plan, each of your goals should include an action plan. If your research shows your prices are too high, for example, you must have a strategy to make them more competitive. Determine who is responsible for each action plan and what resources you'll need to carry it through.

In a time of open book management, it's wise to share the company's marketing strategy with your employees. That will encourage them to buy into the plan and motivate them to meet the stated goals. Conduct a survey before you implement a new program, and follow through with a survey after the plan has been implemented. For example, a survey could let you compare the level of customer complaints to see if they're lower than last year.

A marketing plan's success depends on the extent to which goals and action plans become a daily part of the business. A good marketing plan will help you identify the right prospects for your product or service. Remember, nothing happens until something gets sold.

CHAPTER 10

Finding Financing

The night of October 9, 1996, is etched in my memory as one of the strangest of my life. Late in the evening, I arrived home after traveling much of the day, and my answering machine had 23 messages from friends, family and business associates, all of them demanding to know *When did Earl Graves become a Republican?*

It didn't take long to find out what all of this was about. Because I had been traveling, I hadn't watched the televised debate that night between Republican vice presidential candidate Jack Kemp and Democratic vice presidential candidate Al Gore. But I quickly got a replay from those who had.

It seems that Kemp, who is a friend of mine, had quoted *me* in the debate while laying out the Republican platform. He threw out something along the lines of "Earl Graves, the publisher of *Black Enterprise* magazine, says that one of the greatest impediments to the growth of black business is a lack of access to capital."

I raised a little hell later, not with Kemp's people but with Gore's staff because he missed a great opportunity to get a shot in. He could have scored some points, and maybe gotten a rare laugh, by simply noting "But Jack, Earl Graves is a lifelong *Democrat!*"

Of course, a few weeks later Clinton and Gore soundly defeated the Republican ticket, but I have to admit Kemp's comment did serve to highlight once again what has historically been one of the most vexatious problems facing blacks in business: *How do African American entrepreneurs find financing for their ventures?*

My family sometimes jokes that I am the "poster child" for Chase Manhattan Bank's minority economic development programs because I have done so much business with them over the years. My relationship with Chase got off to a great start only because I had made some powerful contacts while working with Kennedy. Without those networking contacts, I never would have gotten in the door.

After Kennedy's death I secured a $25,000 loan from Citibank to launch my consulting business. In all these years, with the exception of that first loan, I've never had to personally guarantee a penny. I advise you to aim for that same record. To launch *Black Enterprise*, Chase lent me $175,000; $150,000 was debt, and $25,000 bought Chase a 25 percent stake in my business. The magazine turned a profit in the first ten months, and the debt was promptly repaid, which obviously helped establish my long-term relationship with the people at Chase. To buy back the 25 percent equity that they bought for $25,000 cost me more than $500,000 a decade later. (Incidentally, to start a magazine like *Black Enterprise* today, I'd need at least five million dollars.)

For all of my intimate dealings and relationships with top banking executives, even today I constantly have to remind bank tellers and others in the financial services business that I deserve as much respect as their white customers, most of whom can walk in the door and cash a check without catching nearly the flak that black customers encounter.

It is no joke that the number one problem faced by African American entrepreneurs is finding financing for their business ventures. The president of Chase once told me that more than half of the blacks in business had to borrow money from family members to get started. I may be well off enough today that I don't have problems getting bank loans, but that doesn't mean I don't run into racial prejudice and discrimination every time I walk into a financial institution.

Even as I was writing this chapter on how to get financing, I had a problem with a bank teller having to go to her boss to get approval to cash a check. To tell you the truth, I get heartburn every time I go into a bank to get some cash, even though I have a special private banking card given by Chase to its long-time customers. In fact the former president of Chase recommended me for an honorary degree from his alma mater, Brown University. Yet there are bank tellers in the town where I live who run when they see me coming because I raise the roof when they go running to their branch manager to get approval to give me my own hard-earned money. I've been known to call up the executive vice president of Chase and tell him that I am planning to go to one of his branches and that he had better call ahead and warn them that a black man with a low tolerance for prejudice is coming in to claim some cash. I've conducted a few impromptu sensitivity training sessions in banks.

If there is one place where racism is alive and well, it's the teller line of your neighborhood bank, and that racism extends into the loan offices as well. This is nothing new, of course. The raising of capital, the lifeblood of any business, has always been a greater challenge for minority-owned ventures than for white-owned companies. Investors, lenders and potential strategic partners have traditionally been wary of the ability of blacks to launch and sustain a business. It's racist and a major nuisance, but it's a fact of life.

All in the Family Financing

Blacks in business have to be creative and determined to find financing. Philadelphia restaurateurs and nightclub owners Ben and Robert Bynum had to dig into their own savings and refinance a house to get the capital to open their first restaurant, Zanzibar Blue. Had they been white restaurant entrepreneurs, they would undoubtedly have had less difficulty getting start-up financing, particularly since their father, Benjamin Bynum Sr., had run a string of highly successful nightclubs over the years. But even a family history of business success carries little weight for African American entrepreneurs. Which may explain why even though blacks spend $30 billion each year dining out, a mere 4,571 eating and drinking establishments are owned by African Americans in a nation with 407,824 such businesses, according to U.S. Census Bureau figures.

Without a bank loan to lean on, the Bynum brothers pooled their resources, got a second mortgage and, in 1990, opened their richly appointed jazz café, which has become recognized as one of the best in Philadelphia. But again, when the brothers went to their local banks to build upon their success with another establishment, they ran into the number one nuisance factor—their race. Even though Zanzibar Blue was well on its way to financial success, and even though many of the bankers they talked to were in fact patrons of their café, the Bynums could not get a $100,000 loan without signing away nearly everything they owned.

Once again, however, they refused to be denied. They took their profits from Zanzibar and borrowed money from a few close friends to finance their next venture, Warmdaddys, a blues and soul food spot that has been so popular they may franchise it. It is doubtful that any banker will ever have the opportunity to tell the Bynum brothers no again. By the way, I have been to Zanzibar Blue and it is one of the most elegant and comfortable dining establishments I have ever been in.

Using Savings to Elevate Your Business

The six banks that turned down Kenneth W. Mason's request for capital to fund his Chicago-based Professional Elevator Services, Inc. (PES) in 1990 are probably kicking themselves today, just as the banks that failed to see the potential in the Bynum brothers' operation should be. Sales at PES are $3 million and climbing. The company has contracts in six cities, including Boston, Kansas City, St. Louis and its hometown, Chicago.

Mason launched his company with the $10,000 he had socked away in his 401(k) plan while working as a chemical engineer for Westinghouse Elevator. When Westinghouse Elevator was sold, Mason took the buyout and his savings and opened shop in his one-bedroom apartment. In spite of his low profile, he slowly began winning contracts for elevator installations, repair and maintenance, earning $30,000 in revenues in the first year. When he tried to borrow $35,000 from a bank to keep his business going in its second year, he was rejected, so he got the money from a friend. His friend has since been repaid, and the banks are now more attentive to this African American entrepreneur's needs.

Mason closed out his 401(k) account when he left Westinghouse, but corporate employees who plan to stay put while launching a business on the side can usually borrow from company-sponsored savings programs such as the 401(k). As a rule, loans of up to $50,000—the maximum allowed—can't exceed half the value of the 401(k) account. Loans must also be repaid within five years.

Entrepreneurs who can stand the wear and tear of moonlighting often start companies while keeping one foot planted safely in the corporate world. It's one way to hedge your bet and, at the very least, determine if the entrepreneurial life is for you. Another way to self-finance a start-up is by borrowing on margin against the value of your stocks and bonds. In essence, you pledge a portion of your holdings—50 percent, for example—as collateral. Using that formula, you could borrow $10,000 of your $20,000 in stock holdings.

Entrepreneurs can also borrow against the value of their insurance policies. Usually the policy needs to be in effect for at least five years before the loan privilege can be exercised. Should you fail to repay the loan, the amount due comes out of the principal, diminishing the death benefit

The Credit Crunch

Many black entrepreneurs resort to unorthodox financing because commercial banks, some of the best sources for a small business, have traditionally been reluctant to seed a black-owned start-up or early-stage company. Some entrepreneurs have turned to consumer credit or credit cards. The finance rates are higher, but again, black-owned businesses are used to working extra hard to make their dreams come true.

In addition to loans, entrepreneurs can raise money through equity investments. In a nutshell, a business owner, in exchange for cash, allows an investor to participate in the ownership or equity of the company, typically for a limited period of time. In a later chapter I will discuss in detail ways that self-financed or family-financed black firms can take their businesses to the next level though more sophisticated financing mechanisms such as venture capital and initial public offerings.

A poll by the Roper Organization for the *Wall Street Journal* underscores the frustration of black entrepreneurs over accessing capital: 83 percent of them said credit was a very serious problem. An earlier Roper poll found that 70 percent of all black business owners completely self-financed their companies. The figure is only 25 percent for entrepreneurs as a whole.

It's time for lenders and investors to abandon the notion that all African American businesses are mom-and-pops or low-tech, slow-growth enterprises. Black business represents a rich vein of opportunity for lending institutions, investors and would-be partners.

I make it a point to spread my banking business around because bankers, like politicians, will take you and your business for granted if you don't serve notice regularly that you are being vigilant for the best opportunities. We recently refinanced the loan on our Washington, D.C. Pepsi franchise and moved from Fuji Bank to NationsBank to take advantage of a more favorable rate environment as well as to establish a relationship with them in order to take advantage of other benefits. Part of the deal involved creating opportunities for black-owned banks by having NationsBank partner with them.

Despite the obstacles and unfair perceptions contributing to a credit crunch, more blacks than ever are taking the entrepreneurial plunge, according to the Department of Commerce. The number of black-owned businesses increased 46 percent between 1987 and 1992—from 424,165 to 620,912. That's the good news. The bad news is that revenues from black-owned businesses average about $52,000 compared with $193,000 for all U.S. firms.

Margaret Simms, director of research programs at the Joint Center for Political and Economic Studies, which conducted the study for the Commerce Department, says that despite the lagging revenues of African American firms, the news is encouraging. "There are some indications that black entrepreneurship is on the increase. In particular, individuals entering entrepreneurship at this point are forming more cutting-edge businesses, such as upscale consumer marketing or management information systems."

The Five Cs of Credit

Regardless of whether you're borrowing money or raising it through an equity offering, you should be mindful of the so-called 5 Cs of credit before approaching any financial provider. They are . . .

1. **Character.** What is your personal and professional track record in repaying money owed? Remember, businesses don't pay back loans, people do, and that's why lenders, investors and partners look carefully at your personal credit history.

2. **Capacity.** Will your company generate sufficient cash flow to repay borrowed funds? If revenue and profit projections look thin or overly optimistic, don't count on getting the cash.

3. **Capital.** How much money have you invested in the business? Most lenders want you to have a substantial stake in the business, frequently no less than 20 percent. Lenders and equity investors believe there's nothing more motivating for entrepreneurs than to put all of their personal savings, including the equity in their homes, on the line. It keeps the adrenaline flowing.

4. **Conditions.** What are the economic and demographic trends that may affect your business now and in the future? Is your business in a growth industry or in one that risks going the way of the buggy whip? For obvious reasons, entrepreneurs in such high-growth fields as telecommunications, information services and financial services will get more serious consideration.

5. **Collateral.** What is the market value of the asset being pledged? That could include real estate, equipment or vehicles. The more value at your disposal, the more the bank is willing to risk.

Finding the Money Trail

When it comes to finding financing, few do it better than Maceo K. Sloan, chairman and president of Sloan Financial Group, one of the largest African American–owned investment management firms, with $4 billion in assets. Even if a minority-owned firm is up and running, it essentially must start at ground zero every time it taps new sources of capital. Every dime that's being requested must be justified when a black entrepreneur seeks capital, says Sloan, who suspects that most white-owned firms aren't subject to such intensive scrutiny.

The idea of growing minority-owned firms is still foreign to most of America, where, Sloan says, "minority is synonymous with small." Sloan adds that most lenders and investors from the majority community simply aren't used to a black person coming and talking about "real money. You can't blame the lenders and investors for that. It's just a sad fact of life and something we have to get used to. If black entrepreneurs just stand around and moan about the way things are, we'll never get anywhere."

The environment for black entrepreneurialism, he believes, is more difficult today than it was 25 to 30 years ago when a lot of black businesses, including my own, were launched. Today's environment is tough, but not impossible, says Sloan. Despite its flaws and biases, the American economic system is still better than any other system he's encountered in his world travels.

This very astute financier and businessman offers ten tips on accessing capital.

1. Come armed with financial records. Fledgling companies in search of additional capital, perhaps to take them to the next level, will be expected to present the financial performance of their company over the past three years. "If you're serious about getting money, go in there with the financial records of your company from Day One," advises Sloan.

2. Always tell the truth. Lenders and investors can quickly tell when someone is trying to pull the wool over their eyes.

3. Demonstrate a strong growth trend in revenue and earnings. A sales slump is OK as long as you can explain why it occurred. Perhaps the company operates in a cyclical industry.

4. Demonstrate potential earnings in lieu of actual earnings. If the fledgling company can't demonstrate positive earnings, it should at the very least prove that a good potential for positive earnings exists. That's often the case with research-and-development types of enterprises that are ready for the transition to a commercial enterprise.

5. Create and present a "bulletproof" business plan. It should include cash-flow projections, break-even points and financial ratios as well as details of the company's sales and marketing plans.

6. Build a strong management team. Nothing impresses lenders and investors more than managers who have plenty of success stories and a few failures under their belt. Sloan believes there's nothing more eye-opening for entrepreneurs than to watch their money go down the tubes. If that's happened once, they're determined never to let it happen again.

7. Establish an outside board of directors or advisors. Savvy businesspeople who aren't involved in your day-to-day process can provide you and your management team with opinions and perspective on how things are being run. The board of directors or advisors can also bring a wealth of valuable contacts to the table.

8. Be financially flexible. Sloan says you should be willing to give up a portion of your business in the short term to grow and gain share in the long term. "Just because you bring in an equity partner now doesn't mean they will stay your partner forever." (Maceo speaks from personal experience. When Sloan Financial was formed in 1991, a 40 percent stake was sold to American Express. That portion of the business is scheduled to be bought back from American Express by Sloan at the end of 1997, per the agreement.)

9. Deal with sophisticated investors and lenders. People who understand the nature of an entrepreneur's business can better understand why things go wrong when they do.

10. Prove that an infusion of capital won't disrupt the business. When a mom-and-pop operation spreads its wings, it may find itself dealing with a larger, tougher breed of competitor. That can be the death knell for some companies. Savvy start-ups make a rational, even-handed transition to the next level.

Going to the Bank

Raymond J. McClendon, vice chairman and chief operating officer of Pryor, McClendon, Counts & Company, the largest minority-owned and controlled investment banking firm in the United States, says that banks have traditionally lent to black entrepreneurs only "enough money to fail." Minority businesses, especially start-ups, tend to be much more undercapitalized than their white counterparts.

That's not to say that blacks can't ever get their hands on bank loans. "The bottom line is that money is attracted to the best strategies that have the best opportunity to succeed. The sounder your business plan, the more you lower the risk for your investors and lenders, who in turn can offer more favorable terms," he says.

Although banks have traditionally turned a deaf ear to requests for capital from black entrepreneurs, things may be changing. Driving that change is the consolidation taking place in the banking industry. In this more competitive environment, banks are looking for new opportunities, including the growing class of black entrepreneurs in search of capital. Banks can no longer afford to restrict their lending to their own backyards.

Regardless of location, a black entrepreneur with a strong business plan has a far stronger chance of getting serious consideration from a banker. But what do bankers want? Over the course of my 30 years in business, I've found that you can never be quite sure. But here are five key questions to ask yourself. How you answer them can make the difference between landing that all-important loan or getting rejected.

1. How much money do you need? If you want to borrow $50,000, only ask for $50,000. Never ask bankers how much they are willing to lend. It's important to collect the most precise calculations possible and then explain why you need every penny.

2. How will you repay the loan if things go as planned? Will it be from your business's cash flow, proceeds or the conversion of assets? To demonstrate to the banker exactly how you'll make good on the money owed, it is necessary to present at least a year of monthly cash-flow statements and quarterly projections for the term of the loan.

3. How will you repay the loan if things go sour? In most cases you'll have to surrender collateral such as equipment or property. Bankers will consider the market value of the collateral you have pledged against the value of the loan. Regardless of how the bank is compensated, it's important to have a contingency plan.

4. How will the loan help your business? Bankers want to be assured that the infusion of cash into the business will help it build cash flow, expand the sales force or lead to cost controls. Count on a rejection letter if you tell the banker the money will be used to increase your salary or buy a fancy new vehicle.

5. What's your personal stake? If your own finances aren't on the line, bankers won't be interested in risking any of their cash. As I have mentioned, banks prefer a personal investment of at least 20 percent.

It may seem as if there's no rhyme or reason to a bank's lending practices. The fact is, however, that most banks base their lending decisions on several key financial ratios. One of the most important of these criteria is the current ratio, which measures the number of times current assets will pay off current liabilities.

Let's say your current assets total $50,000 and your current liabilities are $20,000. That's a current ratio of 2:5. A ratio of 2:1 or higher is considered to be a strong financial indicator by bankers. Well-run businesses that maintain low inventories and strict credit policies generally have current ratios that bankers find appealing.

It's also important to build a relationship with a banker before you need the money. As I noted earlier, I have worked at developing long-term relationships with Chase Manhattan's top executives in the past and am currently doing it with NationsBank because I consider them part of the team when it comes to my businesses, even if I rarely ask them for loan money.

I try to get to know them as individuals, to find out what interests we may have in common, even what charities their bank is interested in supporting, and I support them too. You have to know what the hot buttons are for your bankers as well as what they are looking for. Business owners can build long-term credibility, for example, by delivering quarterly financial statements. Don't just send the good news. If your business hits a few bumps in the road, send the reports from that quarter as well. Simply explain the situation. Bankers should be made privy to your company's game plan.

Once you've become a borrower, don't just send the quarterly statements. Invite the banker to visit your plant or distribution center. Let the banker meet your key people. Face-to-face contact with the banker helps build a bond of friendliness and trust that will go a long way toward winning approval on the next and undoubtedly larger loan request.

Bankers should also be notified when something significant happens in your business. It could be a major new account, a new piece of equipment or an important managerial hire. And, of course, if there's bad news, don't sugarcoat it. Explain what happened and how it will be remedied.

Loans from family and friends are based more on emotional factors than cold-blooded financial ratios. Nevertheless, entrepreneurs should be just as diligent about the paperwork in securing a loan from a relative as they would be for a bank. Blood may be thicker than water, but don't take it for granted. Why risk touching off a family feud in the event of a misunderstanding over money.

So that nothing is left to chance, a promissory note should detail such elements as the amount of the loan, the date of the loan, the interest rate, the frequency of payments and the period over which the money is to be repaid. The document should be witnessed by a notary, not a family member. The note should also include a contingency plan in the event that terms are not met. Just as the banker would be entitled to some collateral, so should the family member.

Another reason to dot all the i's and cross all the t's when hammering out a family loan is the tax consequences. The agreement must be not only formal but legal as well. Entrepreneurs risk IRS audits if the feds suspect things aren't quite right.

Remember that all bank deposits of more than $10,000 in cash are automatically reported to the IRS. When you deposit Uncle Joe's check for $30,000 in your bank account and fail to report it on your personal or business tax form, you'll have some explaining to do.

The relative providing you with the loan should base the interest rate on current rates in the market. Otherwise the loan might be considered a gift and subject to federal gift taxes. Federal tax laws allow individual taxpayers to give up to $10,000 a year tax-free to any individual. A married couple can give up to $20,000 a year to each individual. Amounts above that can be subject to gift taxes for the borrower.

To be certain you don't run afoul of the tax man, consult section 7872, subsection D of the IRS code. Each month the IRS also publishes rates for loans ranging from short term to long term. Your accountants, too, should be consulted regularly to make certain that they are monitoring your business and keeping you out of trouble, which is what they are paid to do.

Micro-Loans and Big Money

There are many other ways to bypass the big bank, especially when only a few thousand dollars are enough to fuel a start-up. In 1992 the Small Business Administration (SBA) began funding a network of more than 100 "micro-loan" centers nationwide. Local groups such as churches, credit unions and small community banks have served as intermediary lenders or micro-loan centers.

Elmwood Neighborhood Housing Services in Providence, Rhode Island is a micro-loan center that provided more than $20,000 in micro-loans to several budding minority-owned enterprises. The program is sponsored by a local church, several community groups and a local bank. In addition to obtaining micro-loans of up to $2,000, the entrepreneurs are taught business skills by experts from the community.

Having gone through the micro-loan process, entrepreneurs have the confidence and expertise to apply for loans from the big banks. Small businesses may not get rates as favorable as the micro-loans, however. The SBA charges the intermediary micro-loan lender interest based on the five-year U.S. Treasury bond rate, which in 1996 hovered around 5 percent. The intermediary lender is allowed to charge its small business customers an average interest rate of about 10 percent.

Another nonbank source of capital for minority-owned businesses is specialized small business investment corporations, or SSBICs. About 100 SSBICs are funded through a combination of SBA funds and cash from the private sector—banks, corporations, foundations and pension funds. SSBICs, formerly known as Minority Enterprise Small Business Investment Corporations (MESBICs), have helped launch hundreds of black-owned businesses since their creation in 1970. One of the biggest SSBICs in the country is Dallas-based MESBIC Ventures Holding Company, which has $40 million in assets. It has a diverse roster of corporate shareholders including NationsBank, Mobil Oil, Sears Roebuck and Xerox.

The three areas of the country with the greatest concentration of capital available to SSBICs are New York, with $54 million in private capital and $106.3 million in leveraged SBA funding; the Chicago area, with $35 million in private sector funds and $40.5 million in SBA-leveraged funds; and California, with $24.6 million in private cash and $44.6 million in leveraged SBA funds.

Information about SSBIC funding can be obtained from the National Association of Investment Companies (NAIC), 1111 14th Street, NW, Suite 700, Washington, D.C. 20005 (202-289-4336).

I would also advise black entrepreneurs to look for money with economic development groups in their geographic areas. You can find these easily enough by going to the local city hall and asking for the small business bureau or the economic development officer.

Most universities also have small business development programs. Your local library is another obvious place to look for the names and addresses of agencies designed to encourage small business development. Your accountant and lawyer should also be able to direct you to helpful agencies.

Going Country for a Loan

Minority-owned businesses usually don't think of the U.S. Department of Agriculture (USDA) as a source of capital. But it can be, according to Dayton Watkins, administrator of the USDA's Rural Business and Cooperative Services Agency (RBCSA). Watkins explains that his agency provides "credit enhancement" through such intermediaries as banks, insurance companies and nonbank lenders in rural communities or those with populations of less than 50,000.

That requirement doesn't necessarily leave African American businesspeople from big cities out in the cold, however. Businesses that establish some type of presence, such as a manufacturing, distribution or sales center, in a smaller community will be considered. And these are no micro-loans. The agency will guarantee 90 percent of a loan up to $2 million. The entrepreneur is required to have a minimum of 10 percent equity in the business. For loans of $2 million to $5 million, the agency will guarantee 80 percent of the loan, with the entrepreneur providing 20 percent of the equity. For loans of $5 million to $10 million, the agency guarantees 70 percent of the loan, with the entrepreneur putting up 30 percent of the equity.

The average loan guaranteed by the RBCSA is about $1.5 million. The agency expects to have about $850 million in lending authority in 1997. Watkins, who is African American, says it's unfortunate that so few black-owned firms have applied for loans through the program. Only about $30 million has been loaned to black-owned businesses through the program since its inception in 1994. The agency is eager to help black-owned businesses expand into rural areas, says Watkins. One of the goals of the agency is to encourage the intermediary banks participating in the program to take a risk with minority-owned businesses.

To be considered for an RBCSA-guaranteed loan, borrowers

must have an acceptable personal and business credit history. In addition, they must have considerable expertise in their particular industry, adequate collateral to cover the loans if the business doesn't pan out and enough cash flow from the business to cover debt service. Financial projections should be on the conservative side, and there must be evidence of economic growth trends in the chosen industry.

One of the most important criteria is coming to the table with a vision, says Watkins, who encourages minority-owned businesses to consider the RBSCA as an alternative to more traditional SBA-backed loans. Many minority-owned businesses have found the SBA-backed loan process a nightmare and are more than happy to consider an alternative.

The SBA was founded in 1953 to help small businesses grow and prosper through low-interest long-term loans. Although the SBA has helped many blacks get started, including me, it has also frustrated a lot of entrepreneurs and would-be entrepreneurs through its cumbersome application process, which often requires a mountain of paperwork. Both the SBA and the intermediary bank that will actually lend the money require detailed analyses of your business, including cash-flow and research data to back up sales projections. Also required in the application are a management capability summary, a business description and marketing strategy, a personal financial statement and a statement of capital requirements.

The SBA loan process can take three months or more depending on the bank's caseload. Missing paperwork or other complications can prolong the process. In short, it's not easy raising capital through the SBA. To help cut the red tape, entrepreneurs should find an advisor familiar with the SBA loan process. There are a number of former SBA officials who know the drill and can provide valuable advice—for a fee, of course. Paying a consultant familiar with the SBA process a fee of $10,000 to $15,000 to secure a $500,000 SBA-guaranteed loan is money well spent.

In response to a growing number of complaints, the SBA in 1994 streamlined the application process for loans of less than $50,000. Under its LowDoc (low documentation) program, applicants simply need to fill out a one-page document. Approval can be granted in a matter of days rather than months. The LowDoc program has granted more than $300 million in loans, 20 percent of which have gone to minority-owned companies.

The SBA offers free information on business planning and development. The agency also has free pamphlets on how to apply for a loan, crafting a business plan and entering the international export market. The address for the Small Business Administration is 1110 Vermont Avenue, NW, 9th Floor, Washington, D.C. 20005.

Loans "R" Us

Another important resource for minority entrepreneurs is the Small Business Resource Center. It's a joint project of the SBA, the Minority Business Development Agency and NationsBank. The center is designed to be a one-stop shop offering training, counseling and financing for entrepreneurs.

There are other encouraging developments for minority entrepreneurs in search of start-up financing. Some of the credit belongs to the Clinton administration, which has put pressure on Congress to pass bank-sponsored minority-based lending programs. For example, two dozen Los Angeles banks stitched together $10 million to fund the Southern California Business Development Corporation. The program cuts loans averaging $100,000 to credit-starved minority enterprises in such fields as manufacturing, retail and services.

In a growing number of cities, banks and minority-business-development centers have created joint ventures to lend money to minority-owned enterprises. An outstanding example can be found in Nashville, Tennessee, where 14 local banks contributed $10 million for loan packages sponsored by the Nashville Minority Business Development Center. Applicants can qualify for loans of $25,000 or more.

In Orlando, Florida, minority entrepreneurs are assisted in preparing and presenting loan applications by the city's minority business development center. In three years the center has helped 30 minority-owned businesses land more than $3 million in loans.

Small business incubators, which can be found in nearly every big city in America, are designed to provide office space at affordable rates and professional advice for companies in their infancy.

Incubators can expedite the grant and loan process and can also be a source of grant and loan money.

They also offer management training and school their tenants on how to qualify for bank loans and government grants. From tiny seeds grow mighty redwoods. All it takes is entrepreneurial hustle and an infusion of cash. My bottom-line advice on getting the money: Be patient and persistent.

The pages of *Black Enterprise* are full of people who have done it. You can do it too.

CHAPTER 11

Growing a Business

Twenty years ago, my idea of growing the business was simply to get enough cash flow going that I could afford to make the car and house payments by the end of each month. Over the years of publishing *Black Enterprise* and being involved in other ventures, I have come to realize that while finding start-up money has always been the major challenge for blacks in business, it is certainly not the only financial challenge that awaits.

As soon as you find a way to get your company up and running, the next challenge is to keep it going and growing. Taking a young company to the next level while keeping it healthy in the early stages can be just as challenging as the launch itself. African American–owned companies, even though they may be growing at a strong and steady pace, frequently find that a critical infusion of cash is hard to come by.

About ten years ago, I decided to grow my publishing business by creating a black "shelter" magazine along the lines of *Better Homes & Gardens* but with more zip. Letters sent to *Black Enterprise* subscribers to test the waters got a very good response. I was convinced that we had a runaway train with the concept, which was called *Verve* magazine. So my staff and I put together a marketing kit and went out to advertisers to sell the new book. We promptly ran into that old nuisance again, white ignorance.

The only ads we could sell were to cigarette and liquor companies. The manufacturers and product names that were the backbone of *Better Homes & Gardens*—the companies that make refrigerators, air conditioners, paints, fabrics, floor coverings and faucets—wouldn't have a thing to do with a magazine that dared to present African Americans as living in comfortable and well-designed homes. Maybe they didn't want their products associated with blacks, or maybe they thought we all live in rundown shacks by the railroad tracks. At any rate, after more than a year and a half and probably a half-million dollars in research and design, we dropped this effort to grow our business and looked elsewhere for opportunities offering a greater return on investment. As I write this book, there is still no shelter magazine targeted at African Americans.

The problem of how to keep a business going and growing beyond its start-up period is one that all businesspeople—but particularly African American entrepreneurs—struggle with. Again, it is harder for us because of the additional nuisances of racism and discrimination, which make it more difficult to get access to money. But there are ways, my friends, there are ways.

Black Enterprise has reported countless stories of black business owners who have gone to banks in quest of needed additional capital only to be told that their growing concern still does not meet the bank's equity-to-debt ratio requirements. Business owners can minimize that sinking feeling by making the search for capital an ongoing and primary function of doing business. No lender or investor is comfortable about pledging money to a company that appears to be desperate for cash.

You need to be aware that there are a variety of funding options available to growing businesses, ranging from venture capital to private placement to initial public offerings. Let's begin exploring them.

Banking on Business

Jacob R. Miles III, who was featured in *Black Enterprise*, exemplifies the merit of considering a variety of funding alternatives when preparing to take your business to the next level.

Miles used $400,000 in retirement and severance pay from his corporate employer to successfully launch one of the nation's first black-owned full-line toy companies, Cultural Exchange Corporation. Although the Minneapolis-based company sold more than

$650,000 worth of toys in its first year, Miles had a serious problem. He could not raise enough capital to finance the company's rapid growth.

Miles, formerly senior operations director of Tonka Toys USA, quickly ran into the same wall that most blacks encounter when they go to financial institutions for start-up financing. Majority-owned banks and white bankers still don't understand the multicultural or African American markets. They certainly didn't recognize the potential for profits being generated by Cultural Exchange's line of more than 60 toys. They couldn't see beyond Miles's black face to his expertise, based on 20 years of experience as a senior officer at one of the nation's largest toy makers.

Turned away by the banks, Miles toyed with the notion of an initial public offering (IPO) until he learned that Cultural Exchange needed to raise $20 million before investment banks would underwrite the IPO. With IPOs, shares of the company's stock are sold to the public at market value. The price reflects expectations for the company's future growth.

But an IPO can be both expensive and complicated, as Miles found out. Big brokerage fees, government registration, legal retainers and voluminous documents to be filed with the Securities and Exchange Commission can average up to 20 percent of the total amount raised, or higher—all before you sell a single share of stock.

Instead, Miles opted to sell stock to a private group of investors. His private placement of 1.05 million shares of stock at $2 raised $2.1 million. It required him to surrender a portion of the company to investors, but he did not relinquish control. He still controls 65 percent of the company, the investors the remaining 35 percent.

Impressed with Cultural's track record and strong management team, investors were eager to buy into the program. The company was able to leverage the infusion of investor cash to boost its promotional efforts, which was key to landing contracts with such major retailers as Dayton-Hudson, Toys "R" Us and Wal-Mart. Like any savvy businessperson, Miles learned as much as possible about available funding options—including private placement memorandums—and has since made the search for capital a standard part of his company's operations.

Financial Ventures

Venture capital is another potential source of funding for a company looking to expand. Companies seeking venture capital are often successful but small enterprises that have reached a point where an infusion of cash might help them build a new plant or expand their sales force—moves that would allow them to compete on a regional or national basis in addition to the local level.

In exchange for the funding, companies usually give their new venture capital partners a significant say in the operation. Venture capital partners are usually awarded a seat on the company's board of directors. Allowing an outsider to play a role in the business rankles some entrepreneurs. But it shouldn't, because the investor not only brings cash to the party but valuable advice and contacts as well.

Venture capital can be tough to get, however. UNC Ventures, Inc., a Boston-based venture capital firm that has helped more than 50 businesses owned by minorities since 1971, receives about 200 proposals a year. Only 3 or 4 a year are actually funded.

UNC has operated two funds, or pools of capital from corporations, wealthy individual investors and institutions like the Ford Foundation. The funds, which raised some $30 million, were parlayed into more than $1 billion and created more than 7,000 new jobs. UNC's newest fund, UNC Ventures III L.P., will raise more than $100 million to develop at least 25 companies ranging in size from $25 million to $100 million. Lawrence Dugger III, president of UNC, says that the primary focus of the third fund is to provide capital to enable minority entrepreneurs to succeed.

Dugger, who is black, says that UNC has long recognized the serious and chronic lack of capital for entrepreneurs of color. The typical entrepreneur that UNC's third fund is designed to help is an executive with 15 to 20 years of experience who wishes to create an independent business.

One of UNC's success stories appears to have been Envirotest Systems Corporation of Tucson, Arizona. UNC helped black partners Chester Davenport and Slivy Edmonds piece together $57 million in financing to buy Hamilton Test Systems, a $35 million division of United Technologies. Davenport and Edmonds later bought their largest competitor and took their company public. Envirotest has the auto emission testing contracts for the states of

New York and Pennsylvania and has a $1.5 billion backlog of work.

About a third of the companies that UNC has invested in have gone public—the point at which investors reap their reward. The average rate of return to UNC investors over the past ten years has been about 15 percent—not spectacular by venture capital standards but still more favorable than the Standard & Poor's 500 stock index performance for the same period.

Know the SCOR

A funding option for minority entrepreneurs in 44 states is a relatively new method of raising capital called a Small Corporate Offering Registration (SCOR). Under the program, a company with less than $25 million in revenues can raise up to $5 million from public investors but without having to jump through all the hoops and expenses of a traditional IPO.

Entrepreneurs are turning to SCOR because they, rather than investment bankers, Wall Street lawyers and other high-priced advisors, can broker the deal. The business owner prepares all documentation, including a prospectus, prospects for investors and deposits investors' money in an escrow account. It can all be done for about $20,000—or about $480,000 less than an IPO for a small company. Another advantage of SCOR is that it allows entrepreneurs to raise capital from outside investors while remaining in control of their businesses. SCOR was created in 1989 by the Securities & Exchange Commission in response to complaints by small business owners about the enormous time and expense of "going public."

Like venture capital investors, SCOR investors are making a bet that the company will ultimately go public with a formal IPO. Entrepreneurs interested in SCOR should contact their local secretary of state and/or banking and finance department.

One Line That Is Worth the Wait

In the winter of 1995–96, the government shut down and we had 30 inches of snow fall on New York City. There were a couple of things I was extremely thankful to have during this difficult time. One was my four-wheel-drive Jeep Grand Cherokee. But what gave me even greater peace of mind was the line of bank credit for our businesses. Over the years, I have established lines of credit with banks for amounts ranging from $25,000 to several million. Rarely have I had to tap those lines of credit, but I view them as a measure of whether or not you can count on your banker to help when your business needs it the most.

A line of credit from banks is another important tool for growing a business. They are generally used to maintain or expand an existing business—not launch a new one—because banks are most reluctant to lend money to a company without a track record. But a line of credit can put wind in the sails of an entrepreneurial venture. With a revolving line, the most common type of credit line, the business owner can borrow as little as $5,000 or as much as $1 million. The money can be withdrawn and replaced during the course of the year, and credit may be renewed at year's end. By contrast, a regular term loan is a one-time deal with a set payout of one to five years.

But securing a line of credit is no foregone conclusion. John L. Sims, president of Philadelphia-based Tri-State Marketing Corporation, searched fruitlessly for two years to find a $25,000 line of credit for his $500,000-a-year company, which supplies uniforms and career apparel to large companies. Bankers rejected his company's request for credit because his partner had a minor blot on his credit report: two late bill payments within a two-year period. Sims' hard lesson is a reminder of how subjective the loan-granting process is at the nation's financial institutions.

Minority Business Programs

There are several other ways to grow a business without having to hassle with bankers and investors. About 75 percent of the Fortune 500 companies, as well as many smaller companies, have minority business programs. These programs will generally only consider minority businesses that have a track record, as opposed to startups. The larger companies are looking for minority suppliers with a reputation for quality, strong customer service and, of course, fiscal responsibility.

Other opportunities exist for small businesses in telecommunications with federal and local government agencies. The Defense Information Systems Agency in Arlington, Virginia, procures about

$3 billion annually for the Department of Defense in systems engineering and the integration of computer systems. About 12 percent of that is contracted out to minority-owned business.

The Defense Department has a particular need for high-tech equipment and computer technology to help it stay on the cutting edge of developing systems and equipment. Almost all businesses and government agencies need help in upgrading current computer systems to take advantage of new technology.

There is also a growing need for trainers to show government employees how to use new software, according to Joann Anderson, director of the Minority Telecommunications Development Program at the National Telecommunications and Information Administration. "The changes are so swift, not everybody has been able to keep up," she says.

Large corporations and government offices have procurement processes that potential suppliers and service providers must follow to gain access to the wide range of opportunities. Here is an outline of how that process generally works.

Step 1. Contact the agency's procurement officer and ask if there is a current or future need for the type of product or service you offer. Check to see if there is a program to solicit business from minority-owned firms.

Step 2. Usually you will receive an information package about the procurement process, containing forms to fill out about your product or service, references, financial viability and past track record. Fill out the forms and return them. You may be encouraged to seek minority certification from the National Minority Supplier Development Council or a regional chamber of commerce.

Step 3. Your business may be referred to different buyers within the agency or to different corporate offices throughout the country. Your company may also be placed in a database that these buyers have access to.

Step 4. Don't rely on the buyers to offer contracts to you. Sell your business by calling regularly to inquire about opportunities and showing evidence of your company's capability. It can take months or years to win a contract, so you have to view this as a competition.

Financial Tips for Young Companies

Some of the most costly and damaging mistakes made by entrepreneurs occur in the first few months of operation, when a company's culture is being established. There are, however, ways to stay healthy and to avoid common problems. For example, a smart way to update your company's computer equipment is to lease the latest technology in new equipment. This financing technique allows companies to get the needed equipment without a substantial cash outlay, which preserves capital for the present. The equipment is yours for a specified period. There are no burdens of long-term ownership and no problems with constantly having to cut profits by updating for new technology.

Young, rapidly growing companies short on cash flow but high in product demand should also consider a financing mechanism called "factoring." A factor is a third-party investor that buys the company's receivables, thus allowing for quicker payments.

Factoring offers a number of benefits to cash-starved companies, which can use the money to meet payroll, fund marketing campaigns or provide working capital. Essentially, the factor pays you cash right now for the right to receive future payments on your invoices. Factors are generally willing to fork over from 75 to 90 percent of the receivables' net face value. The service fees of factors range between 1 percent and 5 percent.

Financing options are only limited by your imagination. Leave no stone unturned in your search for capital and new ways to grow your business. Not making the search for capital an important and ongoing task in your company is a serious business mistake.

Here are ten other mistakes growing businesses must avoid.

1. Deadbeat customers. Bad debt costs the economy more than $250 annually for every person in the country, according to the American Collectors Association. Figures like that call for strong credit controls, especially for small businesses, which can least afford a backlog of receivables. A 30-day cycle for receivables should be a priority. Don't let 30 days become 90. Solving collections problems before they start is critical because of the nuisance of small claims court, the 30 to 50 percent cut of collection agencies and the loss of good customer relations.

2. Employee theft. Grocers and restauranteurs call shoplifting and internal theft shrinkage. Disturbingly, shoplifting accounts for only 10 percent of most loss. Employee or internal theft makes up the rest. Strong security procedures may inconvenience employees, but they'll more than offset potential losses. You and your employees must understand that you're all in it together. If the losses continue, there will be no business and no jobs.

3. Overdependence on one client. If your biggest client goes broke or changes vendors, your fortunes could sink like a rock. A broad customer base is essential to survival. Never let one customer become more than 40 percent of your business. Savvy entrepreneurs are constantly on the prowl for new accounts.

4. Bad cash management. Resist the temptation to spend income on yourself instead of the business. It may seem like just desserts for all the blood, sweat and tears of running a business, but businesses with the most staying power put as much as possible into working capital. Don't put your company in a position where it always has to borrow money to do business. The cost of money is too high. Sit down with your banker and accountant to establish a cash management strategy. A written business plan can be the best cash manager.

5. Ignoring your financials. You should be intimately familiar with at least two financial statements. The first is the income statement, which shows your revenue and expenses in either a monthly or quarterly period. The second is the balance sheet, which tells you what your assests, liabilities and equity are at a particular moment. It's like a snapshot. Experts recommend generating a minimum of one income statement each month to ensure careful monitoring. Should income fall 10 to 20 percent below projections two months in a row, you need to understand why. Then go to the discretionary expenditures, like office supplies or temporary help, and adjust them.

6. Inadequate insurance. With proper planning, insurance costs can be analyzed and sometimes even controlled. Shop around for a broker who represents more than one insurer, and negotiate wherever possible. Reexamine the legal and tax structure of your business. A sole proprietorship, partnership or S corporation, for example, can write off 25 percent of its health insurance premiums. A C corporation can write off 100 percent.

7. Ignoring government regulations. It's bad business to ignore the government, whether it's the fire department, the local zoning commission, the Occupational Safety and Health Administration (OSHA) or the Environmental Protection Agency (EPA). The more regulated your industry, the more likely there are to be books, newsletters and seminars to help you stay abreast of the latest laws. Government contractors must scrupulously observe government specifications.

8. Inadequate tax planning. Your firm may pay more than a dozen different kinds of taxes. But employment taxes are by far the most important payments a small, growing company makes during the year. Not paying payroll taxes is the single biggest reason companies fail. You must pay. I have heard scores of horror stories about businesspeople who seemed to think taxes were something they could pay later. Then one day they go to the office only to find the door padlocked courtesy of the IRS. Tax management is entwined with cash management. Just as an income statement helps you judge how you're managing your money, so a balance sheet helps you evaluate your tax options.

9. Poor employee management. Miscommunication creates confusion, high turnover, resentment and even employee theft. On the other hand, good hiring practices, clear personnel policies, information sharing and training can spark employee loyalty and productivity.

10. Failure to log onto the technical revolution. Technology can be the great equalizer for minority-owned businesses. A site on the Internet's World Wide Web, for example, allows a small business to present itself on the same playing field and in the same light as a Fortune 500 company. Information technology can be the affirmative action program of the 21st century, if a minority-owned company can harness its advantages.

Ignoring information technology will be like trying to do business without a telephone. Obviously, it can't be done. Technological empowerment must be a top economic priority for African Americans.

I'm convinced that the technological revolution shifts the marketplace in favor of such qualities of nimbleness, smallness, knowledge and entrepreneurism. Companies that embrace technology—particularly the Internet and its multimedia portion, the

World Wide Web—gain a larger-than-life presence. They can market and distribute their product or service to a global audience.

Web sites consist of electronic pages of text, graphics or sound that are connected to one another within the same site or through other sites. A Web page is a publicly available computer file stored on a computer and attached to the Internet. By dialing into an online service, like BlackAmerica Online or America Online, or an Internet Service Provider (ISP), home computer users can access a Web page.

Entrepreneurs can build as many Web pages as they want by setting up their own Web server (computer, software and telecommunications services). They can also rent space on another company's server. There are no definitive cost figures for Web pages. Some companies have spent $500 to develop a small site consisting of six pages of text and graphics, while others have spent more than $100,000 for upwards of 25 pages of text plus graphics such as animation and video clips. The cost of maintaining the page in cyberspace can range from $30 to $500 per page, depending on whether the pages are updated daily, weekly or monthly.

Although it is sometimes difficult to convince white-owned computer and technology companies that blacks are on the Web and into the Internet bigtime, at *Black Enterprise* we have encountered many examples of African American–owned businesses that have successfully ventured into cyberspace.

Backing onto the Information Superhighway

Stephen Jackson first ventured onto the Internet when he discovered the usefulness of the on-line services for sending e-mail to his staff at Jackson & Jackson Management Plus in New York City. He founded the company in 1991 to lease full-time employees to technical firms and professionals like doctors and lawyers. In 1993 he took the next step into cyberspace when he created an electronic library that allowed clients to access information over the Internet.

At the time, he saw the Internet as a device that could help his company trim overhead such as postage, paper and fax costs. He hadn't yet considered the Internet's marketing potential. But by 1995 it dawned on Jackson that he could make big money on the Net by surfing for business prospects. The $5 million firm also began offering Internet training, marketing courses and Web page development. He scrapped the employee leasing component of his company to concentrate on business in cyberspace. It's a decision he doesn't regret.

In the first eight months that he offered the service, more than 800 people signed up for courses. The $129 training seminar provides hands-on Internet exercises, while the $250 marketing seminar teaches participants how to sell their wares over the Net. In addition to his own company's Web site, Jackson has created sites for a dozen small businesses, which sell everything from T-shirts to newspapers on-line. His company's Web site received more than 130,000 hits (the number of times it was accessed) and generated more than $600,000 in revenues during its first eight months.

Jackson believes that companies conquering the Internet today will be in a vastly stronger position to capture the consumer market of tomorrow. But the Internet isn't for everyone, he cautions. On-line businesses must carefully research their market. Nor is the Internet some sort of silver bullet. Poorly run companies aren't necessarily going to succeed just because they've gone on-line.

What's best about the Net, says Jackson, is its level playing field. A small African American company can create a site that is as deep and meaningful as that of a Fortune 500 giant. No one owns the Internet, it's there for the taking, adds Jackson.

Finding New Life on the Net

The Carlos Howard Funeral Home of Norfolk, Virginia, has taken its once-small business global thanks to the Internet. By putting up a Web page on MelaNet, an African American network on the Internet, the company is now selling about 200 caskets a month to buyers in South Korea.

Rodney Jordan, co-founder of Norfolk-based MelaNet Information and Communications Network, says that when he began discussions with Howard about creating a Web site for his funeral home in 1995, there were no other funeral homes on the Net. Howard's was the first. Now there are more than 200 funeral homes with Web sites.

Even though the Carlos Howard Funeral Home no longer has cyberspace to itself, the benefits of the home page continue to accrue. Howard has generated tens of thousands of dollars in business the company might not otherwise have had, because Howard sells caskets at deep discounts. So deep, in fact, that other funeral homes are complaining that he's costing them business.

The Virtual Catalog

The Internet not only exposes a small business to a large, global audience, but it can reduce overhead costs. Karen Pugh, a former creative director for fashion designer Ralph Lauren, is putting her own line of fashions out on the Net. Pugh found that it was cheaper to produce a catalog of her fashions on the Web site of her New York-based company, called KP Studio, than to create a paper catalog. Creative work, paper, postage and other production costs for a paper catalog would run to more than $12,000 a page. Overhead, personnel and material costs would have added another $50,000.

By contrast, Pugh could post a six- to ten-page catalog on the Net for about $500 a page—and that includes the cost of regularly updating the pages to reflect design and price changes. She believes that her business's presence in cyberspace gives KP Studio a distinct competitive advantage in the hypercompetitive fashion world.

A BBS Is Good Business

Another African American pioneer in cyberspace is Idette Vaughn, who operates the Blacknet Bulletin Board System (BBS) from her home in Brooklyn. A BBS, in its simplest form, is a computer that has been left on so that it can field calls from other computers via its modem. With BBS software, people can read posted messages, send and receive e-mail, upload and download software, search databases and exchange ideas.

Unlike the large commercial on-line services, BBSs usually serve local clients. And they're much less expensive to operate. Assuming you have a computer, a BBS can be launched for as little as $600. Vaughn's Blacknet has more than 600 users, who pay a $10 quarterly subscription to access Blacknet, which offers everything from a list of books by black authors and black databases to screensavers.

Information to Grow Your Business

As these African American entrepreneurs have demonstrated, the Internet can be a powerful selling tool. Yet Rodney Jordan believes that a Web site's greatest strength remains its informational capabilities. A Web site allows a company to present itself as an expert, often the first step in building a long-term relationship with a customer or prospect. Jordan recommends that companies establish their expertise by giving away information. Don't give away the store, but offer enough information to pique a prospect's interest.

Going Global

The revolution in communications technology is making international business opportunities easier to grasp for small and midsized companies. High-speed faxes, global 800 numbers, data modems, the Internet and other new technologies are making exports a reality for minority-owned businesses. A study by the Kessler Exchange, a Northridge, California–based research firm, found that exporting is the number one opportunity for small businesses.

There are a number of ways minority entrepreneurs can grow their businesses through exports. The National Minority Business Council (NMBC) offers overseas trade missions and technical assistance to small and medium-sized exporters. NMBC trade missions have visited promising markets in Latin America, the Caribbean and South Africa. Call 212-573-2385.

Black entrepreneurs are in a strong position to penetrate international markets. One reason is that blacks and minorities face less restrictive legislation and discrimination overseas, especially in the Caribbean, Latin America and Africa.

Paul Owsley, director of international government sales for Pro-Line Corporation, a Dallas-based B.E. 100s hair care product manufacturer, believes that market saturation is forcing more African American businesses to look beyond the United States. Pro-Line has been distributing its products overseas for more than 15 years, and international sales now account for 10 percent of the company's $43 million revenue. International sales were up 25 percent in 1995 over the previous year.

American beauty products translate well overseas, with exports of U.S. cosmetic companies bringing revenues of nearly $2.5 billion in recent years. Black hair care products are doing well in this market, with 18 African American–owned companies reporting sales of $70 million.

Taking any business abroad can be an adventure, good and bad. Trade laws, currency fluctuations, politics and cultural preferences are all hurdles in the international marketplace. In South Africa, for example, there is a 100 percent tax on imported products, making it difficult for Pro-Line to compete with local manufacturers. Increasing political stability and economic reform in South Africa have made it more attractive to take the gamble, particularly for African Americans, who may have cultural as well as economic interests in overseas trade. But President Nelson Mandela emphasizes that his priority is to develop local jobs for his countrymen.

Along with Pro-Line Corporation, two other B.E. 100s companies are trading on their ethnicity to make inroads in foreign markets. Black Entertainment Television launched BET International (BETI) in 1993 to target the fledgling international market with a network devoted exclusively to jazz. It is called BET On Jazz: the Cable Jazz Channel. BET has targeted South Africa, Botswana and Zimbabwe as well as Central Europe, North Africa, the Middle East and the South Pacific.

Ebony South Africa is the international entry of publisher and business tycoon John H. Johnson and his Johnson Publishing in Chicago. To avoid paying the stiff 100 percent trade tariff in South Africa, Johnson Publishing teamed with five South African partners. Johnson holds a 51 percent share of the South African version of *Ebony*.

There are difficulties in publishing overseas, but there are also advantages, as Johnson noted in a *Black Enterprise* report. "Black people are the majority in South Africa; so you don't have to convince advertisers that we can cover the market," he said.

None of these companies are yet claiming great financial success in the overseas markets. Costs are substantial in establishing a physical presence and traveling back and forth. International tariffs can range from 15 to 100 percent and add to the bottom line of business abroad. But many African American–owned companies were inspired by the U.S. government's commitment to international trade under late Commerce Secretary Ron Brown, and now they have come to view the overseas market as key to their growth strategies.

Pro-Line, which views the domestic market as saturated, is targeting England and Canada as well as South Africa because of the large number of blacks in those countries. "Our best market is England. There is a high literacy rate, a high enough income and an aesthetic consciousness about what is going on both here and in Britain," says Owsley. Surprisingly, Pro-Line has also found a ready market for its products in Middle Eastern countries such as Saudi Arabia, Yemen and the United Arab Emirates, along with Australia and Malta, where hair relaxers and texturizers have been welcomed by consumers.

Pro-Line, under its hard-driving chairman, Comer Cottrell, and other U.S. companies have taken advantage of the Commerce Department's matchmaker program, which pairs U.S. companies with foreign businesses. Pro-Line has accessed markets in Jamaica and Brazil through this program, run by the International Trade Development Center.

The international market is not limited to large African American businesses. Even smaller companies facing thinning profit margins because of competition in the United States have joined the global market, particularly in the ten areas designated "Big Emerging Markets" (BEMs) by the Clinton administration. These are China, Argentina, Brazil, Mexico, the Association of Southeast Asian nations (ASEAN), India, South Korea, South Africa, Turkey and Poland. BEMs are places where "the growth potential for export opportunities in the post-2000 period has been clearly identified," says Lauri Fitz-Pegado, director general of commercial services at the U.S. Department of Commerce. These regions offer opportunities to American entrepreneurs, particularly in the areas of energy, telecommunications, transportation, privatization and public utilities.

There are of course risks and frustrations involved in venturing overseas. Even South Africa, which has attracted a wave of African American entrepreneurs, is not always welcoming. The 27-year-old son of Sharon Leslie Morgan, joint managing director of Afritel Cellular Systems Ltd., was kicked and punched into unconsciousness one November night by two off-duty police officers as he left a Johannesburg nightclub with a white friend. That is an extreme example, and in truth, it could have happened just as easily in Morgan's hometown of Chicago, but it is wise to remember that there are no guarantees that life will be any better—or less frustrating—overseas than at home.

African American entrepreneurs in South Africa have found that there is a lack of critical skills in the construction trades, in particular, and also in basic customer service. Still, South Africa remains attractive to black entrepreneurs and businesspeople. In 1995 an average of five new or returning U.S. firms opened offices there each month, including Levi Strauss, Ford and Dell Computer.

"Despite the ups and downs associated with the things we deal with, we both view this as one of the best decisions we've made in terms of our careers," says Roberta Coleman, who is working with her husband, Frank, for AT&T in South Africa. "It's a new world, and there are unlimited opportunities here. How many places can you say that about?"

Here are my final tips for taking your business global.

1. Learn everything you can about the country you are interested in so that you can create a global business plan that analyzes its culture, history and politics, as well as the competition you will be going up against. Hone in on key factors such as the buying habits of your target customers; whether you will need a foreign retailer, licensee, subcontractor or distributor; whether a joint venture is desirable; whether you will need a foreign office; and the country's rules and regulations regarding foreign participation.

2. Visit Web sites, read trade journals and check private and public trade promotion organizations to obtain data on countries, markets and potential customers—even before you book a flight anywhere. The Export Hotline and Trade Bank (800-USA-XPORT) offers 5,000 market reports on 78 countries and industries. Also available is information on trade shows, government programs and key contacts.

The Trade Bank lists more than 10,000 companies looking to buy and sell products overseas. Trade journals and magazines that may be helpful include *International Business, The Exporter, World Trade* and *Export Today.* They contain information on trade missions, international seminars, programs, trade fairs, catalog shows and other matchmaker events that will give you the chance to gather information and network.

3. Once you have chosen your international market target country, contact its embassy or consulate as well as the mayor's office in your city regarding sister city programs or foreign visitor hospitality. Some may operate local chambers of commerce. Ask officials to place you on mailing lists so that you can be informed about future conferences or briefings.

4. Join public and private trade missions such as those sponsored by the National Minority Business Council.

5. A wealth of information broken down by industry and region is available through the U.S. Department of Commerce and its Trade Information Center and Global Market Information Service. Both can be accessed by dialing 800-USA-Trade or through the Internet at (http://www.ita.doc.gov).

6. Find out if the country you are investigating has a U.S. commercial trade mission office, and obtain trade brochures or import/export and shipping regulations.

As we leave this subject, let me remind you that growing your business is not an option like growing a garden or growing your hair. (We'll leave the sidburns alone.) If you don't grow your business, it will die. Period. You either grow it or it goes away. Each year that you are in business, you incur new costs and expenses from your taxes and employees, so from Day One you must plan on how to expand your business to meet rising costs. All the companies that I own or have a relationship with have one-year, three-year, five-year and ten-year business plans, at the very least.

The primary strategy at Earl Graves Ltd. is now to focus on the big bang. With my other businesses doing well, I am now looking for significant opportunities that will have a payout over a relatively short period of time. Recently I told my top planners that I would like to see us do one very big deal each year, whether that means a $5 million deal with a good return or a $500 million deal with an even better return.

Afterall, I've hit a homerun with runners on most bases already by anybody's measure. But I wouldn't mind hitting the grand slam before I move on to splitting my time between public service work and private pleasure—say, skiing six months a year.

CHAPTER 12

Strategic Alliances

As we move rapidly toward the next century of business development and entrepreneurship in this country and around the globe,
synergy has become the buzzword among the major players, in the
media and telecommunications industries in particular but also in
most other areas of business, from banking to medical care. Too
often, African Americans have found themselves on the outside
looking in when major mergers, partnerships and alliances take
place. Three African American–owned firms have attempted to
remedy this situation, at least in part, by forming an alliance to create a venture capital fund for minorities in telecommunications.

Bandwidth Consulting, Inc., Pryor, McClendon, Counts &
Company (PMC) and Ark Capital Management have joined forces
to provide advisory services, venture capital funds and private
equity funds to minority entrepreneurs in telecommunications. One
of their primary target groups is the extensive pool of talented
African American businesspeople leaving the corporate world to
launch their own enterprises. And one of their strategies is to help
minority entrepreneurs form strategic partnerships. "A small company that has a good idea or product can align itself with a major
player and generate a significant opportunity," notes Raymond
McClendon of PMC.

Like me, most African Americans who go into business for
themselves do so because they want to make money and be the
boss, but sometimes, when the stakes are high, you can't be the

Lone Ranger. There are times when it makes sense to join forces with someone stronger than you, or at least someone who brings to the table talents or resources that complement yours. Forming strategic alliances or partnerships is one way for both big and small African American business owners to play the game and win. If giant corporations such as Disney, AT&T and others see the value of strategic alliances, we can't afford to stand alone.

Strategic alliances aren't just for the titans of business, industry and technology. An increasing number of small- and midsized black companies have successfully used strategic alliances with larger white-owned and black-owned companies to grow their businesses. *Ujammaa*, the Kwanzaa principle of cooperative economics, is routinely becoming part of the way African American companies do business. It's an encouraging development and an important strategy as black-owned businesses march toward the 21st century.

Finding a Way to Make It Pay

Strategic alliances come in a variety of forms. There are joint ventures, supplier development agreements and licensing deals. The alliances can be struck in two basic formats—on or off the balance sheet. An on-the-balance-sheet alliance, for example, is when two companies pool their resources to capitalize a new venture. Each company puts up $500,000, and voilà, there's a $1 million company. Off-the-balance-sheet alliances typically don't disturb the capital structure of either partner. Two companies join hands to work on a special project, but neither company has to put up any of its equity.

Attention needs to be paid to the type of legal entity that will be used to form the joint venture. Most are either partnerships or limited liability companies (LLC). This latter form of corporate entity is recognized in every state except Hawaii and Vermont. An LLC allows for the pass-through of income and loss to individual owners and avoids the double tax imposed on corporate earnings.

Whatever they're called, strategic alliances occur when two or more firms join forces to do something they could not do on their own. When done right, the combination creates a synergy that defies simple mathematics. One plus one can often equal three. And black and white can lead to green. A number of black-owned companies have struck successful partnerships with white-owned companies.

John Bolling III, the African American president of A.L.L. International Clothing, Inc. in Dallas, formed a strategic alliance with Critic's Choice Graphics Ltd., a white-owned company that makes T-shirts, jackets, caps and athletic clothing. They signed a five-year deal to produce and sell A.L.L.'s Brikama Apparel product line of African shirts and other clothing in 650 stores nationwide, including J.C. Penney, Pier One Imports, Marshall Fields and Dayton Hudson.

Such alliances, when carefully put together, can be a win-win situation because the black-owned company gains access to new markets and distribution channels while the white-owned company can diversify its customer base or fulfill minority participation requirements stipulated in a growing number of commercial and government contracts.

Bad Strategy, Bad Business

Strategic alliances are not without their pitfalls, however. There are no guarantees that the arrangements will be successful. An ill-conceived alliance can drive both companies out of business. An exit strategy must be agreed upon long before the partners actually begin doing business. Exit strategies can include a planned external sale, an initial public offering or a cross-buyout agreement.

To keep a deal from going sour, partnering companies must agree on a clearly defined business purpose. The two companies must be on the same page in terms of the strategic alliance's customer base, the type of product or service being offered, the vendors being used and the prices. The partners must also have a clear understanding of each other's roles and the controls used to guide the alliance.

Companies uneasy about any of those issues probably aren't good candidates for an alliance. Carefully crafted agreements between black-owned and white-owned companies can also prevent the sense that the often smaller black-owned partner is selling out. What the black company is really doing is buying into a business strategy that's a proven winner.

Black-owned companies that have any lingering doubts about the benefits of strategic alliances should consider a survey conducted by Coopers & Lybrand, the giant New York–based accounting and consulting firm. The survey found that firms participating in joint ventures are growing 37 percent faster per year than their nonparticipating peers. Companies involved in an international joint venture are growing a whopping 63 percent faster than non-participating firms.

The Coopers & Lybrand survey was based on interviews with the CEOs of 428 product and services companies identified as the fastest-growing U.S. businesses over the past five years. The companies, from every sector of the U.S. economy, ranged in size from $1 million to $50 million in revenues.

Besides faster growth and shared economic risk, the CEOs responding to the survey identified product development and the acquisition of marketing and distribution expertise as among the key benefits of strategic alliances. The CEOs estimated that an average of 13.9 percent of their company's current revenue growth was derived from the joint venture. Figures like that have convinced me that if the 1980s were the decade of mergers and acquisitions, then the 1990s will be known as the decade of strategic alliances. It's a trend in which a growing number of African American–owned businesses have taken part.

Let me introduce you to seven black-owned companies that have struck successful partnerships with larger, white-owned and black-owned companies. The results speak for themselves.

Working an Alliance with a Net

NetNoir, Inc., a digital Afro-centric content company based in San Francisco, struck a strategic alliance with an industry giant to help put itself on the map. E. David Ellington, co-founder and chief executive officer of NetNoir, approached executives of America Online (AOL), the nation's largest on-line service, with the argument that it couldn't genuinely call itself "America" Online until it had established a major Afro-centric component.

Ellington's argument won over Ted Leonsis, AOL's president, who orchestrated the purchase of 19.9 percent of the equity in Net-Noir and allowed the company to become the major black content supplier on AOL. NetNoir is billed as the "cybergateway to Afro-centric culture." Its business page, for example, features information about seminars, publications and directories of interest to black audiences.

NetNoir, a start-up with a value of about $6.5 million, intends to become one of the nation's leading new media companies by creating, distributing and archiving distinctive Afro-centric programming and commercial applications in interactive media such as CD-ROM, on-line services and the Internet. Ellington, a lawyer with a specialty in international entertainment and multimedia/new technology law, believes that NetNoir would never have reached its goals without partnering with AOL, which bought into Ellington's concept and into his company as a minority partner. The on-line service's infusion of cash and its subscriber base of more than 5 million people have helped take NetNoir to a level it could not have achieved on its own, while still allowing Ellington to call the shots.

Ellington offers the following advice to black entrepreneurs when considering a strategic alliance with a larger white-owned company.

- **Ask for the moon.** Ellington wanted NetNoir to be the primary Afro-centric content provider on AOL. That's what he pitched and that's what he got.
- **Look for a compatible corporate culture.** Although AOL is substantially larger than NetNoir, both companies think like entrepreneurs. A small entrepreneur-driven company could become quite uncomfortable trying to conform to a company with a slow-moving bureaucratic culture.
- **Find a champion at the larger company who is sensitive to minorities.** Ellington says he found one at the top at AOL in Leonsis, who grew up with many black friends in New York. Leonsis firmly believed that giving NetNoir a prominent place in cyberspace was the right thing.
- **Do your homework.** Or, as Ellington says, "Make sure your package is tight." Ellington presented AOL with a 55-page business plan, including 30 pages devoted strictly to numbers. Even with that, your oral presentation must be carefully rehearsed.
- **Grease the skids.** Ellington networked for months and months to get word of his company to Leonsis and AOL chairman Steve Case. By the time he called them, they had both heard about NetNoir and were eager to learn more.

An Arch Alliance

While Ellington took the initiative in approaching the giant in the on-line industry, sometimes giants will seek out smaller companies to suggest some type of strategic alliance. That was the case when fast food king McDonald's knocked on the door of C.H. James & Son, Inc., a B.E. 100s fourth-generation food service company based in Charleston, West Virginia. Charles H. James III, the company's chairman and CEO, is a fine young man from my sons' generation and one of our most promising business leaders.

McDonald's was looking to diversify its supplier base by including more minority firms, and after reading a feature about C.H. James in *Black Enterprise*, a McDonald's official called James and suggested that the next time he was in Chicago he drop by McDonald's suburban Oak Brook headquarters because they were "pre-qualifying" some minority-owned suppliers. In about the time it takes to get on an airplane and fly to Chicago, James was there. If no plane had been available, he would have flown under his own power.

He naturally leaped at the opportunity to form an alliance with the giant of the fast food industry, but McDonald's wanted it their way. Company officials asked to see three years of the company's financials, tax records and credit reports and wanted to know all about the people in charge. Of course they liked what they learned and eventually paired James up with Golden State Food Corporation, a Pasadena, California, $1 billion-plus food service concern that had a supplier agreement with McDonald's.

Golden State and C.H. James then created North American Produce, Inc., to supply precut produce to more than 1,400 McDonald's restaurants in the western United States, Alaska and Hawaii, with exports to emerging markets in Mexico and the Pacific Rim. Under the agreement, C.H. James & Son Holdings owns 51 percent of North American Produce, and Golden State 49 percent. James became the president and CEO of the new company. McDonald's is not an equity party in the deal.

Before a smaller black-owned company can ever be considered a possible strategic alliance partner of a larger company, it must have its house completely in order. James says that when a larger company goes looking for a smaller partner for a strategic alliance, it will often look for the following:

- **A clearly defined business plan or business model.** C.H. James & Son fit the bill because its core competency for more than a century had been food distribution.
- **A market presence and reputation.** A member of the B.E. 100s, C.H. James & Son had won numerous awards for enterprise from the U.S. departments of Agriculture and Commerce as well as from the Small Business Administration.
- **Capable personnel.** C.H. James's managerial roots went back four generations.
- **A strong financial track record.** C.H. James had been growing at the impressive rate of 30 percent a year for the past five years.
- **A healthy balance sheet.** The company had no long-term debt.

Creating a strategic alliance is only half the battle. Successfully operating one is the other and perhaps more challenging half. James says that once the joint venture was established, he realized he couldn't be as hands-on as he first thought and began to delegate authority to a team of middle managers. Freed of day-to-day managerial responsibilities, he was able to focus on more strategic issues facing the company.

James identifies five pitfalls to avoid when nurturing a strategic alliance.

- **Failure to build a relationship of mutual respect and trust before entering the agreement.** It's important that the partners get to know each other out of the office by, for example, sharing a game of golf, a dinner or attending a sporting event together. That kind of away-from-the-office exposure will give each partner a stronger sense of their respective character and ethics.
- **Failure to recognize the difference between negotiating the deal and running the venture.** Establishing a business is very different from running one.
- **Failure to bring in the right kind of legal assistance.** Although general practice attorneys may claim to have expertise in mergers and acquisitions, they usually don't. Spend the money to hire a lawyer with merger and acquisitions experience. Most hail from Wall Street–based firms.

■ **Failure to understand the impact a strategic alliance can have on each company's core business.** An already thinly staffed company could buckle under the pressure of vastly expanded markets and financial demands.

■ **Failure to recognize that a joint venture is like a marriage.** The ones that work succeed because of time and patience.

Comic Strategies

Milestone Media, Inc., is a multicultural comic book company that grew through a strategic alliance with a much larger publisher. Milestone offered its African American, Latino and Asian American superheroes to a much greater audience. I'm particularly proud of this company because one of its co-founders, Derek Dingle, is a former managing editor of *Black Enterprise*.

Dingle, who calls me his "second dad," left *B.E.* in 1990 to become a senior writer at *Money*, a Time Warner publication. I took that as a compliment because I had helped him grow and develop his talents. Dingle not only did well in developing that magazine's small business coverage, but cultivated contacts with Time Warner that led to the successful strategic alliance between Milestone Media and DC Comics, a unit of Time Warner.

New York–based Milestone, launched in May 1992, serves as a model of how a small black company can benefit from a link with a much larger company. Dingle resigned from *Money* to become president and CEO of Milestone, which struck up a marketing and distribution deal with DC Comics, the nation's second-largest comic book company behind Marvel. He and three other partners pieced together more than $300,000 in personal savings to launch the start-up.

One of the partners was Denys Cowan, a boyhood friend of Dingle's and one of the nation's top comic-book artists. As fourth graders, they would draw their versions of black superheroes and sell them to their friends. These two wasted no time in developing a sense of entrepreneurial hustle. The two other founders were Michael Davis, a veteran comic book artist who drew for both DC and Marvel, and Dwayne McDuffie, a former editor for Marvel who later became a full-time freelance writer for Marvel and Harvey Comics.

The Milestone Media/DC Comics partnership serves as an example of an off-the-balance-sheet alliance. Milestone did not relinquish any of its equity to DC but reaped a number of benefits from the alliance. For starters, multimedia giant Time Warner printed, marketed and distributed Milestone's comic books through about 8,000 retail outlets. Rather than being shunted to some distant corner of a remote comic-book store, as many small independents are, Milestone's books are displayed on racks adjacent to DC's big guns like *Batman* and *Superman*. Visibility like that at the point of purchase is difficult for small-time operators to get, unless they visit every outlet and rearrange the displays themselves.

Milestone has gained visibility not only in the stores but in other critical venues. For example, Sky Box International, a maker of nonsports trading cards, produced two sets of cards based on the Milestone characters Icon, a conservative black attorney and superhero, and Hardware, a techno-wiz who challenges a corrupt and racist employer who exploits him and his inventions.

The Time Warner connection also gave Dingle and his colleagues the opportunity to go to comic book dealer meetings where they can make their case for books featuring multicultural superheroes. His presentations helped break down the resistance in retail channels to nontraditional comic book heroes. During one meeting with comic book dealers, Dingle was told that black was not the right color for comic book superheroes. He countered by noting that the skin tones of comic book heroes range from green to purple to orange. So why not black?

Customers seemed to like the new hue of superhero. Milestone sold 3.5 million copies of its comic books in its first year. Milestone's fans range from film director John Singleton to U.S. Supreme Court Justice Clarence Thomas.

The partnership is hardly a one-way street, because DC Comics has gained a toehold in the growing market for multicultural comic book fare. Milestone's arrangement with DC is not unlike that of an independent film production company hooking up with a major Hollywood studio, such as Spike Lee's arrangement with Universal Pictures. Derek is quick to point out that Milestone has retained total creative control of its products. Milestone has also retained the copyrights on its characters and has the final say on all merchandising and licensing deals that DC arranges on Milestone's behalf.

Milestone did cede control of such business matters as distribution and marketing to DC Comics, which initially was responsible for 100 percent of Milestone's sales. That figure is now about 75 percent, as Milestone has begun developing some of its own sales channels.

Tackling a Reluctant Partner

Even when a smaller company is going strong, it can be hard to convince a larger company to match up in a strategic alliance. But when you have the determination of former pro football star Charlie W. Johnson, there is no mountain that can't be moved.

Johnson is president and CEO of Active Transportation Company, a Louisville-based firm that specializes in hauling cars, automotive parts and trucks. Johnson, who played in the National Football League for the San Francisco 49ers and the Baltimore Colts, wanted a piece of the action at Ford Motor Company. Johnson was no stranger to Ford, having worked as a supervisor at a Ford plant in Louisville while completing his degree at the University of Louisville after his playing days in the NFL.

Eating fast food to save time and money, Johnson made countless six-hour car trips between Louisville and Detroit to, as he put it, "get into the Ford mainstream." But so did a lot of other transportation companies, many of them larger than Johnson's fledgling firm. Ford officials politely told Johnson that they were aware of his company's reputation for reliable on-time delivery, but there were plenty of other companies with equally sterling track records.

His persistence finally paid off when a manager in Ford transportation told Johnson of a much larger trucking firm than his own that was equally aggressive about trying to land some of Ford's business. The manager told Johnson that he wasn't going to throw any business their way, because the firm had no minority partners and Ford at the time was committing itself to more diversity in its supplier base. But a light went off in the Ford official's head, and he suggested that Johnson's small minority-owned trucking outfit team up with the larger white-owned company.

It proved to be a match, and Johnson's Active Transportation struck a deal with Jupiter Transportation Company of Kenosha, Wisconsin, with annual revenues of about $250 million. Johnson structured a deal under which Active owned 60 percent of the equity and Jupiter 40 percent. Active's business with Ford skyrocketed, going from about $200,000 a year in 1985 to more than $5.3 million in 1987.

The strategic alliance with Jupiter also gave Active access to the larger company's infrastructure, including computers and accounting systems. By 1990 the alliance was doing $47 million worth of business with Ford. On November 11, 1994, Johnson along with three business partners purchased Jupiter for about $80 million. By 1995 Active's revenues topped $350 million, making it the largest minority-owned vehicle transporter in North America. The same year Active received the Minority Economic Development Award and was recognized as one of the ten outstanding businesses of the year by the *Minority Business Report*.

Mindful of his company's early struggles, Johnson has made a commitment to buy goods and services from smaller minority firms. In 1995 Active purchased $25 million worth of product from smaller minority-owned firms. Johnson has also spearheaded an effort among large and midsized companies in Louisville to create a $9 million venture capital fund to help seed the development of small entrepreneurial ventures.

Johnson's advice is simple: "Sell yourself, find a niche and develop a strategic partnership with a Fortune 500 company."

The Big Get Bigger through Alliances

Former NBA great Dave Bing is another retired professional athlete who teamed up to grow his business. He is also one of those athletes who planned carefully for his life after sports. Although he no longer plays professionally, Bing is still a man of steel and he is still running strong. He is the owner or principal owner of three manufacturing concerns that comprise the Bing Group: Bing Steel, Bing Manufacturing and Superb Manufacturing. Chrysler, Ford, General Motors and Toyota are among the Bing Group's major customers.

Bing, whose company ranks high in the B.E. 100s, is a strong proponent of using strategic alliances to grow companies. Like many entrepreneurs, Bing said he can't always bring a lot of cash to the table. What he does instead is let third parties bring the cash to him in exchange for a portion of the equity in his companies. Bing sells only a minority stake in his companies so that he can continue to call the shots—or at least most of them. For example, he sold a 25 percent stake in Bing Steel to a German conglomerate. In exchange, Bing got a $1.7 million piece of equipment that allowed his company to expand its production capacity and improve his balance sheet. Bing alerted his customers and prospective customers to his company's additional capacity, and the orders began to flow.

Bing Steel, which he founded in 1980, is projected to top $100 million in sales in the next year or two—up from about $65 million in 1995. Bing was introduced to the German steel-making concern by officials at General Motors, which was putting pressure on its tier 1, or leading, suppliers to incorporate more minority-owned companies into their supply chain. The German firm, which was trying to get a toehold in the U.S. market, was told by GM that only by striking an alliance with a minority-owned firm in the same field would it be given serious consideration for future business.

Despite the incentive, crafting the deal between the Germans and Bing Steel wasn't easy. Not only were there cultural, language and demographic differences, but the Germans were reluctant to let Bing have the upper hand in the deal. Bing and the German company eventually struck a five-year deal that includes an exit strategy. Bing can buy back the portion of the equity he sold the Germans. They do not have the option of buying Bing out. A shrewd negotiator, Bing is in the process of selling a minority stake in his Superb Manufacturing, Inc., a stamping company, to a larger white-owned company in South Carolina.

A series of joint ventures is helping to drive growth at Bing Manufacturing, which Bing predicts will become the largest of the three companies in his group. Bing owns 40 percent of Bing Manufacturing. His two partners are Forest Farmer, the former president of Chrysler's $3 billion Acustar subsidiary, who owns a 35 percent stake, and Mel Farr, a former Detroit Lions star and car dealer, who controls 25 percent of the company's stock. Farmer serves as Bing Manufacturing's president and CEO.

Within a year of its launch, Bing Manufacturing had entered into two joint ventures. One is with a large Canadian company. Under that agreement, Bing Manufacturing, which has primary control of the venture under a 55-45 split, will make the foam that lines automobile headrests and armrests. Plans call for the construction of a new manufacturing plant from which the foam products will be exported to automobile plants around the world. The second joint venture is with a major automobile seating manufacturer.

Bing says the best way to grow is by giving up some of your company's equity to a strategic alliance partner, but he cautions that companies should be very careful about giving up control. Always insist on retaining the upper hand in any deal, he advises. If you can't, it's best to walk away and look for another candidate.

A Joint Venture for Mutual Benefit

Bob Johnson and his daughter, Rhonda, own a 51 percent stake in Johnson Bryce, Inc., that allows them to call the shots on a day-to-day basis at the flexible packaging manufacturing company in Memphis, Tennessee. Controlling the other 49 percent of the equity in the joint venture, whose sales topped $15 million in 1995, is Bryce Corporation, a $250-million-a-year packaging equipment manufacturer based in Atlanta. The joint venture, created in 1991, was the product of about a year's worth of negotiations between Johnson, a former vice president at Sears Roebuck, and top executives at Bryce. Nearly $6 million was pooled to create the new company.

Bob Johnson was named chairman and CEO of the venture, and Rhonda Johnson became the on-site manager with responsibility for day-to-day operations. Bryce Corporation is hardly a silent partner, however. Decisions about major capital expenditures are usually made in joint meetings that include the Johnsons, Bryce president and co-CEO Tom Bryce and some of his top executives. Bryce is quick to point out, though, that the joint venture is a completely separate entity.

The joint venture's board of directors, which includes the Johnsons and Bryce Corporation executives, maps the company's long-term strategies. Under the agreement, Johnson Bryce leases and operates an 18,000-square-foot Bryce plant in Memphis. Bryce Corporation lent the start-up its engineering expertise and helped install the plant's extrusion laminating equipment, which applies a hot seal to food packages.

Johnson Bryce, which has more than 60 employees, can boast of several blue-chip customers like Frito-Lay and Procter & Gamble.

The company makes snack-food bags for Frito-Lay and produces a polyethylene overwrap for P&G's Always product line.

In addition to engineering and manufacturing expertise, Bryce supplies such support services as accounting, benefits administration and graphics for an annual fee. Tapping Bryce Corporation's infrastructure helps the joint venture to remain mean and lean. Outsourcing such services would greatly increase Johnson Bryce's overhead.

Rhonda Johnson says that there was no way she and her father could have successfully launched the business without a strategic alliance with Bryce Corporation. It would have been very difficult to sell a bank on the viability of a high-capital/low-margin venture without a larger company's backing.

It wasn't the first joint venture for the Johnsons, however. In 1989 the father-daughter team struck a deal with another flexible packaging maker—Chicago-based Bagcraft Corporation of America. As they would later do with Johnson Bryce, the Johnsons bought a 51 percent controlling interest in Bagcraft's Atlanta manufacturing plant and took managerial control. The new venture, called Bagcraft-Atlanta, Inc., got out of the starting gates quickly. Its first-year sales were $11 million, including $8 million from Frito-Lay, which had been seeking to increase its use of minority businesses by matching them up with its existing roster of packaging suppliers.

But no sooner did Bagcraft-Atlanta have things rolling than Frito-Lay radically changed its packaging specifications. The only way the venture could retain its largest customer was through a massive plant renovation. The cost would prove too much, although the Johnsons continued to nurture their relationship with the giant snack-food manufacturer. A year later, the Johnsons were back in business as Johnson Bryce and resumed their supplier relationship with Frito-Lay.

Building Together with a Strategic Alliance

When Anthony "Tony" Thompson, owner of a small St. Louis construction company called the Kwame Building Group, joined forces in 1994 with Atlanta-based H.J. Russell & Company, the nation's largest black-owned construction company, his struggling business struggled no more. Thompson, who had been a successful project engineer for Monsanto Chemical and Anheuser-Busch, incorporated his own construction management company in 1991 while still working for Anheuser-Busch. Among the projects this architectural engineer and MBA handled while at A-B was the multimillion-dollar expansion of its Newark, New Jersey, brewery.

While continuing to work by day at A-B, Thompson spent the next three years landing construction management contracts for several small projects in the St. Louis area. His company provided construction management services for the St. Louis YWCA's Head Start building and the renovation of the St. Louis Regional Medical Center. He took off the life jacket and made the full entrepreneurial plunge in 1994 when he resigned from A-B to devote full-time attention to the Kwame Building Group. Unfortunately, he soon discovered that most people in the local construction industry didn't believe that a small black-owned construction management firm could handle big-time projects.

Despite his expertise and major corporation experience, Thompson realized his fledgling operation needed the resources and track record of a larger construction management outfit to land the big contracts. He also decided not to rely on minority participation requirements as his major means of winning contracts.

A strategic alliance was the answer, but his search for a suitable partner in St. Louis turned up empty. Researching back issues of *Black Enterprise*, Thompson read that H.J. Russell & Company, the nation's largest black-owned construction management company, had a reputation for mentoring smaller black-owned companies. This information led him to Michael Russell, vice president of the Atlanta firm, who was intrigued by Thompson's seemingly outrageous proposal to strike up a partnership.

Russell believed the environment for black business in St. Louis was moving in the right direction with the election of Freeman J. Bosley, Jr., the city's first black mayor. H.J. Russell's alliance with Kwame would help it establish a beachhead there while Thompson and his small firm could use the vast resources of the larger company to win bigger contracts.

The strategic alliance began paying dividends right from the start. In April of 1994, Russell/Kwame was awarded a $100 million contract by the St. Louis Housing Authority—the largest construction management deal ever awarded a minority firm in St. Louis. The new partnership also won a contract to serve as the construction management company for the expansion of the St. Louis International Airport.

Under the agreement between the two firms, the Kwame Building Group receives 25 percent and H.J. Russell 75 percent of the revenues they jointly generate. They also agreed to assist each other in lining up construction management opportunities in their respective cities.

Thompson believes the 25-75 percent revenue split is fair because Russell is taking on the risk of a smaller firm and it eliminates the need for Kwame to hire much additional staff or add resources. As Thompson says: "Who better to teach me than one of the better-managed construction service companies in the country, black or white. The guidance and training that my staff and I receive from H.J.Russell has been invaluable."

Our very future as businesspeople in this nation depends on our ability to work together so that we prosper together. Alliances are our last best hope as we near the end of one century and the dawn of a new one. Cooperation and mutual support will get us from where we are to where we want to go.

If we are to survive, if we are to grow, if we are to assume our rightful place in the national and global economy, it will be through our commitment to working together with mutual understanding and respect. There is no other way.

CHAPTER 13

Building Personal Wealth

Early in our marriage, when Barbara and I were both working, we overextended ourselves because I wanted more than we could afford. Like many people, we got a little crazy with the credit cards, and one day we realized that we were fighting the tide of debt. It was a real slap in the face, but it awakened us to the reality of personal finance. We had to stop using credit cards entirely and pay off the debt. I think we did it by paying $150 a month for a year or more, but we dug our way out and then started living more within our means. Today I rarely make a financial move without consulting my accountant, who has a background in investment and financial planning. No one can afford to be casual or sloppy when it comes to personal finance.

Many African Americans mistakenly believe that once they cross some mythical salary barrier—$30,000, $50,000, $100,000, $250,000—they have it made. They're convinced they are wealthy and then they try to live that lifestyle. I've seen many people spending money like they had a pass key to Fort Knox, only to find out later that they were really living paycheck to paycheck. It's not how much you're making, it's how much you're keeping. It's not how much you're spending, it's how much wealth you are building.

True wealth is measured by your net worth, which is what you own and how much it would be worth if you had to cash it in or sell it. It's a measure of assets minus liabilities. You build net worth, true worth, when you put less of your money toward things that decrease in value—such as cars, clothing and low-interest invest-ments like passbook savings accounts—and more money into income-producing investments such as stocks and mutual funds. Another way to build net worth is by investing in appreciating assets such as real estate and income-generating businesses.

I built my wealth by growing businesses and investing carefully in real estate. I believe that entrepreneurship is the ultimate smart money move and the surest path toward wealth for African Americans. Far fewer blacks than whites benefit from inherited wealth or assets. Entrepreneurship is the primary way to create the sort of wealth that can be passed on and built upon by succeeding generations.

As you know by now, I believe, as my parents did, that the only way African Americans are going to be able to command the respect and power they deserve in this country is by amassing wealth as individuals and leveraging it as a group. That means not only saving and investing wisely, but putting your money to work for the good of the entire community by doing business with black-owned banks and financial service companies, buying stock in well-run black-owned companies and developing an all-around philosophy of thinking black while staying in the black.

To that end, I have dedicated myself to seeing that my money works hard for me through my investment portfolio, and *Black Enterprise* has offered personal financial and investment advice from the beginning. There are no guarantees that every investment you make will be a good one, but if you have a well-considered and con-stantly updated financial plan, I am convinced you will build wealth.

A Business Plan for Building Personal Wealth

We need to think of our personal finances as a business and approach them with the same focus and deliberation we devote to our businesses and careers. Just as any successful company has a business plan, you should have a personal financial plan. To acquire wealth takes planning, a good sense of timing and undoubtedly some luck. The sooner the planning process begins, the greater the likelihood that you will build your savings to finance whatever you dream of—a second home, a secure retirement or a college educa-tion for your children.

I realize that many entrepreneurs and fast-trackers in the corporate world are so absorbed in their business they don't have time to think about building net worth, but that can be a serious mistake. The longer you delay the launch of a well-designed financial plan, the more distant your dreams become. That's why more financial pros are advising even the most timid investors to begin their financial journey immediately.

Here are four steps that anyone serious about building wealth should take now:

Step 1: Set specific goals.

Ask yourself such questions as Do I want to retire early? Should I invest in my child's college education? Or do I want to buy a house in the next six months?

Next comes the hard part. Attach a time frame and a dollar amount to each goal. Ask yourself a second round of questions: At what age do I want to retire? In how many years will my child begin college? How much will the new house cost?

Ideally, you should set up a separate investment account for each goal and prioritize your goals according to the projected timetable. By assigning different accounts to each goal, you diversify your portfolio while creating an easy way to monitor and track investments.

Step 2: Identify financial obligations.

Once the right mind-set has been established, your second step requires taking a hard look at your financial responsibilities and prospects, with an eye toward determining how realistic your goals may be.

If you are in your mid-30s and plan to retire at 50, you better be well on your way to creating your nest egg. Otherwise it's too late. The wealth-building process should have begun in your 20s. Creative and realistic thinking is vital at this stage of financial planning.

Creating scenarios—best and worst—helps you face your various financial obligations and challenges. If you know your goals and have established their order of importance, then creating a cash-flow chart won't seem so onerous.

Step 3: Assess your tolerance for financial risk.

Having determined what you want, ask the fundamental question: What am I willing to put on the line to get it? The lower the risk of an investment, the lower the return and the longer it will take to achieve the goal. With goals that are less immediate, you can assume more risk.

Those with a low tolerance for risk tend to be wary of the stock market. But avoiding equity investments is not the answer if you are looking for growth or income. By ruling out the stock market, including stock mutual funds, you severely limit your choice of liquid investments that can grow with the economy while not being tied directly to interest rates. Smart investors park their money in a broad range of investments.

Step 4: Stick with the plan.

"Those who fail to plan, plan to fail." The old saying is true. That's why deciding who you are, what you want and what you are willing to risk is so important. It is also critical that you continue asking yourself those questions because of the changing circumstances of your personal and business lives: Where am I at this point? Where do I want to be in five years, ten years, twenty years? What do I have to do to get there? And what am I willing to risk? Financial planning may seem daunting, but few things you do offer the rewards of wise investments. They can change your life.

Monitoring Cash Flow

Earlier in this chapter, I mentioned the importance of tracking your cash flow. That does not mean that you stand and watch all your money pour down the drain. I know of one prominent African American whose accountant told him that his income was very high but it was like water flowing through a faucet and directly into an open drain. He was making a huge amount of money, but it was going out just as fast as it was coming in because he was not paying attention to the flow.

This is a critical underlying step toward devising a successful financial plan. Your finances must be in order before you can hope to succeed at long-range financial planning. Keep in mind that your personal cash-flow statement and your monthly budget are not one and the same. A budget is a record of anticipated income and planned expenses. Your cash-flow statement is a regularly kept record of actual income and expenditures. It's designed to help you keep track of exactly how much money you have on hand at regular intervals—usually at the beginning and end of each month.

A budget and a cash-flow statement can give you the information necessary to achieve financial goals. You must determine where you are before you can plan for the long range. I recommend setting aside a day at the end of each month to document the past month's actual expenses and to devise a budget for the next month. With all of the cash-flow information in front of you, it is easier to identify and reduce unnecessary spending. The hard part is making a record of every expenditure. It takes some discipline, but once armed with that information, you will be less likely to run out and buy that new stereo system or the latest CD-ROM, the sort of impulse buying that is the undoing of most personal budgets.

A Financial Planner Can Set You Straight

When you take the time to analyze your expenditures each month, it becomes much easier to spot the problem areas and to determine if you are living beyond your means and why you are doing it. Not everyone has the self-discipline to do this. It can be painful to see your spending habits. That's why it can be helpful for many people to enlist a financial planner.

Although more focused on long-term financial goals than short-term spending habits, a financial planner can help you get a handle on your finances. A financial planner can offer advice on employee benefits, investments, retirement, insurance and tax and estate planning strategies.

Some financial planners specialize in one or more areas such as estate planning, retirement strategies or tax planning. Some planners handle a certain type of client—for example, small business owners, doctors or female executives. You should take the same care in selecting a financial planner that you would in choosing a personal physician. It's important that you establish a bond of trust with the planner so that he or she fully understands your goals and the strategies that best suit your income and your personality.

To protect yourself, make sure the planner you select is either a

Certified Financial Planner (CFP) or a Chartered Financial Consultant (ChFC). Request a disclosure statement that will tell you the planner's education, experience, fees and services. Here are some other tips on working with a financial planner.

■ **Clearly understand how the financial planner is to be compensated.** Commission-based planners don't charge for their advice, but their recommendations may be biased because they earn from 0.5 to 2 percent of whatever you invest. Fee-only planners don't sell commissionable investments but earn their money by charging hourly rates of $100 or more.

■ **Don't agree to a contract before the planner has actually begun working on a plan.** This allows you to document the scope and nature of the services to be provided. You also have the right to see more than one type of written plan.

■ **Ask the planner for worst-case and middle-of-the-road investment scenarios.** Don't buy into pie-in-the-sky promises of high rates of return. Ask about the planner's track record with investors similar to you.

The Seven Deadly Sins of Investing

The more you know about investing, the less likely you are to commit mistakes that could jeopardize your financial future. A poll of investment professionals found that the seven deadliest sins of investing are . . .

1. Failure to do the proper homework on investments and goals.

2. Not taking advantage of such sure-bet opportunities as your employer's 401(k) savings plan. Many employers will match up to 50 percent of your contribution. Leaving this option unfunded is like leaving found money on the sidewalk.

3. Failing to plan adequately for the passing on of your wealth. Remember, you can't take it with you. Create a plan to pass along the wealth to someone else, be it your wife, children or favorite charity.

4. Being too conservative with long-term investments. You can't build wealth with investment instruments that don't do better than the rate of inflation. Playing it too safe can make you sorry later.

5. Delaying the start of your investment plan. Time is on your side when you're young. If you're serious about early retirement or other enviable financial achievements, start now.

6. Failing to get professional advice. Even the most astute entrepreneur should tap the advice of an expert.

7. Failing to set aside at least three to six months' worth of savings in an interest-bearing account. When things go wrong—and they inevitably will—this fund will help cushion the blow and spare you from making any desperate money-management moves.

Playing the Market

A few years ago, a hot new restaurant concept named Boston Chicken went public. There was a lot of talk about this stock being a real hard-charger, so I bought it, and so did my son Butch. At first Boston Chicken climbed so fast it set records and made headlines. Butch realized that it had climbed beyond its real value and got out. His wise father, however, blinked. I "forgot" to sell off my stock, and by the time my memory returned, it had gone south.

Now known as Boston Market, the restaurant chain is doing well, but it left me with a few wounds in its early days because I played for the short-term gain without paying adequate attention. Generally, I have found that one of the surest ways to build wealth is through investing in stock, but it is unwise to play the market in a style unsuited to your needs, lifestyle or the amount of time you can devote to monitoring it.

Michael Jordan got into baseball, realized it wasn't his game and got out. For me, it was Boston Chicken and trying to time its rise and fall in the market. That is just not my game. I have done very well, however, by investing in AT&T, the oil companies and other blue-chip stocks. These you buy and hold over the long term because, while the stock market may go through some bumps and declines, it has moved higher and higher over time. The buy-and-hold strategy puts you in a position to profit from the long-term upward trend of the market. This strategy can produce substantial returns without having to monitor the performance of your stocks on a daily basis.

Generally, the blue-chip stocks—or those of the nation's leading industrial companies—are the best candidates for the buy-and-hold strategy. An advantage of the buy-and-hold strategy is the compounding effect that a dividend reinvestment plan can have on your return. Many companies offer shareholders a plan that does not pay them in cash but in the form of additional common shares. Dividend reinvestment plans offer small investors an easy way to build wealth. The plans work best when the company has a solid history of dividend payments and steady price appreciation. I have invested heavily in the stocks of the companies on whose board I serve. As an outside director, it keeps me meaningfully focused on how the stocks are doing. Also, as a director, it is an obligation. Fortunately, in the last five years, they've all done well.

I have found that another smart long-term investment strategy is dollar-cost averaging. Using this strategy, you invest the same amount of money in a stock or mutual fund at regular intervals—monthly, quarterly or semiannually. You buy the security regardless of its market price at the time of each stock purchase.

Consistency and the amount invested are the key ingredients of the dollar-cost-averaging method to minimize pricing and timing risk. When the price of a security falls, your purchasing power expands. When the price of the security rises, your fixed investment buys fewer shares. Over the long run, the cost of each share is lower than the average price per share during the investment period. Like the buy-and-hold strategy, dollar-cost averaging is based on the steady increase in the value of stocks over the long term. Building wealth is no short-term proposition. Commitment is the key.

Here is some well-founded advice on how to build wealth through dollar-cost averaging:

1. Invest over the long haul—from $7\frac{1}{2}$ to 10 years. This recommendation is based on the market's cyclical history. In the past 100 years, there have been about 40 recessions, occurring about every $2\frac{1}{2}$ years. Continuing to invest through the downturns will allow you to maximize dollar-cost averaging.
2. Invest at regular intervals—preferably monthly or quarterly.
3. Invest regardless of the stock price.

4. Choose high-quality stocks or mutual funds. Look for companies with a history of regular dividend payouts and the potential for capital appreciation. Dividend reinvestment can further boost the returns on dollar-cost averaging.

Investment experts believe that the money set aside for dollar-cost averaging should be money for wealth-building, not everyday money.

Investment Strategies for Building Wealth

I've learned that your approach to the market can be just as important to financial success as the actual moves you make. There are two different styles of investment management—value and growth. You can use each style individually, or use them both to create portfolio magic. Combining value and growth strategies helps you enhance investment return while reducing risk.

Growth stock investors believe that future earnings are key. Expectations are that over the long run, a company's stock price will rise along with its earnings. Growth stock companies, many of which are found in the high-technology, telecommunications and biomedical fields, are expected to experience strong growth in future earnings. But when a growth company's earnings fail to live up to expectations, the stock price can drop. Many of Wall Street's high-flyers can be extremely volatile. Ask yourself how much risk you can handle without losing sleep or feeling uncomfortable.

More conservative players prefer the value style of investing, which places less emphasis on projected earnings. Value-oriented investors and managers favor stocks with a proven track record.

The price/earning (P/E) ratio is a company's stock price divided by its earnings per share over the past 12 months. It's the most common method of determining a stock's value. P/E ratios are like golf scores—the lower the better. For example, a company with a stock price of $20 and earnings of $1 per share has a P/E of 20. Value-oriented investors bank on share price increases occurring when Johnny-come-lately investors start to buy after the stock has started rising.

Value investing has produced some impressive long-term results for some investors. There are risks, however, as my experience with Boston Chicken shows. For example, you can buy your stocks at the wrong time; the company may never reach its full valuation; or it may take so long to reach its potential that the return is insignificant and is eroded by inflation.

Once you grasp the difference between growth and value investing, you will be able to choose a comfortable style and use it as a tool to manage risk and improve the returns in your portfolio. If you are investing without the assistance of a broker or financial planner, you will need to do your own homework. One of the best ways to learn about a stock is by reading the company's annual report. Here are a few tips.

1. Read the shareholder's letter describing the company's past performance and future prospects. The letter will normally note whether the company fulfilled its target goals. Be wary of a chairman who fails to mention any potential problems on the horizon. Beware too of hype over new products and services. It usually takes three to five years before a new product affects the bottom line positively.

2. Study the balance sheet. Divide assets by liabilities. A ratio of at least 2:1 indicates that the company can probably handle its debt.

3. Examine the company's inventories. Rising sales, earnings and dividends generally signal a winner. But if inventory is outstripping sales, be careful. The company is producing more than it can sell.

4. Don't be fooled by rising revenues. If expenses are rising faster than revenues, the company will be unable to report a profit. That should be a caution signal to you.

5. Determine the company's source of earnings. If profits are up, find out why. In this era of downsizing, companies can squeeze out profits without increasing their sales. If profits are down, determine whether it's because of a price war, poor management or other factors.

6. Note the company's return on equity—its profit rate. This important yardstick measures the company's ability to make money. A return on equity above 15 percent is good. Compare that with the company's earnings from previous years.

7. Be skeptical when reading. Phrases like "Integrating this year's highs and lows proved challenging" probably means that sales were up but profits were down.

Mutual Funds

People who lack the time or interest to sift through the minutiae of individual stocks are better off investing in mutual funds, which pool investment contributions from shareholders to buy stocks. Mutual funds also buy bonds and other investments. Investors in mutual funds own shares of a mutual fund company, which is essentially a portfolio of investments.

With an initial investment of from $250 to $2,500 you become part owner of that portfolio. Each fund of dozens or even hundreds of stocks is professionally managed, meaning that you don't have to do all the homework. The advice doesn't necessarily come for free, however. The sales fee, or load, can be as much as 5.75 percent of the amount you are investing. Many funds don't charge any load, while some others have lower fees, ranging from 1 to 4 percent.

Before you buy into a fund, you should at the very least read the fund's prospectus, which spells out the fund's investment objective, management fees, shareholders services and past performance. If you have already purchased shares in a mutual fund and want to know how well or how poorly you are doing, there are two ways to find out. One way is to wait until your statement arrives in the mail. Some funds provide monthly statements, others issue them quarterly.

You can also calculate your gains or losses yourself. To do that, determine how many shares in the fund you own. You bought a specific number of shares initially, but with dividend reinvestment, the number of shares you own has grown. Once you have figured out how many shares you own, check the latest net asset value (NAV) listed for the fund. You can call the fund's manager to find out. Almost every fund has a toll-free number. Multiply that figure by the number of shares you own to determine the value of your holdings.

To determine how much you have made or lost on your investment, go through the same procedure, only this time calculate the value at the time you made your initial investment. A comparison of then and now will reveal whether you are a winner or a loser.

The diversity of a mutual fund's stock holdings helps spread your risk. The nation's largest fund, Fidelity Magellan, holds shares of more than 700 different stocks, for example. There are now more than 5,000 different funds, which come in a variety of flavors. There are global funds, small company growth funds, socially conscious funds and balanced funds. In my opinion, mutual funds may be the best investment in town.

More conservative investors prefer income funds that invest in well-established companies. These funds provide a steady stream of income as well as some stock price appreciation. For the bold at heart, there are aggressive growth funds, which hold shares in high-tech concerns, or start-ups, which may someday join the ranks of the Fortune 500. Aggressive growth fund managers also invest in underpriced stocks ripe for a turnaround and in potential takeover stocks, which can produce a huge run-up in price. There's risk involved, but the returns can be quite handsome. Every April, *Black Enterprise* lists the top mutual funds. The objective ranking is based on each fund's five-year total return compared with similar funds.

If you plan to invest your money only in mutual funds, you probably don't need a stockbroker. But if you plan to invest heavily in individual stocks, a broker becomes a must. There are two types of brokers. Full-service brokers can help you buy and sell securities, do research and offer you advice. Most full-service brokers charge such hefty commissions (at least $25 every time you buy or sell) that it's not economical to start an account with just $100. Full-service brokers also like to trade in round lots of 100. At that rate, you'd need a minimum account of about $25,000.

Discount brokers won't be nearly as expensive, perhaps charging only a third of what their full-service counterpart might charge, but then you don't get nearly the level of research or advice. Regardless of whether you get professional advice, remember that patience, combined with the power of compounding interest, dividends and appreciation of the shares in the fund, can help you build wealth. Successful investors strike a balance between the need for long-term growth, current income and the ability to sleep at night.

There are mutual funds and investment vehicles that allow you to invest in good conscience. A politically correct investor might consider the Dreyfus Socially Responsible Growth Fund co-managed by my longtime friend Mace Sloan of Sloan Financial Group and Stephan A. Jackson of NCM Capital Management Group. This mutual fund features companies that do not promote such social vices as smoking, drinking or gambling, and it gives a good return too. The $460 million fund posted a one-year growth rate of 36.19 percent in the first quarter of 1996, putting it in the top 13 percent of all growth funds and in the top 6 percent of all equity funds at that time. Although socially responsible funds are limited in their span because of restrictions on choosing company stocks, this one includes technology stocks that are environmentally friendly, as well as such strong stocks as Gillette, Johnson & Johnson and Regal Cinemas, the eighth largest movie exhibitor in the country.

Another form of investment similar to mutual funds is the unit investment trust, or UIT. Unlike mutual funds, UITs are a fixed investment. One that has been recommended to *Black Enterprise* readers is the American Diversity Growth Trust UIT, which has a fixed portfolio of 25 stocks representing firms popular with African American consumers, or stocks in which blacks hold senior management positions, such as Tommy Hilfiger Corporation, Fila Holding SpA and Gucci Group N.V. It includes five publicly traded stocks of black-owned companies: BET, Granite Broadcasting, Carver Federal Savings, United American Healthcare and Caraco Pharmaceuticals. Other stocks in the portfolio are Avon Products, Citicorp, Walt Disney, The Gap, Reebok, Estee Lauder, Fannie Mae, Nine West, Time Warner and Wal-Mart.

The American Diversity Growth Trust is a five-year investment open to the public. The minimum investment required is $1,000, unless you buy it for your IRA, which will require an investment of $250 or monthly payments of $50. I mention it here because it is a new way to buy and invest in black-owned and black-friendly companies, which I believe should be a key element in any African American's personal financial philosophy.

The Security of Bonds

One investment option that won't cause you to lose sleep is a U.S. bond. Buying bonds from the government is one of the safest, most inexpensive ways to invest. Treasury bills, notes or savings bonds are backed by the full faith and credit of the U.S. government. Unlike corporate bonds issued by companies, there is almost no chance that Uncle Sam will default on paying you your interest at the bond's maturity. Treasury bills and savings bonds are affected by interest rate changes, so the prices and yields may fluctuate before you cash them in.

Let's look at how you can profit from investing in Treasuries, or T-bills, which are securities with maturities of one year or less. The ones most commonly bought by investors are three- and six-month T-bills. Offered in denominations of $10,000 to $1 million, T-bills are issued at a discount from their face value. You pay the face value minus the interest. When the bill reaches maturity, you collect the full face value.

Take the example of a $10,000 T-bill. If the one-year rate for a particular week is 7 percent, you would pay $9,300. When the T-bill matures a year later, you collect $10,000—the full face value. The 7 percent is called the discount rate. The advantage the T-bill has over a corporate bond is that you only have to pony up $9,300 instead of $10,000. You can also count on being paid the interest.

You can buy T-bills through your bank or your broker, but make sure the transaction fee or commission doesn't erode your profit. The cheapest way to buy Treasuries is to go through the Federal Reserve Bank in your area.

U.S. savings bonds are another investment option. The Series EE bond is an appreciation-type security that accrues interest for 30 years. The purchase price is half the bond's face amount. For example, a $100 bond costs $50. The bonds are available in denominations of $50, $75, $100, $200, $500, $1,000, $5,000 and up. Savings bonds are available from the Federal Reserve or your bank. They can also be bought through your company's human resources department.

Taxing Strategies

U.S. government instruments like bonds are free of state and local taxes. Your capital gains are subject to federal income taxes, but your liability is deferred until the bonds mature. Serious wealth builders must keep the tax man at bay. I am not advocating anything illegal.

I'm suggesting that your investment strategy include a tax strategy as well.

The first rule of tax-wise investing is to maximize contributions to your retirement plan. IRS-approved plans and 401(k) employee plans let you save pretax dollars and defer taxes on their investment income until you withdraw the money—usually after reaching age 59½. Retirement accounts are almost unbeatable even without an employer match. Let's say you invest $2,000 a year. If you are investing in a taxable account and you're in the 36 percent tax bracket, your $2,000 investment is reduced to only $1,280 once the taxman is done with you. But put that $2,000 in a tax-free account and the entire amount is yours to keep upon reaching retirement.

Next, consider the advantages of tax-deferred compounding. Take the case of a 39½-year-old investor planning to retire in 20 years. Assume that the investor earns an average of 8 percent a year on the account. At the end of 20 years, the taxable investor has $42,865, and the tax-deferred investor has $91,524.

Another tax-free play is municipal bonds, the debt of state and local governments. Most interest income from muni bonds and muni bond funds is not federally taxed. If you live in the state issuing the bonds, you may be exempt from state and local taxes as well.

Buyers of individual stocks can reduce the tax bite by investing in companies that retain most of their earnings rather than paying out large dividends. That's because the federal government taxes dividend income at a different rate than capital gains. Income stocks, such as utilities, return most of their earnings in the form of dividends. By contrast, growth stocks retain all or most of their earnings because they invest the profits for research and development purposes to fuel the company's future growth. The payoff with growth stocks doesn't come until you have sold your shares.

Another way to shelter investment income from current income taxes is to buy an annuity. You do, however, pay taxes on the amounts actually paid to you by the annuity. Sold by insurance companies and most recently by banks and brokerage firms, annuities share many features with Individual Retirement Accounts (IRAs). Investment income compounds on a tax-free basis, and there are penalties for withdrawal before age 59½. Annuities also have insurance features that guarantee a return of principal to beneficiaries.

Conservative investors find annuities appealing because they protect against loss of principal. High-income investors also like them because they can be used to shelter more income than IRAs allow. It pays to do your homework because the insurance feature of annuities can be expensive. Generally, it costs about 1.25 percent of your annuity investment a year. Most annuities also have stiff back-end loads or penalties, starting at about 6 percent before phasing out completely after six or seven years.

There are several types of annuities worth considering. There are single-payment deferred annuities, which require you to make a lump-sum payment. The more common type of tax-deferred annuity allows you to make smaller regular payments over a number of years. Fixed-income annuities invest primarily in bonds. Rates are set periodically based on market conditions. Variable annuities are similar to mutual funds because they invest in a wide range of instruments, including stocks and bonds.

Annuities can be customized to your needs. With a straight life annuity, for example, you receive an income as long as you live, once you reach a specified payout date. But when you die, your beneficiaries get nothing. The straight life annuity provides the highest possible payout while you are alive. If you want your beneficiaries to receive payments for 10 to 20 years after your death, you must stipulate that in the contract.

There are a number of ways to get a bigger tax break from your charitable gifts. If you are planning to make a gift to a nonprofit organization, don't cash in your securities to make the contribution. That's because selling the securities at a profit would trigger a tax liability on the gain. If you give the securities directly to the charity, however, you can claim a deduction for their current value while avoiding the tax.

Let's say you make a gift of $1,000 to your church or another IRS-approved charity. The tax deduction, in the 36 percent tax bracket, would trim your tax bill by $360, making your out-of-pocket cost $640. But let's say you donated $1,000 worth of stocks to your church, for which you paid $750. The deduction is the same, but your out-of-pocket cost is $250 less.

Tax strategies don't need to be complicated. What counts is how much capital you can preserve for major expenditures such as retirement and the financing of college for your children.

Many people are in the unenviable position of having to fund retirement and college savings simultaneously. That's why every dollar counts.

Investing in Higher Education

Just like saving for retirement, the sooner you begin the college savings process, the better. Investment advisors say you should establish a college savings fund the day your child is born. Besides borrowing, there are a number of ways to foot the bill for college. They include saving money through cash-value life insurance and prepaid college tuition plans.

Orenettia Todd salted away $64.40 every month for five years to fund her granddaughter Avia's college education. By the time her granddaughter entered college, her tuition and fees were paid off at a two-year community college and four-year state university thanks to Florida's prepaid college tuition plan. Todd is one of 6,000 African Americans enrolled in Florida's Prepaid College Program. Under the plan, money put down on prepaid tuition contracts is invested in stocks and bonds by an autonomous non-profit organization, which administers contracts for tuition and dormitories.

Prepaid tuition plans are available in Alabama, Alaska, Florida, Massachusetts, Michigan, Ohio, Pennsylvania, Texas and Virginia.

Another option for those who live in a state that doesn't offer a prepaid college tuition plan is to use a cash-value life insurance policy to save money to pay for college. Charles Harris, for example, pays a monthly $175 premium for his $300,000 universal life insurance policy. He will generate $2,100 a year, or $18,900 by 2004—the year his son, Scott, will reach college age. At that time, Harris can withdraw the $18,900 tax-free because the money is a return on premiums. His policy earns an interest rate of 6.25 percent. As Harris puts it, "People talk about using bonds and mutual funds, but this option had a double advantage to it. One, I'm providing protection for my family, and two, I can take some funds that have accrued from that account."

The downside to using a life insurance contract as an investment vehicle is that it requires a long-term commitment. And it's best not to let the policy lapse, because you'll lose your tax benefits.

Financing Retirement

If building wealth for four years of college sounds like a challenge, consider the task of setting aside enough money for a retirement that could last 25 to 30 years—and that's for people who retire at 65. The joint life expectancy of a retired couple in good health is age 90, according to retirement specialist Bruce Temkin.

For many people, retirement will last nearly as long as their working careers. Whatever your retirement dream, it's probably going to take more money than you realize. With employer pensions becoming more the exception than the rule, it will be up to you to finance most of your retirement. Despite all the scare stories, your retirement income will include Social Security benefits. But the benefits will hardly provide for an extravagant lifestyle. If you'd had the maximum amount of wages withheld for Social Security taxes most of your career and were to retire this year at age 65, you could expect to receive a benefit of about $15,000 a year.

I've mentioned the importance of building wealth through a 401(k) account or an IRA. Entrepreneurs may be able to fund retirement through the sale of their businesses. Whatever route you choose, make a plan and stick to it. The race isn't to the swift but to the steady.

CHAPTER 14

The Business of Family

I believe that economic development is vital to the black community and that more African Americans should consider entrepreneurship not simply as a career choice or as a way to make money but as a way of life for them and their children. But the family, and the principles and values that hold this society together should not be neglected in the pursuit of business or career success. Rather, they should all be equal parts of your approach to life.

I think each person has to make his or her own decisions about how to live and what faith, if any, to follow. I don't preach about it, but I do believe that without my family and my faith, I would never have had the strength to fight all of the battles I've had to engage in. I've found that the ministers I have known well, including the late Rev. John Coleman of St. Philip's Episcopal Church in Brooklyn; the late Rev. Leonard Anderson, Episcopal chaplain at Morgan State; the late Right Rev. Henry B. Hucles III; the Rev. W. Franklyn Richardson at Grace Baptist Church in Mount Vernon, New York, and the Rev. James Forbes at Riverside Church in Manhattan have been great resources for me and my family over the years.

It is the responsibility of all African Americans to help our young people—our hope for the future—to understand the opportunities that entrepreneurship and business offer them just as our parents paved the way for us. Black children must be shown that there are opportunities beyond the streets, gangs and crime. The way to do that is to incorporate business into their lives.

Our children grew up in a business environment. Sometimes they benefited from it in unusual ways, such as with one of the most successful and enjoyable sales campaigns undertaken by my staff at Earl Graves Ltd. It had nothing to do with the publishing world, Chrysler, Pepsi-Cola, South Africa or business in general and everything to do with my belief in family and the importance of leading a balanced life as a key to success. The product that we were packaging and selling, you see, was my eldest son, Butch.

Butch as a Brand Name

At Yale University, Butch was the all-time leading scorer on the basketball team and named the school's top scholar-athlete at graduation. Going into his junior year, Butch was playing so well that he began to think he might have a shot at his boyhood dream of playing professional basketball in the NBA. He had the skills to make it, most people agreed, but for all its prestige and grand academic traditions, and despite having produced some great athletes over the years, such as former football players Levi Jackson and Calvin Hill, Yale is not a renowned showcase for sports talent.

In the first two years of his college basketball career, Butch was the star of an average team with a mediocre record. Because of the team's poor performance overall and Yale's lack of status in the athletic world, it was likely that the only professional scouts in the stands would be those from Price Waterhouse and Merrill Lynch, which was fine with me. But Butch wanted to test his athletic skills against the best before he got down to more serious business.

I agreed that he deserved a chance. So I summoned all the top creative marketing talent at Earl Graves Ltd., as well as that at the Graves family residence, and announced the launching of a special sales campaign aimed at getting my eldest son his fair shot at a pro basketball career. There were a lot of smiles among the staff members at that meeting, but no one was surprised. They had already become accustomed to organizing bus trips for our family and friends to Butch's games.

Family Assets

Family is a priority in my business. It always has been. It always will be. To head a successful and legitimate business, I believe you have to be grounded in values, principles and relationships. I also believe you have to have a wider frame of reference than the room around your desk. You have to be involved in life, in family, in your community and in the world around you. Far too many people in business see their personal lives and their careers as competing aspects of their lives. I don't. They are each parts of the whole, with family being the most important. I cannot imagine being able to conduct business or taking any joy in it without a family to go home to—my wife and sons, and now my daughters-in-law and my grandchildren.

Success can sometimes be nearly as lethal to black families as struggle. I know many African American men and women whose professional accomplishments have been offset and even undermined by family turmoil.

Years ago, when we moved to Westchester County, which is home to many affluent white corporate executives, one of the greatest fears that Barbara and I had was that our sons would lose track of their black identities. We also did not want them to feel that life was going to be easy for them simply because they grew up in a relatively affluent setting. One of the ways we instilled our sons with the work ethic was to require them to take care of the yard and landscaping all year round, which is a considerable job given the size of our yard and all of the trees in it. I think we did pretty well in teaching them responsibility and hard work. In fact, to this day my son Johnny refuses to do yard work at his own house because we made our point so strongly.

But Barbara and I had no part in another lesson that was imparted one fall day when my sons, then teenagers, were raking the grass out front. Suddenly a stranger, a white man whose car had broken down, came walking up the driveway and asked them, "Is anybody home here?"

Johnny, the future lawyer, took the case: "You see me standing right here and you ask me if anybody is home? What am I, a *nonentity*?"

Even upon realizing that he was speaking to residents of the house, not the gardening crew, the guy insisted upon putting both feet and hands in his mouth: "How was I to know that you lived here? You don't see anybody else around here doing their own yard work."

Fortunately for our visitor, I arrived in time to keep my sons from dismantling him and his car. If my goal in having my sons do the yard work was to keep them from forgetting who they were, this was but another lesson.

The Family Foundation

I believe that if you are to succeed in the dog-eat-dog business world, particularly if your skin color is always going to set you apart, then you are going to need a deep reservoir of strength and determination. You are going to need principles and values, those guidelines that determine how you lead your life. Most important, you are going to need the lasting and unconditional love of a family.

I don't mean a family in a gilded picture frame that smiles out from a corner of your desk. I mean a family in which you are actively and deeply involved—a family in which you know the names of best friends and girlfriends, the batting averages, the inoculations, bumps, bruises and shoe sizes, the teachers, the Scout leaders, the favorite colors, the heroes, the secret fears and dreams.

That is your most important business, and if you have it in order, the rest is icing on the cake. Believe me, it's true. You will know it's true if your family business ever hits a crisis, because all other business stops when that happens. I've seen it happen and I'm certain you have too. A sick child, an unhappy marriage—these things can destroy a business career if the foundation of the family has not been well constructed and maintained.

On the other hand, there is nothing more gratifying to me than the bond of family. It means a great deal to Barbara and me that our sons and their wives and children eagerly include us in their vacation plans—and I'm sure it has absolutely nothing to do with the fact that we pay the fare. I'll never forget the time that Michael promptly dumped a girlfriend after she announced that she did not enjoy going on trips with him and his parents and brothers.

Now I'm not saying that you have to be married or to have children to be successful in business. Not everyone can be that lucky.

And I understand that there are some out there who don't share my enthusiasm for the traditional family life. I won't argue about lifestyle choices. But I do maintain that it is vital to your business success that your life not be an undisciplined, solitary scramble from one day and one paycheck to the next. You have to have the personal side of your life together to support the professional side. You have to be there for others so that you know they will be there for you.

Selling a Son

I wanted to be there for Butch. I wanted to help him go after his dream of playing professional basketball. I knew there were far greater accomplishments ahead of him, but I knew he understood that too. He had made me proud, and now I wanted to help build his pride in his own accomplishments. So I launched the campaign to market Butch to the professional ranks.

Shortly after that initial meeting, sportswriters, professional basketball scouts, coaches, assistant coaches, agents, trainers, mascots and ball boys all across the National Basketball Association began receiving weekly postcard updates providing the game-by-game performance statistics of one Earl "Butch" Graves Jr. of Yale University's basketball team. The Butch highlight videos soon followed.

Don't think that I didn't go to the network for this campaign. No stone went unturned. Anyone who knew a coach, a sportswriter or an usher heard from me. As a result of this full-court press, Butch started getting the sort of attention generally reserved for 7-foot-8-inch Pac 10 All-Stars. I'll wager you haven't heard of too many other Ivy League ballplayers on mediocre teams being featured on the *Today Show* or in *Sports Illustrated.* We sold both on the concept of contrasting Butch's relatively unsung but high-scoring college career with that of a star at basketball powerhouse Syracuse University—I can't seem to remember his name. I do know that Butch had far better stats, but the other guy had a well-oiled media machine and easy access to the ravenous New York sports media.

As a result of our off-court press, and Butch's own considerable skills, he played in the NBA for one season. After being drafted by the Philadelphia 76ers he played for the Milwaukee Bucks and then

Cleveland, before deciding to hang up his sneakers and shoot for an MBA at Harvard. He is now executive vice president and chief operating officer of Earl G. Graves Publishing.

Family Matters

My other two sons, both of whom were also college athletes, are also key players in my business ventures. Johnny, my second son, is a Yale Law School graduate, which doesn't surprise us, since as a youngster he regularly appointed himself to represent his brothers in the Graves family court ("Dad, just why can't we go to the movies tonight?"). Today he serves as vice president for business ventures and legal affairs at Earl G. Graves Publishing. He is also in charge of our highly successful Golf and Tennis Challenge. My youngest son, Michael, a University of Pennsylvania graduate and the only football player in the family, heads up our Pepsi-Cola bottling franchise in Washington, D.C.

The fact that my sons are involved in the business is, I believe, the result of our love for each other. It is perhaps my greatest achievement that they all want to build upon what their mother and I have created. All of them have had lucrative offers elsewhere, and all of them had to prove themselves worthy of the positions they now hold by working up through the ranks. I think Michael is still trying to clean off the Pepsi syrup from his days of hauling cartons on a sales route.

I am enormously proud of my sons and their families. I have also been blessed with a partner who has been my most trusted and wisest business partner, advisor, critic and confidante. Barbara has been involved in the family business from the start. Over the years she has run every department at the magazine with the exception of sales. It is difficult to put into words all the contributions she has made and continues to make. I wanted to write an entire chapter on Barbara, but they told me to save that for the best-selling autobiography. In truth, I could write a book—a series of books—about all Barbara has meant to me.

Publishing a magazine for black business professionals and entrepreneurs has not gotten any easier over the years, and in recent times, there have been many nights when I came home exhausted, beaten, bloodied and bruised from the daily battles against racism and ignorance. No matter how down I've been, she has always raised my spirits, cleaned me up and sent me back into the fray.

Barbara had an office for years at our headquarters in Manhattan, and when she wasn't called away to her first duty with the children, she was an extremely active and influential part of the business. That's why I've refused to dismantle her office, even though, for the most part, she now chooses to work out of our home, a luxury she deserves to enjoy. But not having her around the office has created a void for me personally and professionally.

She has always provided me with a guiding sense of perspective and balance. Her values and principles have kept me on track over the years. It was Barbara who taught me, through example, what true integrity is. Around the time we launched *Black Enterprise*, ours was among the few black families, if not the only one, living in Armonk, New York, and there was a controversy about a plan to build low-income public housing in the town. Many of the white residents objected to the housing because they did not want more blacks in town. I had not paid a great deal of attention because of business matters, but Barbara made sure I got with the program and that the city fathers were informed about where the Graves family stood on the issue. I had said, "Barbara, I have enough battles in the office." Her response was, "We are going to fight this one too."

I'm not saying you have to have a spouse to be successful in business or to have integrity, but I don't know how people do it alone or without partners who are fully engaged in all aspects of their lives. In fact, I know very few successful businesspeople who do not have a solid family life. My earliest role models and mentors and friends have all had successful families who have been major parts of their lives.

Along with my philosophy that a successful business is built more upon personal relationships than on a driving need for money, I don't believe in keeping family and loved ones separate from business, because, first, I think that is impossible—what happens in one aspect always affects the other—and, second, I think African Americans in particular have to use all the assets at their command, including their families.

This philosophy has always been reflected not only in the way we have raised our children, but also in the pages of *Black Enterprise*.

You will find very few issues of the magazine over the years that do not have a story and photographs relating to family matters, whether it is tips on financing childen's college educations, selecting a good summer camp or family vacation spots or teaching children basic business principles.

Kidpreneurs: Teaching Business to Our Children

My concern for family involvement and establishing a business tradition for African American families is behind one of the more exciting projects we have undertaken in recent years, our Kidpreneur Konference program. It was established in recognition of the increased importance of preparing the next generation of African American leadership for economic empowerment and professional excellence. Kidpreneur is an innovative program committed to developing the entrepreneurial potential of each child.

Our aim is to inspire African American young people to view entrepreneurship as an option for success and to teach them the skills required to become successful business owners. We seek to teach them the rich traditions of African American entrepreneurship in this country and to provide them with the ability to develop skills for business ownership by giving them experiences that deepen and extend their pleasure in learning.

Although still in its infancy, the Kidpreneur program provides a challenging business curriculum while stressing the importance of building friendships with children of similar interests and ambitions—networking in kneesocks. Each child in the program obtains a sense of self-worth while experiencing learning. Our primary goal in the Kidpreneur Konference program is to provide a warm yet competitive environment while meeting the exploratory and creative business needs of children of all intellectual levels and ages.

The program strives to balance business learning with oratory, real-life math applications and recreational skills. With a dedicated team of business owners and consultants as instructors, it is designed to teach children and young adults the merits of entrepreneurship through hands-on exposure and interactive activities. It offers three levels of instruction: Futurepreneurs (ages 7–10), Junior Executives (ages 11–13) and Future CEOs (ages 14–17).

The Junior Executives program helps participants understand the principles of entrepreneurship. Through educational play, pre-teens are exposed to business basics. Special emphasis is given to the characteristics and qualities of an entrepreneur as well as to choosing the right kind of business, setting goals and getting started. The Future CEOs program allows teenagers to explore the world of entrepreneurship by becoming business owners. Teenagers choose partners, create an organizational chart, raise capital, write a business plan and market their products in this program.

I believe it is crucial for young people to understand early on that business is an option and that owning a business is a real possibility. I think we need to start at a very early age and continue through their childhood and into young adulthood. We must convey to them the message that black people can not only be on the radio, we can own radio stations; that black people can not only be construction workers and engineers, we can own construction companies that build cities.

My longtime friend and frequent advisor Dr. James P. Comer, who is director of the school development program at the Yale Child Study Center and a leading child psychiatrist, says it is critical to introduce the opportunities of business to young people very early on because economic development is so vital to the African American community. Comer and others have noted that the entrepreneurial route is one of the greatest ways out of poverty in this world. Schools and education are crucial, yes, but in a capitalist society it is economic activity that drives political, social and other economic change.

If your child grows up outside the economic mainstream, it becomes nearly impossible for that child to compete economically as an adult. That has been one of the traditional problems in the black community because we have been shut out of the economic mainstream. Our leaders have attempted to address what is essentially an economic problem with social solutions, and many blacks have been able to attain middle-class lifestyles as long as the economy provided blue-collar industrial jobs that did not require a lot of education. But when the economy shifted to service and information, those blacks who had jobs in Rust Belt factories and other industrial facilities around the country were cut out of the economic mainstream in great numbers.

Other blacks, including many of the children of blue-collar African Americans, gained access to education through affirmative action programs. Those who attained education have gained access to jobs and government contracts to some degree because of those same affirmative action and set-aside programs. But we need to expand the opportunities for more blacks to enter and successfully negotiate the mainstream. We need the black community to include more business owners, more people who provide jobs and accumulate economic power. With that will come the sort of clout that other racial and ethnic groups have acquired by forming alliances with police and politicians, bankers and business leaders.

African Americans must have access to capital to compete, and the way you do that is by building your professional class. We need to strengthen and enlarge that class. For too long we have been limited because owning a business has simply not been a tradition for enough of us. Two few of our children have been exposed to working in family businesses, hearing conversations about business or seeing blacks who own and operate businesses in their neighborhoods.

To address this lack of exposure, we need to create activities that introduce and empower our young people to move into the economic mainstream. Dr. Comer tells me that if we can do this, if we can show more young people the opportunities of the business world, it might very well reduce the illegitimate economic activity that has seduced so many. The stronger the attraction of legitimate opportunities, the more young people will resist illegal and irresponsible activities.

Comer says that young people who enter the legitimate economic mainstream find structure for their lives, set goals and build knowledge. They don't fall into the trap of waiting for life to come to them. Instead, they learn to make things happen for themselves through hard work, determination and initiative.

How can you encourage your children and help them understand the possibilities that exist for them in the business world? Well, first of all, as a good parent, you pay attention to their needs and provide the guidance and structure that are so important if they are to become responsible, confidant and secure people.

Growing an Entrepreneur

Here are a few suggestions, gleaned from our Kidpreneur experiences and from the Graves family scrapbook, on how to raise a future business executive:

I. Be there for your child.

The most important way to develop the entrepreneurial spirit in your child is to practice good, caring child-rearing, which means being there when your child needs you, modeling good responsible behavior and providing strong guidance for your children.

Believe me, if I never sat through another Little League game in my life it would be just fine with me. At that level, baseball is like watching ink dry on the page. But Barbara and I made the effort to be there, coaching and cheering on our sons, because we felt our enthusiastic involvement was important for them.

I am very traditional in my belief that a child needs parents, not hired baby-sitters. I don't think anyone else can truly provide what children need. I understand that it's not always easy or even possible in today's society, where the traditional family situation is no longer a given, but so often people become caught up in their own pursuits and think their children can be raised on autopilot. It does not work that way, and the crime statistics reflect it.

It's also true that no two children are alike, and generational differences must also be taken into consideration. My sons, Johnny in particular, questioned everything as they grew up. They were also the generation that questioned our involvement in Vietnam. I was of the generation that believed in serving my country without question. Johnny taught me something else. I now understand that it is indeed possible to do your homework with the room around you vibrating from the stereo speakers and somehow have a successful academic career while graduating with your eardrums intact.

2. Don't panic if you aren't perfect.

Because of increased awareness today about the importance of child-rearing, parents often become uptight about every situation, every circumstance that their children present. Dr. Comer's traditional advice is "Don't worry." It's inevitable that you will do some things wrong and make some mistakes, but that's OK. You have to use common sense and apply good values to rearing your child. The important thing is to think about your approach and to be observant of the effects of your approach and judgment as you go along.

3. Outline your expectations.

Parents too often assume their children know what to do and how to act, but children don't come into the world knowing the rules. You can't presume that your children know what is expected of them in every situation. It is your responsibility to tell the child.

A friend of mine was recently struck by this when he noticed that his children did not respond well when they were introduced to adults. Both tended to look down and mutter responses, seemingly overcome with a suddenly developed shyness. My friend took his children aside and explained what he expected of them in future situations. He asked them to look into the eyes of the people they were being introduced to, speak clearly to them and respond to questions. His children responded immediately to his directions, making it clear that they simply had not known how to act. Once the expectations were outlined, they eagerly met them.

4. Communicate with your children.

Children need to understand, and they need to be understood. Dr. Comer advises that you think of your child as constantly moving from the highly dependent state of infancy to the final independent state of adulthood. The child is always developing and refining skills. At first the child's very survival depends upon your communication and guidance ("Don't touch that, it's hot!"), while later they need more subtle communication to guide them through the briarpatch of the teenage years ("I think that skirt is a little short for a formal dance").

At the same time, children are moving from a consciousness that is survival-oriented, totally self-absorbed and irresponsible into greater awareness of people and the surrounding world, developing compassion, empathy, responsibility and the desire to act independently. Dr. Comer advises us that this is as it should be. Nature equips them for survival; our job is to give them guidance and skills to work within society's rules and help them develop the strength of character that will enable them to deal with all that life hands them.

5. Teach them the difference between what they need and what they want, and show them how to work and save to attain their rewards.

It's important to teach children early on that they need to work for their rewards, not only to counter the dangerous desire for instant gratification but to instill in them the sense that they can improve the quality of their lives through their own actions, that they can count on themselves, which is a very important attribute for the entrepreneur, and for black entrepreneurs in particular.

When you take your children shopping, place limits on what they can have, help them understand the difference between what they want and what they need. Tell them how much you have to spend and let them help you work within those limits to buy the essentials. Giving them an allowance when they're around seven or eight years of age helps them understand the limits of money—how they can use the allowance wisely and how they pay the price when they spend unwisely.

6. Let them in on the planning.

To nurture independent thinking and confidence in your children, allow them to help plan and organize events, and encourage them to be flexible as those plans are carried out. If you're planning a family vacation or a business trip, allow them to participate and offer ideas and suggestions. This is a wonderful opportunity for children to gain confidence in their ability to plan and carry out activities and to develop a sense that they can make things happen in life. Owning and taking responsibility for pets is another example, as is creating and tending to a garden, both of which are hobbies that can be developed into entrepreneurial activities later.

7. Listen. Listen. Listen.

I know a couple who both work in their home in a neighborhood where most parents—both husband and wife—work outside the home. On school days, when the other children in the neighborhood come home to baby-sitters or an empty house, my friends, who are the only adults around, are often besieged with neighborhood children just wanting an adult to talk to, to relate what happened to them in school that day.

Listen to your children. Let them know that what they have to say is important, that they have good minds and good ideas and relevance in your world. Dr. Comer tells a story about the time he and his wife were stumped over how to buy the vacation home they wanted. Their 12-year-old daughter came up with a plan in which they would make the down payment and then rent the house to friends to help make the monthly payments. "It turned out to be one of the best investments we ever made," he recalls.

8. Introduce children to technology.

It is imperative for African American young people to be exposed to computers. The cost is dropping rapidly. Before a family invests in a big-screen television or stereo system, it might be wise to consider that the return on an investment in a home computer will be far greater. It isn't important that your child have a state-of-the-art multimedia system. It is important that he or she learn to feel comfortable with basic computer functions.

Many public libraries and schools offer on-line access free of charge, and used computers are increasingly available for very reasonable prices. Ideally, children should have access to a computer at home, where they can become familiar with it at their own pace and where family members can explore the on-line world together.

9. Teach your children the basics of investing in the stock market.

Building wealth is vital for African Americans, and for too long blacks have neglected the greatest tool for doing that—the stock market. It is never too early to start coaching young people on the complexities of buying and selling stocks. Programs for teaching children are springing up around the country, and black families cannot afford to be left out. This is one area that can pay dividends, whether you use real money or play money. Here are a few resources to help you educate your children about the stock market:

■ The AT&T Collegiate Investment Challenge is a nationwide educational stock-trading competition in which more than 20,000 students participate, each starting off with an imaginary $500,000.

The student who turns that into the highest stake at the end of the competition wins.

- The Securities Industries Association sponsors the Stock Market Game, a ten-week simulation game that uses actual stock market data. Young people from the fourth grade through college can participate.

- Stocks and Bonds: The Stock Market Game. Avalon Hill sells board games that mimic the stock markets. The object is to make money, of course.

- Pit. Parker Brothers makes this game, which simulates the commodities exchanges. You win when you corner the market.

10. Expose your children to successful African American entrepreneurs and businesspeople at an early age.

They must understand the full range of possibilities for their lives. Take your children to places where they can see African American professionals who own their own businesses. Give them the autobiographies of successful black people to read and discuss. Show them publications (such as *Black Enterprise*) that highlight African Americans competing and succeeding in the business climate.

Let them see that people just like them are in the game of business. If possible, take them inside the inner sanctums of a black business to get a sense of what it takes. They don't have to understand everything that goes on. The exposure to blacks thriving in a business environment is the most important thing. Too many African American children simply do not know that they have choices in the business world. It's up to parents and all black entrepreneurs and professionals to expose our young people to career options in the business community.

Many black organizations and black-owned companies have modified the Take Our Daughters to Work Day to include young black males. The New York Association of Black Journalists, for example, has conducted a concurrent program called Brothers Back to School, in cooperation with some of New York's public schools. On the same day that most of the girls are out at businesses in and around New York, black men from a variety of professions are recruited to speak about their career experiences to the boys back in the classrooms.

11. Share the responsibility for all black children.

In my old neighborhood in Brooklyn, you didn't have just one mother and one father, you had a parent behind every tree, on every porch stoop and on every bus. If you acted out of line, there was always an adult there to tell you or to tell on you. In too many of our communities, that has been lost. We need to regain that sense of shared responsibility for all of our children. I encourage you to be concerned not only about your own children succeeding in the business world, but about all children that come within your range of influence.

African Americans must do whatever we can whenever we can to help as many of our children as possible become contributing and valued members of society. Those of us who have experienced success in the business world in particular need to share our gifts by serving as mentors, role models and big brothers and sisters. Johnny and Michael have both mentored young people since their college days, and they and their young charges have benefited substantially. In addition, Michael just created a program in Washington, D.C., to encourage and reward high school graduates.

I'm proud that my sons feel responsible for helping others find their way. We all need to understand that it's not simply a moral duty, it's also part of a strategic plan to nurture success throughout the African American community by instilling a positive spirit in our young people so that they can see the greater possibilities for their lives. Even those businesspeople whose goods or services do not directly benefit the black community are important because their status and influence in the world affect the way other racial groups perceive and relate to all of us.

Business Is Kids' Stuff

Exposing young African Americans to the option of business ownership should be a priority for all black adults. Emmanuel Modu, director of the Center for Teen Entrepreneurs, is one of the leaders in the growing field of kidpreneurship, or youth entrepreneurial education.

In 1995 he left his job as a senior treasury analyst for Merrill Lynch to launch Gateway Publishers in Newark, New Jersey, which publishes business and personal finance books. Modu also conducts

Teen Business camps each summer at the campuses of the New Jersey Institute of Technology and Rutgers University in Newark. Campers learn about finance, marketing, stocks and bonds, job-seeking skills, business plans and more. In recent camps, 20 teens managed a portfolio of $2,000 in stocks and launched their own gift basket business.

For help in finding other kidpreneur programs, contact your local NAACP, Urban League or National Business League. Check with social service organizations such as the YMCA/YWCA and Boys and Girls Clubs. Colleges and universities often offer programs for children through their continuing education divisions. Many school districts, professional associations and some churches also have programs.

Keep in mind that good kidpreneur programs should offer . . .

- Instructors who have owned and operated a business or business owners from the local community who work as mentors with students
- A solid curriculum that explains business concepts in a way children can understand and relate to
- Funding that includes start-ups so that children can gain hands-on experience owning and operating a business
- An active, knowledgeable, committed program administrator and board of directors

Most programs combine an academic curriculum with hands-on experience, making it challenging and fun for children to learn business skills while at the same time nurturing the entrepreneurial spirit in African American children and showing them that owning a business is something they can do.

Kidpreneur programs do a great deal of good, but they are not a substitute for personal commitment to mentoring your children and those in your community.

I will never forget mentors of mine, such as Dr. Wilfred Bryson, head of the economics department at Morgan when I was there. He monitored my senior thesis. But, more important, he challenged me throughout college and afterward to do and be my best. Here are a few ways each of us can help in the mission to nurture future business leaders and entrepreneurs in the African American community.

- Arrange for tours of nearby black-owned businesses for African American students at local schools.
- Recruit at least one black college student for an internship at your company.
- Let a young person shadow you as you go through your workday.
- Sponsor student memberships for your professional association.
- Organize tours of colleges for children in your neighborhood.
- Join or organize a mentorship program for a school in a black neighborhood.

Exposure to job options can make the vital connection between reading, writing, interpersonal and computing skills and the incentive that kids can relate to: the profit motive.

Illiterate slaves once risked their lives so their children could learn to read and write; later, Freedom Schools were launched in the South to prepare a generation for full citizenship. In the same way, today's black professionals must teach young people how to earn, manage and generate wealth to help create a better future for all African Americans.

The more black people succeed in business and become economically independent, the greater the impact on the lives of all of us. The more undeniable our clout and status, the more difficult it becomes to scapegoat blacks politically, economically and socially. As we build wealth, we must use it to support the development of the young people who will lead us in the future. Our young people must become successful members of the economic mainstream, for the good of our community and our country as a whole. Remember, our children are the vessels of our hopes.

CHAPTER 15

Standing in Harm's Way

On a January morning in 1990, I arrived at my office and found a message atop my daily call list from fellow publisher John Johnson in Chicago. I dialed his number right away, and when he came on the line, Johnson was cordial as usual but quickly got down to business.

"You are going to be getting a call from Chrysler," he said matter-of-factly. "I'm going off their board, and I told them I had only one recommendation for my replacement."

He didn't wait for me to ask.

"I told them it had to be Graves," he said.

Immediately I flashed back to the early days, when Johnson had tested me time and again. I thought too of how our rivalry had grown into a friendship based on mutual respect and cooperation. Over the years, we had become strong allies bonded together by our belief in economic development as the key to true freedom for African Americans. We were much stronger in our mission as friends than as rivals.

For example, when lower-echelon employees at Hyatt Hotels had refused to purchase advertising in *Black Enterprise*, Johnson had gone with me to meet with the CEO of the hotel chain and helped facilitate the business we would do. By recommending me for the Chrysler board of directors, Johnson had proved once again that he lived as he preached. He has repeatedly shown that commitment, as I believe each of us must if all of us are to compete in the white-dominated business world.

I feel that a large part of my role as publisher of *Black Enterprise* is to be a catalyst for black economic development in this country. When I can act as an instrument to make it happen for legitimate and reasonable people, I do it. I try to be helpful and put people together, whether it's finding a candidate for a trustee position at Howard University or reaching out to the CEO of Motown Records to save a company that was at the forefront of black economic development in the early days.

When Johnson recommended me for the board of Chrysler, he was telling me that I had proved to him that I was willing to do as he had done: to stand in harm's way when necessary to clear a path for others of our race to compete and succeed in the game of business.

Getting on the board of directors of Chrysler was an incredible opportunity for me at that time. Although the nation's number three auto maker had experienced difficulties, it was still one of America's greatest and most recognized companies. And under CEO Lee Iacocca (who was succeeded, to Chrysler's benefit, by current CEO Robert Eaton and vice chairman Robert Lutz) it was on its way to staging one of the nation's greatest comebacks as well.

I realized that this was an opportunity to learn an entirely new field of business and to have an impact on an industry that employed millions of African Americans. I was thrilled and grateful, but I tried to sound professional and as matter-of-fact as Johnson when I thanked him and asked what had made him select me as his successor. I'll never forget his reply: "Because I know you won't ever forget you're black, and that you'll take care of me," he said. "You will take care of all of us."

Blackballed for Black Advocacy

Johnson was speaking of all African Americans who are fighting for their share of opportunities in the business world. He was talking about our responsibility to help each other survive and succeed in the white-dominated business world, no matter where we are.

Several years ago, I had an experience that is still quite common for African Americans everywhere, even those who have penetrated the highest levels of the white business world. I was turned down for membership in the Winged Foot Golf Club. It was one of the proudest moments of my life.

My sponsor for membership was an executive vice president of Chase Manhattan Bank, where I had done more than a little business over the years. He was more torn up over my rejection than I was, to tell you the truth. I felt I was turned down because I was perceived as being too vocal on issues affecting African Americans. I had publicly chastised a bank in Westchester for redlining, and at a United Way speaking engagement I had chastised local clubs for not having black members.

I believe I also rankled the membership committee at Wing Foot when I told the committee members that I would try to get as many of my friends inside the club's gates as possible. Of course, that's exactly what all the white members do, but when an African American said he would endeavor to do the same thing, their response was no, thank you very much.

Being black means that if you're fortunate enough to get a seat on the board of Chrysler, or of the Boy Scouts of America, for that matter, you make sure you do what you can whenever you can to represent the interests of the entire African American community. It means that if you're on the board of American Airlines, as I am, you act as a responsible advocate for minority hiring and promotions, and you work to see that the executives in the corporation understand the black consumer market.

Let me illustrate for you once again why leveraging our resources is vital to our survival, not just in business, but in this society. Microsoft Corporation launched Windows 95 with a $600 million marketing and advertising blitz aimed at consumer markets in 22 countries, but only at the white consumer markets. You and I apparently didn't count.

If you don't have a problem with that, you should. Even if you have never touched the keyboard of a home computer, which would be career and intellectual suicide in itself, you cannot afford to be marginalized as unworthy of the attentions of Silicon Valley or Madison Avenue. That would make you the modern version of Ralph Ellison's *Invisible Man*.

The Rewards and the Responsibility

Too often, corporate America benefits from the money spent by African American consumers without respecting or making any commitment to that market. If corporations get our money without working for it, why should they change their ways? They won't, unless you and I demand it.

They don't have to contract with minority-owned suppliers or dealers if we don't demand it. They don't have to hire us, train us or promote us if we don't demand it. They don't have to buy advertising in our publications, put us in their ads or hire us to design their advertising campaigns if none of us is willing to stand in harm's way to demand it.

Blacks in business have a primary responsibility to take care of their businesses. But they have an equal responsibility to make a contribution, whenever possible, to the economic development of the entire community. We have been disadvantaged as a race, so whenever we find ourselves in a position to open opportunities for each other, we must do it, whether that means making the right introductions for someone, serving on the boards of historically black colleges and universities or contributing to the United Negro College Fund.

If you're going to reap the rewards of success, you have to accept and live up to the responsibilities it brings. If you're black, that means that eventually, and perhaps frequently, you're going to find yourself in harm's way. You may have to stand up in a meeting with your bosses or fellow board members and give them hell for discriminatory hiring or promotional practices or for failing to respect and commit to the black consumer market. You may have to stand up for a fellow minority employee, risking your job in the process.

Tom Porter did it for me when he helped pave the way for my meeting with Learson at IBM. John Johnson did it for me when he told Chrysler that I was his only choice to succeed him on the board. You better believe I do it on the boards I sit on and within the organizations in which I have a voice. That is standing in harm's way, and it is the responsibility of all of us.

Reaching Up and Reaching Down

Blacks in business must look our for one another, no matter where we are in relation to one another. In other words, you don't have to be a CEO or corporate board member to make a significant difference. In 1996, *Black Enterprise* named as its Executive of the Year Roy Roberts, a Magnolia, Arkansas, barber's son who had risen to be general manager of the Pontiac-GMC Division of General Motors. My staff doesn't select people for that honor if they haven't shown a willingness throughout their careers to reach out and help others. Roberts, who has surely done that, offers us a reminder that it works both ways.

Even today, he tells movingly of how more than a decade earlier in his career, when he had just taken over as plant manager of General Motors's North Tarrytown, New York, assembly facility, he was confronted by a black employee. Now, Roberts has long prided himself on his relationships with employees. He had spent his first three weeks on this job meeting every one of the workers in the plant. He had even sent every one of them a personal Christmas card. So he was more than a little taken aback when this worker, Reggie Harris, came into his office and confronted him with what sounded like a challenge.

"You're a good guy, but you don't know crap about building a car, do you?" Harris asked his new boss.

Roberts, who had once worked on the assembly line of an aerospace parts manufacturer but began at GM after college as a management trainee, admitted to Harris that he didn't have intimate knowledge of the automotive assembly line, to say the least.

The line worker nodded and said, "We're going to teach you." Over the next several weeks, Harris and several other black workers in the plant did just that. After hours, they took Roberts through the process. "They taught me how to build a car," he recalls. "They wanted me to succeed."

Those assembly line workers may have worn blue collars, but they had more vision and a deeper understanding of what it's going to take for African Americans to secure economic independence in this country than many executives I know. It's going to take that kind of spirit of cooperation.

Roberts has never forgotten what those black factory workers did for him by reaching up to give him a hand and make him better at what he does. Today he sits on the board of directors of the United Negro College Fund and speaks around the country on leadership, diversity and individual responsibility. He talks the talk and walks the walk. "The only thing I can do for GM that none of my white counterparts do—none of them—is bring to the table the black experience, and that's critical," he insists. "I've seen many black executives lose touch with that." And, he adds, it has been their downfall.

Standing Tall

No matter where you are in your career or business, there is always something you can do and someone you can help in order to strengthen the entire black community. None of us can afford to say, "I've got mine. You get your own." Anyone with that attitude—and we all know people who have it—should be aware that the day will come when he or she will need help and there will be no one there.

The attitude that all African Americans in business must adopt if we're all going to compete for opportunities is that of mutual assistance. If you reach the upper rungs in your own business or in the corporate world, you must feel duty bound to reach out and point out. Why are there no black lawyers in the firms we deal with? Why does this airline have so few black pilots? Shouldn't some of these contracts go to black-owned subcontractors? Open doors, ask questions, push the point when it needs to be pushed. That is standing in harm's way. It is our only way if we are to be in this game.

The racists will say, Why should blacks get preferential treatment? Why should we allow you to become millionaires? Your response to that is that we don't want to be given anything. We only want the opportunity to run the race wearing the same track shoes they wear, rather than combat boots.

Affirmative action was intended to make opportunities available, not to guarantee success. Anyone who has administered it otherwise has corrupted the intent. Anyone who says it is something else is wrong. We don't need guarantees—the pages of *Black Enterprise* are proof of that. We only want to be free of the discrimination and racism that persist at all levels of business—and of which the Texaco tapes are proof.

It is abundantly clear that the bottom line today is this: The vast majority of white America doesn't much care about whether you and I succeed in business, or even whether we make it home tonight. Nor should they, necessarily. That leaves you and me with each other, and if I get mine and say the hell with you, that makes for two lost people.

What Can You Do?

We must ask ourselves continually what we can do to help those coming up behind or working alongside us. Here are examples of how anyone can contribute to the creation of greater opportunities for all African Americans in business.

1. Be an opportunity spotter.

If you hear of a job opening and you know of qualified people, alert them to the opportunity, and if you are in a position to help them, go to the company's personnel department and recommend those you think are qualified. If no blacks are interviewed for the job, it is your duty to find out why by going to the supervisor and inquiring. You don't have to be confrontational. Simply ask what you can do to make sure that blacks are given the same opportunities to succeed as others in the workplace.

2. Be a quiet champion for fair treatment.

No matter what your business or where you work, you can be vigilant not only about opportunities for African Americans, but in those instances where you can improve treatment of blacks. If you're working at a bank and it's discriminatory in making loans to blacks, let your superiors know that even if they are not concerned with fairness, they are missing a business opportunity by failing to recognize the importance of the black consumer market.

You can make your point with statistics rather than shouting or open confrontation. Show them the numbers. In the year 2000 you may not be able to sell "Do the right thing" to employers. That dog won't hunt. But if you show them that it makes business and financial sense to include African Americans, they will be more inclined to see the light.

3. Monitor charitable contributions by your business or corporation.

If you see that agencies and charities that benefit African Americans are not part of the giving strategy, push for inclusion by making the point that contributing to the betterment of black America is helping to build the nation's overall strength. Again, it isn't about being charitable to African Americans in need, it's about acting responsibly for the good of all Americans.

4. Try to help others understand the value of sharing the responsibility for fairness.

I have been serving on corporate boards for 25 years, and there are times when it is simply better for someone else to carry the fight against discrimination and racism. Sometimes you don't have the necessary clout. Sometimes you may not be in a position to raise the matter. At those times, rather than doing nothing, go to someone you trust within your organization and help him or her see how it would benefit them and the overall welfare to champion the cause.

Over the years, I have occasionally been surprised and delighted when other board members, including white men and women, have stepped forward and said, "Earl, let me run with this one for you." I think that is terrific. It says to me that they understand that it makes sense socially and economically to provide opportunities and share the wealth with all people.

On the flip side, through the years I have encountered far too many white women in business who have benefited from affirmative action but feel no duty to help other minorities gain access. Rather than be accused of generalizing, let me note here that, without exception, the white women I have served with on corporate boards have always proved to be the most concerned about discriminatory hiring and employment practices. I've seen many of these intelligent and dynamic women stand in harm's way.

5. Stand together.

At all times, and particularly in periods of downsizing, do your best to ensure that African Americans are not cut out in disproportionate numbers. Most of the major corporations, including AT&T, Xerox, IBM and the auto companies, were very careful in this regard in the early 1990s, but that doesn't mean there weren't others who tagged the last hired to be the first fired. Step forward and make the point that it is extremely difficult to find good people and also to maintain diversity.

6. Do not be afraid to take a stand.

Those I recognize as having stood up for fairness and inclusion have generally done very well in their careers. Selfishness doesn't last. Uncle Toms don't last. Fearful people don't last. It's rare for the individual who only cares about himself or herself to get very far in the modern business world where relationships are so important. Those who stand up for their beliefs and values are more respected and universally seen as leaders.

I receive a fresh offer to serve on a corporate board at least once a year, and I doubt that you will find anyone who would describe me as a shrinking violet in matters of race (you certainly won't after this book). I'm outspoken on discrimination, but I'm also a champion of shareholder value and business success. Driving shareholder value is the first responsibility of any director.

But let's be frank: African Americans are not invited to join the boards of white-owned companies because the world has run out of smart white people. We are expected to add a unique business perspective and a fresh dimension, just as women are. That is a strength to be leveraged, not a deficit to be hidden away.

Those Who Have Taken a Stand

I am not an assimilationist, I am an equal opportunist. I want smart black people who work hard to have the same opportunities as smart white people who work hard. In truth, because of the era in which I started my business, there were as many whites as blacks who reached out to help me, and they did it for the right reasons—because they believed that economic development and self-sufficiency in the black community were good for the entire country. To this day, several of the white businesspeople I know and work with frequently take the unpopular stand on behalf of African Americans. I respect and appreciate their courage.

It's true also that there have been times when blacks who could have helped me in business went south. There will always be those who, having reached a level where they can help a lot of people coming up, instead snatch the ladder up behind them. Clarence Thomas is probably the most glaring example of a black person who has forgotten who he is. I'm sad to say I can think of many others who have been afraid or simply unwilling to stand in harm's way.

I'm tempted to name those African Americans in business whose only interest is protecting the crumbs they have gathered for themselves. There are those who would love to see me point the finger and condemn other blacks, but it would do no good to cause them further embarrassment and grief.

It is a far better use of this space to salute those successful men and women who have laid it on the line time and time again because they saw the opportunity and understood their responsibilities. Some of the names, and their deeds, you'll know well. Others will mean little to you. But I want you to witness them here nonetheless and know that their actions have made some true difference on my behalf and yours.

Ron Brown Stood in Harm's Way

Although people in government, public service and civil rights organizations are expected to stand in harm's way as part of the job description, there are those who have been exceptional champions, among them the Rev. Jesse Jackson; former U.S. ambassador to the United Nations Andrew Young; California congresswoman Maxine Waters; the late Berkely Burrell of the National Business League; former U.S. solicitor general Jewel LaFontant; former governor of Virginia Douglas Wilder; former New York mayor David Dinkins; UNCF president and CEO Bill Gray; the late Floyd McKissick Sr., president and CEO of the Congress on Racial Equality (CORE); New York congressman Charles Rangel; the late Whitney Young, former executive director of the National Urban League; NAACP president Kweisi Mfume; National Urban League president Hugh Price; and former Atlanta mayor Maynard Jackson. And, of course, there was the late U.S. secretary of commerce Ron Brown.

One week after my friend of 20 years and his fellow travelers lost their lives in the crash of a U.S. military plane in the mountains of Croatia while on a trade mission, those closest to him gathered for a traditional African American homecoming at the Metropolitan Baptist Church in Washington, D.C.

At the service, the Rev. Jesse Jackson noted that sometimes on such occasions there is a tendency to glorify and exaggerate the honoree's accomplishments, to "hallucinate a life," as he put it.

Jackson added that there was no need to build upon Brown's accomplishments and character. His life needed no embellishment.

It was unfortunate, but not surprising, that his death and the reviews of his accomplishments were overshadowed in much of the media by the arrest of a man suspected of being the Unabomber. Over time, however, I'm certain that the world will become more aware of Brown's contributions than it ever was during his lifetime. He was underappreciated by many, but not by the blacks who knew him and what he stood for.

Brown was a champion for African Americans in the business world. He showed the majority community that he could play their game and be a leader in it, but he never forgot his home base. When we formed the Mobilization for Economic Opportunity Political Action Committee (MOPAC) to defend affirmative action and other government policies that had enabled us to push open the doors of opportunity a bit wider, he stood with us. When my black partners and I joined together to help create the Pepsi-Cola Company of South Africa, it was with Brown's encouragement and support.

He believed in black entrepreneurship, and he never missed an opportunity to encourage it and stand up for it. Many of us who knew him during his too brief lifetime benefited from his vision and leadership and courage, but we are few compared to those who will benefit in the future without realizing who their benefactor was or how many times Brown had to stand in harm's way so that their path would be clear.

As secretary of commerce, he made it a point to emphasize that America's diversity is its strength. Many white CEOs, unaccustomed to dealing with large numbers of minorities in professional settings, were bowled over by Brown's well-integrated team, which forced them to consider whether they had done enough to promote minorities within their own organizations. Through Brown's advocacy, many minority entrepreneurs were showcased and given opportunities to compete for contracts. He led trade missions to five continents that reaped more than $80 billion in foreign deals for U.S. businesses, and on every trip, black businesspeople and entrepreneurs were in attendance.

Brown's life benefited every African American in this nation, whether by direct deed or mere example. He rose to the highest levels of power in the country, but he always remained true to who he was and, by extension, to who and what we all are. His personal and professional impact transcended race, but his ego, his purpose and his greatest pleasure remained grounded in his family and the community from which he sprang. Even as his opponents and his peers scoffed, Brown held fast to the tenet that American business cannot thrive if its minority-owned businesses cannot thrive. He stood in harm's way.

Global Advocate for Black People

Perhaps the greatest example we have today of an African American in public service who stands in harm's way without any thought to his own personal interests is Randall Robinson, founder of TransAfrica, and the individual American who deserves the most credit for Nelson Mandela's rise from prisoner to president of South Africa.

Six years before Mandela was released in February 1990, an act of civil disobedience created the momentum to set him free. Robinson's TransAfrica, a lobbying group for Africa and the Caribbean, galvanized the worldwide anti-apartheid movement when he led a group of African Americans refusing to leave the South African embassy in Washington, D.C., until Mandela was freed and apartheid dismantled.

He and U.S. Civil Rights Commissioner Mary Frances Berry and former Washington, D.C., delegate Walter E. Fauntroy were then the first of more than 5,000 people to be arrested for peacefully protesting apartheid over the next two years. Two years after that protest, the U.S. Senate overrode President Reagan's veto to impose sanctions on South Africa, effectively throttling the racist regime and forcing it to let Mandela walk out of his cell and ultimately into the presidency of the nation that had imprisoned him.

Robinson barely paused to bask in that incredible triumph on the world stage before resuming his efforts on behalf of black people around the globe. His hunger strike brought worldwide attention to the plight of the people of Haiti. Whether there, in Ethiopia or in Kenya, like Martin Luther King Jr., Robinson understands that as long as injustice against blacks is tolerated anywhere in the world, we all are threatened, and whenever blacks are allowed to thrive in the world, we all benefit.

"Our potential as black people is to harness our power globally," he has said.

> Then our [African American] business communities will trade with those [African and Caribbean] communities, invest in those communities, and we will all be healthier for it. But beyond that, we should care about the black world because it is the right thing to do. If we love ourselves, we love Africa and the Caribbean. We are indissolubly joined.

I could not have said it better. If you love yourself, you will stand in harm's way for other African Americans. If you do not love and respect yourself, then you will probably not feel any need to work for the greater good. It is your decision, and it is on your conscience.

Fighting the Good Fight Front and Center

Very few African Americans have lived as courageously and fought as tirelessly for the rights of blacks and all human beings as my friend, the late Arthur Ashe. His long-term battles with his health cut short our revelry in his superior athletic skill. But we were then blessed with the time and opportunity to discover that he was a truly great man.

He never backed down from his responsibility for standing in harm's way. In fact, he greeted it with an unflagging energy and eloquence rarely seen. Through his courage and exemplary leadership, this man of dignity and honor helped and inspired many others along the way.

Finding the resolve to stand in harm's way is tough enough to do in our own backyards. To do it as Ashe did from within the constant and often unforgiving glare of a celebrity spotlight can be even tougher. Yet there are those who steadfastly rail against the economic injustices leveled at African Americans, frequently putting their valuable and vulnerable public personas at risk in the process. These champions, whom I greatly admire, include entertainers such as Bill Cosby, Ruby Dee and Ossie Davis, Danny Glover and Oprah Winfrey; filmmakers Spike Lee and Mario Van Peebles Sr.; and journalists Ed Bradley, Bryant Gumbel, Charlayne Hunter-Gault, Gil Noble and Carl Rowan.

Keepers of the Flame

We all have people in our lives who have laid it on the line for us in one way or another, earning our admiration and respect, reassuring us—even during the darkest moments—that we were not alone. Most of their names will never make the headlines or appear in lights. But their deeds have indelible impact nonetheless.

Darwin Davis is such a person. A senior vice president at Equitable Life Assurance Company, he's a superb businessman, but he's also a great human being and a quintessential example of an African American who has repeatedly reached out to help others gain access to opportunities. So far is Davis's reach that I was in Germany skiing once when a dark face on the mountain caught my eye. My face apparently caught his attention as well. My fellow black ski enthusiast and I stopped, introduced ourselves and exchanged pleasantries.

"Where are you from?" he asked me.

"New York," I replied. His eyes lit up.

"Oh, you must know Darwin Davis," and he proceeded to regale me with stories of how Davis had mentored and inspired him.

Whether in the workplace at Equitable, where he established a black executive's support program, or in the community, where he has contributed his time and money to everything from the Alvin Ailey dance troupe to the NAACP and the Urban League, Davis is an example for each of us to follow. Here are several others. While the list may seem long to you, I have surely missed some—they escaped either my attention or my memory—but those who stand in harm's way don't look for approval from me or for public commendation. They do what they do because they are who they are: men and women of courage, honor and conscience.

Lee Archer, retired vice president, Kraft General Foods Corporation

Clarence Avant, chairman, Polygram Records

Dr. Fred Black, retired executive, General Electric Corporation

Joe Black, retired executive, Greyhound Corporation

Alvin Boute, retired chairman and CEO, Independence Bank

William Brooks, vice president, General Motors Corporation

Matthew Brown, president, Big Apple Tire Company, a
Goodyear dealership

Kenneth Chenault, president and COO, American Express
Company

Sandy Cloud, president and CEO, The National Conference of
Christians and Jews

Johnnie Cochran, attorney

Joyce Coleman, vice president customer service, TWA

Dr. Walter Cooper, retired chemist, Eastman Kodak

Maurice Cox, vice president, Pepsi-Cola Company

Darwin Davis Sr., senior vice president, External Relations,
Equitable Life Assurance Company

Richard Dennis, retired director of human resources, AT&T
Corporation

Thomas Dortch, CEO, Luxury Cars of America; national president, 100 Black Men

Al Dunmore (deceased), Chrysler Corporation executive

George Edwards, retired president and COO, National Black
Network

H. Naylor Fitzhugh (deceased), Pepsi-Cola Company executive

Ann Fudge, president, Maxwell House Coffee

Paul Gibson, former vice president, American Airlines

Richard Greene, former president, current chairman of the
board, Carver Federal Savings & Loan

Darryl Grisham, chairman, Parker House (sausages)

Elliot Hall, vice president and director, Ford Motor Company

Ira Hall, director, telecommunications business development, IBM

Dorothy Height, president, National Council of Negro Women

Robert Holland, president and CEO, Work Place Integrators

Mannie Jackson, president, Harlem Globetrotters International

Yvonne Jackson, senior vice president, Worldwide Human
Resources, Burger King Corporation

John Jacob, former National Urban League president, now executive vice president, Anheuser-Busch

Bob Johnson, CEO, Black Entertainment Television

George Lewis, vice president and treasurer, Philip Morris

Christopher Mack, senior vice president, Citibank

Henry Parks (deceased), founder and former CEO of Parks Sausage Company

Richard D. Parsons, president, Time Warner

James Perkins, senior vice president, Federal Express

Alan Pinado Sr., former vice president, New York Life Insurance Company

James Plinton (deceased), former vice president, Eastern Airlines and Trans World Airlines

Colin Powell, retired chairman of the Joint Chiefs of Staff

A. Barry Rand, executive vice president, Xerox

Frank Roselle, former executive with Mattel Ameron

Brenda Scofield, director, Pfizer Inc.

Wayman Smith, vice president, Anheuser Busch Company

Percy Sutton, founder and chairman emeritus, Inner City Broadcasting Company

LeBaron Taylor, senior vice president, Corporate Affairs, Sony Music Entertainment, Inc.

James "Tank" Tyler (deceased), vice president, Connecticut General Life Insurance

Abe Venable, retired executive, General Motors Corporation

William Watson, retired executive, Great Atlantic and Pacific Tea Company

Charles Williams, retired executive, Schenley Company

Christopher Womack, senior vice president, Alabama Power Company

If, at the end of your business career, you haven't in some way applied whatever clout or connections or knowledge you have acquired to furthering the economic development of the entire black community, you haven't done what these men and women have done. And you haven't lived up to your responsibility.

CHAPTER 16

The Ten Greatest Challenges Facing Black America

On a weekday in May of 1995, a tall black man in a business suit stepped off the 6:42 A.M. commuter train from suburban Westchester County to New York's Grand Central terminal into the waiting arms of two plainclothes police officers. The policemen asked the man if he was carrying a gun, then searched him as he stood spread-eagled in front of the stream of morning commuters getting off his train. That man, as you may already know, was my eldest son, Butch, who was then senior vice president of marketing and advertising for *Black Enterprise*.

When Butch asked the police officers who they were looking for, they said they were looking for a black man with short hair. "Well, that narrows it down to about two million people in the city," said Butch, who was released after the highly embarrassing and infuriating two-minute search.

Later we learned that the officers were acting on an anonymous letter received a week earlier from a commuter who said a slender-built black man, about 5-feet–10-inches tall and with a mustache, regularly carried a concealed gun on that train. Butch is 6-feet-4 and weighs 225 pounds. He is clean-shaven. The only two things that Butch had in common with the suspect were his gender and his race.

The frisk-search of my eldest son in front of his fellow commuters enraged our entire family and brought a media firestorm on those involved. The *New York Times* carried a frontpage story and an editorial. Even the normally trite *People* magazine was moved to feature an eight-page story titled "Under Suspicion: Doctors, Lawyers, Athletes or Laborers—Black men in America have concluded from bitter experience that police see them all as potential criminals."

The sad truth is, there was no news in this story, not for African Americans who live with racism every day. *People* told the stories of a number of professional and middle-class black men, including Butch, who had been assaulted or even killed by cops for little reason other than the color of their skin and the prejudice against them. (It wasn't *People*'s cover story, by the way. That was devoted to the startling news that some white actor named Pitt had a new girlfriend.) There probably would have been no mention in *People* or any public outcry if what happened to Butch had happened to some poor black kid from Harlem. It became a minor cause célèbre only because Butch came from a well-known family of means and because the racism was so obvious.

Many friends and acquaintances contacted us to offer support and tell us how shocked and disturbed they were by what had happened. Although we were angered, we were not surprised. This was something Barbara and I had long before prepared ourselves and our sons to handle. For our family and for most African Americans the incident with Butch only served to underscore what we knew all too well.

Racism continues to poison the quality of life of African Americans of all classes, professions and educational levels. What white people don't realize is that it is poisoning their lives as well.

In a recent *Black Enterprise* reader survey, 82 percent of the respondents said that police brutality is a major problem for African Americans. Black America was not surprised at what happened to my son, just as it was not shocked at the Rodney King video or the black church burnings or the blatant racism and incredible lies of a white Los Angeles cop during the O.J. Simpson trial. What happened to my son, a bright and personable family man, only served to add a footnote: You can graduate from Yale University. You can graduate from Harvard Business School. But you can't graduate from your blackness.

Butch kept his cool during the incident. I'd like to think it was at least in part because over the years I tried to prepare my sons for such encounters. From the time that each of them was licensed to drive a car, I began cautioning them each time they left our house, "Remember, the policeman is not your friend." It's sad but true that this is advice given by many black fathers and mothers to their children, especially their sons.

It's a challenge we face as black parents. On the one hand, we want our children to take pride in their black identity and to obey and respect the law. On the other hand, we have to teach them that too many people will automatically equate their blackness with intellectual and moral inferiority at best and violent criminality at worst—even when presented with clear evidence to the contrary. It's not unlikely that many of those people will wear a uniform and carry a gun or a club.

When it was reported that I had told my sons to be wary of policemen, former New York mayor Ed Koch responded by saying "No wonder this happened. Earl told his kids that the cops are not their friends. Black people are telling their children to be on the lookout and to beware of authority." Koch missed the point. I have never told my sons to defy authority. They have achieved a great deal already in life because of their ability to work well within society. Because they are still alive, it's equally clear they have taken to heart my warnings that they can never assume that racism will not be a part of their lives.

I guess what frightens me most as I ponder where we are today is that my sons and their wives and my grandchildren will not be spared the fight that my generation and those before mine fought. It's such a damnable waste of energy and talent. I look at my beautiful grandchildren and I can't help but think of all the aggravation they will go through. It's not a matter of whether they will be called "nigger." It's only a matter of when—very soon, in most instances.

Now that I have provided you with the tools and information to help you succeed individually in the business world, I am going to lay out for you the challenges we face as a race of people. I would like you to keep these challenges in mind as you focus on your personal success. I want these challenges to motivate you toward your own goals and toward the betterment of the African American people. I want these challenges to move you to take an active role in

protecting the gains that have been made and ensuring that we continue to move forward, not only as individuals but as a race.

This may mean supporting a political action committee by leveraging your economic clout to back candidates and causes favorable to African Americans. It may mean putting your hard-earned money back into the black community where it can do far more good for you and for others. It may mean standing in harm's way in your own career or community when injustices and inequities threaten other blacks.

The Rev. Martin Luther King said, "Being a Negro in America is not a comfortable existence. It means being a part of the company of the bruised, the battered, the scarred. Being a Negro in America means trying to smile when you want to cry. It means trying to hold on to physical life and psychological death . . . it means having our legs cut off and then being condemned for being a cripple. . . . "

His words still apply. These are very challenging and disturbing times. The so-called race card seems to be back in play, whether as blacks are downsized in far greater proportion than whites or as racist cops deal from the bottom of the deck. The modern world roils with conflict among races, religions and ethnic groups over both real and perceived differences in access to goods, services and resources. Whether the conflict occurs in Somalia, South Africa or South Central Los Angeles, the tension mounts between those who have traditionally held economic power and those who have been locked out and are now attempting to wrestle their share.

For African Americans, the struggle goes on in spite of all we have gained. I fear that the economic gains and professional advances many of us have achieved in the past 25 years may come to be thought of as only the short-term achievements of a brief "golden age." I fear our grandchildren will be left to fight the same battles all over again unless we meet these challenges by leveraging our resources and together building economic resources that cannot be taken away, denied or marginalized. No one is going to do it for us.

The Ten Greatest Challenges Facing African Americans

1. Racism in America

As I wrote this book, more than 40 black churches were burned down in what some described as a "mysterious" series of crimes. It's

no mystery. Black and white, we know the source of it. Racial hatred always burns, whether on a crude cross in a black family's front yard, behind the door to the executive suite at Texaco or in the smoldering resentment of a fired white worker who feels that his job was cut to make way for some undeserving damned *nigger.*

Embers or flames, the fire is always there. It burns in the California Civil Rights Initiative aimed at destroying affirmative action policies that were created to counter discrimination. Its glow can be seen in the continuing judicial assault on the record of 41 black representatives in Congress as, for the second time in three years, the U.S. Supreme Court strikes down legislative districts created to eliminate American apartheid.

Racism continually fires the rhetoric of national politics. Blame the welfare queens, parade Willie Horton, cite reverse discrimination, study *The Bell Curve,* return to "traditional values" of bygone days when blacks knew their place and it wasn't the voting booth, the college classroom or the corporate office tower. The torch bearers misrepresent the impact and intent of affirmative action and minority business development. They rule vindictively from a high court of corrosive conservatism. They create malicious legislation to turn back the clock and set back a major segment of the population in its honest effort to contribute to the world by strengthening itself.

In the United States, perhaps no area of public policy debate symbolizes the struggle for racial equality and equal access to opportunity more than the heightened assault on affirmative action. Make no mistake, this is a battle for the survival of African Americans. Every facet of our lives—education, housing, economics, employment—will be affected by the outcome of this war. We cannot afford to be silent. We must vote. We must communicate with our elected officials at all levels. We must use our collective dollars to support those who endorse equal opportunity for all.

W.E.B. DuBois said the 20th century's struggle would be that of the color line. As we move toward the beginning of the 21st century, America's struggle has broadened to include gender and ethnic conflicts over jobs, education and business opportunities. If equal employment opportunity laws are enforced and efforts to achieve workforce diversity are genuine, affirmative action continues to be America's most potent weapon against the persistent and pervasive discrimination that has blocked our people from full realization of equal opportunity and our share of the American dream. Now there are very real threats to seize that weapon and a national debate that has been seriously clouded by misinformation and obfuscation.

Affirmative action, as I see it, is very simply the public and private sector process of encouraging qualified African Americans to take positions in fields or areas where they've been excluded or underrepresented. Let's face it, white people have been benefiting from their own form of affirmative action for generations. Whether it's farm subsidies handed to white farmers by their white politicians, oil depletion allowances won by white lobbyists for white oilmen, or top corporate jobs given to white executives by their white old boy networks, the truth is that white affirmative action has been around for a long, long time in this country.

When relatively new affirmative action programs for African Americans are threatened, our economic viability is threatened. We cannot operate our businesses if we are marginalized. Affirmative action has provided some modest assurance that we will not be shut out or ignored. It is true, certainly, that without affirmative action the magazine that I have published for more than a quarter-century would not exist, and neither would the thousands and thousands of African American success stories we have told in it.

African Americans have continued striving for our share of the wealth in this nation, but every generation, every fresh wave of talent and intellect and energy faces the same barriers of racism and prejudice. Blacks are going to school, working hard and pursuing the American dream, but to a large degree they are still not reaping benefits anywhere near those of whites. For too many blacks, the great dream of economic independence and social equality remains a myth.

Economist Margaret Simms cites figures that show that the median income of college-educated African Americans, $46,980, is only 86 percent that of college-educated white Americans, $54,680. Obviously, we are still not on an equal footing.

There is no denying that affirmative action combined with access to higher education has spurred achievement and moved us closer to a level playing field for pursuing opportunities. Between 1984 and 1994, the number of black airplane pilots and navigators increased by 650 percent, the number of dentists by 311 percent and the number of black civil engineers by 173 percent. Those numbers are still not anywhere near where they should be. But now the Great Equalizer is under heavy assault. It is not just the churches that hatred is burning.

Most of us thought that the answers had long been clear to the questions of whether colleges and universities should be allowed to set aside scholarships for minorities, whether cities should be allowed to give minority contractors a competitive edge in bidding for public projects, whether the government should encourage corporations to hire a specific percentage of workers of diverse racial and ethnic backgrounds. In the 1970s and 1980s, the federal government and the Supreme Court said yes, but today the questions are again apparently open for debate. Again, blacks are apparently fair game for the racist with a match, the cop with a hatred, the Congressman with an ultraconservative agenda.

As I noted previously, all of the white women I've served with on corporate boards have stood up for equal opportunity, but far too many white women in business—and they have benefited more from affirmative action than African Americans—are doing little to speak out against the attacks on it. Why? Because they realize that while it opened the doors for them, when those doors slam shut, it will be blacks who are locked out, not white women. This grates on me, particularly when I run up against white women executives who sometimes feel it is their duty to prove that they can be even more exclusionary and mean-spirited than their white male counterparts.

Recently I've seen news stories about white women being denied access to top corporate positions, but where are the stories about blacks and Hispanics? They aren't even on the screen. We fought in World War I as pilots on the Allied side in segregated units, but today there are more white women commercial pilots in the airline industry than black men. How can that be? How can we allow it?

Corporate America needs to understand that blacks do not buy the idea that diversity can be accomplished by simply bringing white women into the white male fold. Diversity is not bringing your neighbor's wife, or your own wife or daughter, into the business. White women in business need to understand that doors opened for them because African Americans fought and bled and pried those doors open, so when they attempt to slam the door on black men and women, or stand idly by, it is both immoral and unethical.

When I write of minorities, I am referring primarily to blacks and Hispanics and other racial minorities who have been denied access, not to white women. True, they have struggled, but they have not experienced *our* struggle. It's also true that we have included them in our fight for equality in hiring and promotions. If they can't bear to help us now, they should at least have the decency to stand out of the way and let us enter.

Whether it is raised in the board room or on a campus, the concept of affirmative action is as divisive today as it was three decades ago when President Lyndon Johnson signed Executive Order 11246 and made affirmative action a reality. The Republican-controlled 104th Congress and the conservative U.S. Supreme Court have turned up the long-simmering opposition.

Conservative radio talk show hosts and writers contend that affirmative action is impossible to implement without quotas. They say affirmative action quotas are synonymous with workplace diversity. Worst of all, they make the patently racist assumption that more productive and more qualified white males are being displaced by incompetent minorities and women, sneeringly described as "the protected class." In fact, the opposite is more often true. More qualified minorities and women are passed over in favor of less qualified members of the original "protected class" of white males. It is also true that blacks have to bring more to the table than their white counterparts simply to get a seat.

Affirmative action is a very small price for this nation to pay to begin making up for the heavy damage inflicted by two centuries of slavery, segregation, discrimination and racial prejudice and to counter what continues today. Contrary to the glassy-eyed rhetoric of conservative critics, black workers are still the last hired and first fired. Blacks make up the only group of employees who suffered a net employment loss during the recession that began in July 1990 and ended in March 1991. During that period, blacks lost a net 59,479 jobs and saw their share of positions in the workplace drop for the first time in nearly a decade. They experienced employment drops in 36 states and in six of the nine major industry groups, according to the results of a 1993 *Wall Street Journal* study of Equal Employment Opportunity Commission figures.

Affirmative action opponents say it has failed to eliminate poverty in the black community, but it was never meant to be the ultimate solution to poverty. Nor was it set up solely to address the problems of African Americans.

Across America, however, corporations are quietly abandoning minority employment goals, or "quotas," as some have chosen to describe them. When the smoke from the downsizing guns cleared, affirmative action had been replaced with the nebulous concept of "cultural diversity." Without the force of law behind it, apparently the goal of cultural diversity is to create a workplace where workers of diverse backgrounds feel appreciated and get along. It sounds wonderful, but in effect, cultural diversity policies dilute the goals of affirmative action. They have not translated into jobs for blacks or other minorities.

Cultural diversity programs too often are the talk without the walk. In fact, corporate diversity initiatives seem to be benefiting every ethnic minority group except African Americans. The *Wall Street Journal* study I mentioned earlier showed that every other group, including whites, gained jobs during the 1990–91 recession. Despite the claims of conservatives, there is no evidence that market competition—without affirmative action regulations—will eliminate discrimination. Without a government mandate to push for minority hiring and promotion, corporations mouth platitudes about diversifying the workplace without making any concentrated efforts to do so.

A recent study by New York's Queens College characterized the majority of large companies in the New York metropolitan area as passive about diversity issues. At the same time, the number of contract compliance reviews by the U.S. Department of Labor has declined steadily over the past five years. The watchdogs are doing less and less watching.

In the 25th anniversary edition of *Black Enterprise*, we looked at a group of 25 African Americans from the class of 1970 who were the first to benefit from some of these programs. "Blessed with ambition, determination and strong families who instilled in them the value of education, the 11 women and 14 men interviewed for this article became first-line beneficiaries for a new program dubbed affirmative action," we wrote. The article noted that the most striking aspect of this group was that although more than half were first-generation college graduates, they had as a group attained a relatively high and consistent level of success. All but four held graduate degrees; some had more than one. Their salaries ranged from roughly $45,000 to nearly $600,000 a year, and 14 of the 25 were earning more than $100,000 annually.

Carol Oliver, 46, of Chicago was one of those featured in the story. A top student, she was among the first large class of blacks to enroll at Northwestern University. After graduating with a degree in sociology, she went to work with Blue Cross/Blue Shield of Illinois as a benefits counselor. She obtained a Master's degree while on the job. She became one of the company's first black female managers and has mentored many others. In spite of her hard work and high academic qualifications, Oliver readily acknowledges that "I would not have been offered the chances I was without affirmative action." She said that the current threat is tragic because parity has not been achieved in the workplace.

"The glass ceiling for me is lower than it is for others," she says. "That's a fact validated and reiterated virtually every day in some specific way. No matter how much they're 'giving' us, they're giving themselves more. We must never forget that."

Affirmative action has not yet achieved what it was intended to achieve. That same sentiment was echoed in the interviews with others in the class of 1970. Lawyers, business executives, successful people by any standard, they all voiced concerns about whether the opportunities they had been able to seize might be drying up, not only for themselves, but for those behind them—their children and grandchildren. Their concern, their anger, their fear is very real.

To achieve, we must be able to dream and form a vision. If we are continually denied opportunity, our dreams dwindle and our vision fades. What can we do about the attack on affirmative action? We must demand that corporations be sensitized to how their hiring and restructuring strategies affect African Americans, not just the vague, ill-defined group of workers known as "minorities."

Finally, we must return to the principles of equal opportunity that were a business priority before affirmative action was tarred and feathered during the Reagan-Bush era. This must be a top priority of our political leadership in this country and of our corporate leaders as well. That means, among other things, aggressively enforcing antidiscrimination laws and providing retraining and placement services to African Americans displaced by downsizing.

I long for the day when we all enjoy real economic opportunity in America, a time when there is no need for affirmative action and other special efforts to create opportunities for those Americans who have never had them. Although a relatively small number of us have succeeded—often by making our own opportunities—we cannot claim victory or abandon the fight for full equality and true freedom. We must respond to these bald-faced attempts to co-opt the American dream of equal opportunity. We must rebuff those who would limit, then neutralize the potency of our voting power. We must fight off the attacks on our hard-won economic gains of the past quarter-century.

We will be heard and heeded. But we must attack the fires of racism with our best weapon—our collective strength.

2. Leveraging Our Might

Though I contributed to its funding, business kept me from attending the historic and compelling Million Man March in Washington, D.C. Two of my sons, Johnny and Michael, did go, and they were as moved by the experience of being there as I was watching it from afar. There were many social and political factors involved in the march, but to me the most important aspect was the symbolism of a million black men coming together in a show of solidarity and strength. That made me proud, and it gave me hope for our future.

The television and newspaper images of the march showed a million black men who were well disciplined, organized and happy as well as proud to be with each other. They marched and stood together, showing they cared about each other. Many of them brought their sons. Some brought their fathers too. Media images of all of those proud black men sent the message to others around the world: *You are not alone.*

Those same images validated much of what I have written here. The march emphasized one of the primary messages I want to convey: Our only hope as African Americans in this hostile world is to march, work and strive together. If we don't leverage our collective economic, political, spiritual and cultural power, we can never expect to control our own destiny in this country.

We have to leverage our strengths to force open the closed doors, whether these doors lead to union jobs, corporate positions, gated communities or private schools. We have to form a united front of all black men, women and children and march for true equality—economic equality. We have to force the world to understand our significance and our importance in every aspect of society, but particularly in the world of commerce. If they want to do business, they can't ignore us. They have to hire us. They have to sell to us. They have to contract with us.

We must make a renewed commitment to black consumer activism to demand the respect that our buying power deserves. Before we buy their products, we need to ask Microsoft, Intel, Sony, Polo by Ralph Lauren and Acura (just to name a few) to prove that they understand the true economic value of the African American market. How many black professionals and executives do they employ and at what levels of management? Do these companies offer vending opportunities to black-owned businesses?

We need to challenge them to respect us as consumers and as players in the business world. E-mail them. Write them. Telephone them and any other company that grabs for your dollars without acknowledging your importance. If we really made up our minds that we were going to boycott a hotel because they weren't hiring African Americans as managers or legal staff, desk clerks or maintenance chiefs, we could force their hands. If we pulled together to support each other publicly every time one of us ran up against racism or the iron ceiling, we could change things.

That was the strategy behind my decision to move the 1996 *Black Enterprise* Golf and Tennis Challenge out of California, where Governor Pete Wilson's vitriolic rantings against affirmative action have burned the ears and seared the souls of African Americans across the country. Moving an event in which more than 1,000 of the nation's top black business professionals spend more than $2 million locally should send a clear message to the state's business leaders and its governor that California's assault on affirmative action will not come without a price. If Wilson wants to play the race card, African Americans will call him on it, and raise the stakes.

We have not done this enough in recent years. Perhaps we have been too distracted by our individual struggles, but we need to restore communal spirit and bring discipline to our dealings with those who threaten our progress and our economic viability. Everywhere I turn these days, it seems, we have given up too much ground.

I have a vacation home in Sag Harbor, a beautiful community on Long Island with a significant population of blacks, both year-round and as summer residents. It bothers me that most of the faces you see working in the fronts of shops and restaurants on Sag Harbor's main street are white, while the people mopping the floors and stocking the shelves in the back appear to be black. When I ask the storekeepers why, they are affronted that I dare to bring the subject up.

In a poll of our readers, *Black Enterprise* found that 46.7 percent said they spent less than 10 percent of their earnings with black-owned businesses. Only 16.2 percent said they spent between 20 and 49 percent of their incomes with black-owned businesses. The question comes up time and time again: Why don't we support each other in our businesses and our purchases?

We cannot afford to take the attitude "I've got mine and I'm not rocking the boat." Too often we are short-sighted, expecting an immediate return, when we should act with the long-term benefits of the greater community in mind. What sense does it make to send your sons and daughters to the finest schools for the best degrees if they cannot graduate and enter the market at a level befitting their training and knowledge?

In the 1960s, when black ministers carried the cross of leadership for civil rights and the elimination of Jim Crow, we came together behind them. In the 1970s, when black community activists led demonstrations and marches for better jobs, housing and education for African Americans, we marched with them. In the 1980s, when black elected officials were swept into the U.S. Congress, state capitols and city halls across the nation, giving a generation of African Americans its first real taste of political power, we voted for them and supported them.

Now, in the 1990s and beyond, we must come together again to defend and protect the gains we have made and to make sure that we continue to move forward. At the heart of all of those battles was the fight for economic equality, the right to compete and have equal access to the opportunities that are this nation's greatest promise. African Americans have the same rights to these as other Americans, but we have not leveraged our power as the Jewish people, the Irish, the Asians and others have—by tapping into the collective strength of their business and financial power.

As the Rev. Martin Luther King Jr. said, "Injustice anywhere is a threat to justice everywhere." Blacks in business do not exist in a vacuum. While most of our time is spent—as it should be—in making certain that the bottom line is taken care of, we also need to be watchful of what government is doing, not just to our business opportunities but to the viability of African Americans in this nation. We need to let the politicians know we are watchful. We cannot afford to take anything for granted, not the Democrats, and certainly not the Republicans.

Now more than at any time, African Americans have the leadership and collective wealth that if properly leveraged can give us the clout to attack racism on all fronts. Racism is more insidious than ever, and we have to come together, as we always have, to fight it.

We should never give our support simply because we have traditionally given it. It has to be earned. We must make our voices heard and our weight felt in the political process. That is why the Mobilization for Economic Opportunity Political Action Committee was founded on May 10, 1995, by the CEOs of the nation's top African American–owned businesses to ensure that the interests of businesses that create wealth and provide jobs for the black community are represented in Washington, D.C. Its mission is threefold:

1. to support candidates who support us and oppose those who don't
2. to educate the American public with the truth about affirmative action and set-aside programs
3. to conduct a major lobbying effort on behalf of affirmative action, set-asides and other programs and policies that benefit African American business and the black community in general

The success of black-owned businesses demonstrates the continuing vitality of the American dream. Through the development and growth of such businesses, societal disparities in income and wealth are narrowed, hopes for individual achievement are realized, and national purpose is reaffirmed. It's time we got angry and leveraged our clout, as we did in Miami after city leaders there snubbed Nelson Mandela by refusing to have an official welcoming ceremony for him. African Americans boycotted that tourist town. We used our collective economic clout to demand a stake in Miami's tourism economy, and we got it in the form of a $37 million Sheraton Suites Hotel owned by four black Miami-area businessmen.

Our fight has always been about economics and the real freedom that economic equality brings. That fight is even more urgent now. As my friend Maceo Sloan, a member of the MOPAC steering committee, said recently, it's time we stopped expecting "the man" to do it for us. What are we going to do for ourselves? As a racial community, blacks constitute the ninth largest population in the world. We have an annual collective income of more than $400 billion, but we invest far too little of it in our own community. We can blame no one for that but ourselves. It's time to stop making excuses. We have a right to be heard and treated fairly in this country, but we don't stand together and demand it.

MOPAC is about putting our nickels and dimes and quarters and millions together so we can go to our politicians as other special interest groups have done for decades and say, "If you aren't thinking the way we think you should be thinking, then maybe we will give this money and our votes to your opponent in the next election."

In the past, we have expected others to do the lobbying for us, but we can't do that now. We must do it ourselves, for ourselves. It's time to step up. We will not stand idly by while policies and programs necessary for black business development, and therefore economic opportunity for all African Americans, are destroyed. On the contrary, we must—and will—do everything in our power to ensure that African Americans are full and equal partners in the American economy.

We have fought together for our civil rights and for our political empowerment. Now it is time we battled for economic equality and equal access to opportunity. Here and now. Black community leaders, activist ministers, politicians and others must continue their efforts to achieve true freedom and equality for African Americans. We have accomplished much already, but it is clear that there can be no lasting social, legal or political justice unless we leverage what we have attained to attain more.

3. Developing a New Generation of Leaders

Hardly a day goes by that I don't hear some black person somewhere ask: Where is the next Martin Luther King? Who is going to lead us into the next century and beyond? Where are our leaders of the future? Our polls show that African Americans have far less confidence in their leaders today than they did even five years ago. Why? Because so few of them are willing to come forward and be heard.

The challenges facing us in many instances are the challenges we have to face ourselves. Nobody's going to do it for us. It may be that we don't need another Martin Luther King. The nature of our struggle has changed. We fought the righteous battle against racism. We had some victories and we had some defeats. It seems clear to me that now we need to take the battle to the field of economics. There will be no further interest in our demand for moral justice until we have the economic clout to fight for it.

In the 25th anniversary edition of *Black Enterprise*, we saluted 25 individuals who blazed the trail in black business. They ranged from Howard Naylor Fitzhugh, the first black Harvard MBA, who founded Howard University's Small Business Center and later became a vice president of special markets for Pepsi-Cola, to our Entrepreneur of the Century, Arthur G. Gaston Sr., whose first business was selling rides on the swings in his grandparent's Alabama backyard. Up to his death at the age of 103, he was active in enterprises that included an insurance company, a savings and loan, and two radio stations.

Others included publisher John H. Johnson, investment banker Travers J. Bell Jr., banker Alvin J. Boutte, banker and entrepreneur Berkeley Burrell, Soft Sheen Products founder Edward G. Gardner, record producer Berry Gordy Jr., banker Richard T. Greene, Parks Sausage CEO Raymond V. Haysbert Sr., insurance executive Jesse Hill Jr., former Atlanta mayor Maynard H. Jackson, Johnson Products founder George E. Johnson, Black Entertainment Television founder Robert L. Johnson, North Carolina Mutual Life Insurance Company CEO William Kennedy III, the late financier Reginald F. Lewis, former Congressman Parren J. Mitchell, business dean Sybil C. Mobley, Parks Sausage founder Henry G. Parks Jr., insurance broker Ernesta Procope, builder Herman J. Russell and Oprah Winfrey.

In the same issue, we also listed 25 leaders under the age of 35. We did this because we need to nurture new A.G. Gastons, John Johnsons, Ron Browns and others to lead us into the next century.

Without great leadership, our institutions become moribund and our local, national and global presence diminishes. We always need to have fresh thinkers and daring leaders unafraid to stand in the line of fire for just causes and noble purposes. And most of all, we need to encourage young men and women of vision who can show all of us the way.

We need African American leaders to step forward, and we need to practice leadership on a daily basis as individuals. We need teachers, doctors, ministers, fund-raisers, business owners and workers everywhere to practice leadership by acting for the good of their fellow blacks whenever and wherever necessary. If you are in a position to hire or promote people, look out for your own. Help them get where they deserve to be. That's leadership. If you are a minister, preach self-preservation and self-determination rather than simply exhorting the faithful to count on personal salvation in the next life. If you are a teacher, reach out to your troubled black students, don't shirk from them in fear or disgust. That's leadership.

If you are on the board of directors of a company that isn't doing all it can to hire and promote African Americans, stand up for them. Tell the board what they need to do and show them how to do it. Inform them that it makes good business sense to hire the best and the brightest African Americans, not because it's the right thing to do from a social perspective, but because it's the wise thing to do from a business perspective. Dynamic blacks in business can bring fresh ideas and a greater vision to a company, just as our creativity has brought greater energy into film-making and our athleticism has pushed the envelope in sports worldwide. It makes good sense for companies to welcome African Americans into their ranks for what they add to the mix. Drive that point home. Use your perspective, your experience, your guidance to improve the lives of those blacks within your sphere of influence. If more of us lived our lives like that, no one would have to ask where our leaders of the future were going to come from. If more of us lived like that, the answer would be obvious.

4. Sustaining our Black Institutions

Just as some of our major weapons in the fight against racism are threatened by hostile conservatives, so are some of the institutions that have historically empowered African Americans to use those weapons. The NAACP, the Urban League, the Southern Christian Leadership Conference, Operation PUSH, the United Negro College Fund and TransAfrica—these are among our greatest resources as a people, and each of them faces challenges today that are as great as any in their history. If we are to leverage our power, we need these institutions. We need to be vigilant in protecting them from outside attacks and the hostile environment that exists.

Each and every organization that brings blacks together and taps into our collective strength is vital, but I doubt that anyone would disagree that the NAACP is the nation's most important civil rights organization. Nearly 40 years ago, when I was an economics major at Morgan State, I wrote my senior thesis on the importance of the NAACP. My passion for that thesis was so great that I ended up recruiting almost every student on Morgan's campus into the organization. Since then, I have supported the NAACP unfailingly in its trials and triumphs. The trials have been many in recent years as the NAACP has struggled with rapid change, internal strife and increasing assault from the conservative and arch-conservative political factions.

But a new era began when former Maryland Congressman Kweisi Mfume, with whom I have a long-term friendship, announced that he had accepted the position of president and CEO in December of 1995. I counseled him to accept the position at this crucial time in the existence of the NAACP. For too long, African Americans had been without a defense system as effective as the Anti-Defamation League is for the Jewish people.

The NAACP is vital as our first line of defense. But organizations are empty shells without the support of the people around whom they are built. The black professional class that thrived under the programs fought for by the NAACP in the past must now rally to support it by committing money, time and ideas. The same is true for other traditional black empowerment organizations. This is not the time to be selfish and focused only on individual goals. We need to help each other.

Those who may have become disenchanted in the past with the NAACP or other organizations representing their interests should take another look, and if those organizations have not changed to meet their needs, they should dig in and help change them rather than abandoning them. They may have lost strength and focus, but like the NAACP, they can be reinvigorated if each of us takes an active role so that all of us can continue the fight.

If we are to look anywhere for inspiration in that fight, it would have to be toward South Africa, where the presidential victory of the great Nelson Mandela changed a nation and inspired the world. Still, the world was not struck color-blind. No matter how high some may rise, none is allowed to forget that we are measured by color and race above all else.

African Americans in business are certainly not immune to this. They cannot divorce themselves from the fight. They must support those institutions committed to advancing the well-being, concerns and battles of black people everywhere. Through its efforts to achieve a more progressive U.S. foreign policy toward Africa, TransAfrica awakened blacks in America to their inherent responsibilities to their brothers and sisters in Africa and, hopefully, to each other.

5. Building Pride in Our History and Culture

Far too many young people today have no real understanding or sense of respect for our history as a race of people. Their perception of their race and of themselves is too often negative. We have not preserved the sanctity of our history as a people. We have not ensured that it is taught properly in our schools and in our churches. We have not taken measures to guarantee that our children know the vibrant and proud African and African American heritage that is theirs. How many of them can speak knowledgeably about Harriet Tubman, Frederick Douglass, Marcus Garvey, Fannie Lou Hammer, A. Phillip Randolph, Whitney Young, the Buffalo Soldiers, the Tuskegee Airmen, the 369th Regiment, Thurgood Marshall, Barbara Jordan, A.G. Gaston or Henry Parks?

How many of our young people fully understand the history of our enslavement, which has had such a lasting and profound impact on our development? When the Holocaust surfaces as a topic of conversation, it is always discussed reverently as the great injustice and horror that it was. When slavery or institutionalized racial injustices against African Americans are brought up, whites often roll their eyes or dismiss the subject as ancient history unworthy of discussion. Often blacks, too, seem embarrassed, as though slavery was something we brought upon ourselves, or volunteered for.

It is a common theme in black circles, this disparity between blacks and Jews. Our relationship is a complicated and often confounding one. We are united in our shared histories of oppression, rejection and racial hatred, yet there is a vast difference in how we have responded to adversity and prejudice. The Jewish people have leveraged their combined strength to the fullest. They teach respect for their history as an oppressed people so that their young people will always remember and fight to get what is rightfully theirs to seek. African Americans, on the other hand, have participated in our own marginalization by neglecting to teach our history. If we do not honor our own history and persuade others to do the same, as the Jews have done, we will never rise above it.

The people I named as important figures in our history should serve as inspirations and role models for our young people. If the lights of their examples are allowed to diminish, we will exist in darkness with nothing to guide and inspire us. Our young people will be left with no role models except the soulless pop icons selected for us by Madison Avenue. It is up to us to save and teach our history at the same time that we pursue a modern agenda.

6. Restoring Our Communities

Rear Admiral Anthony Watson, who graduated from the U.S. Naval Academy in 1970, grew up in Chicago's notorious Cabrini-Green public housing project. A few years ago he returned and was walking through his old neighborhood when he paused to talk with a young black boy about seven years old. The admiral asked the boy what he wanted to be when he grew up.

"Alive," the boy replied.

"I never forgot that," Watson says now. "A seven-year-old should not be preoccupied with staying alive."

Admiral Watson is right. We have lost our grip on civilized life. In far too many of our communities, the focus is on survival day to day, rather than striving for tomorrow. Whether it is in Gary, Newark, East St. Louis, Harlem, Liberty City or my old Brooklyn neighborhood of Bedford-Stuyvesant, the deterioration is shocking.

Where thriving black communities with theaters and churches, shops and restaurants, doctor's offices and dance halls once stood, now lie the skeletal remains of something that once was vital. We waited too long for help to arrive. Even when this country did declare a War on Poverty under President Johnson, the commitment was not really there. The real money goes to defense spending or the space program or some Congressman's pork barrel project.

The condition of our cities is one of the crucial issues facing the nation. For African Americans, most of whom live and work in urban America, the quality of life in our cities serves as a key barometer of our overall economic advancement. Thanks to the efforts of black mayors such as Maynard Jackson, Tom Bradley and the late Harold Washington, the connection between the health of our cities and our economic empowerment is stronger than ever.

Economic studies have shown repeatedly that the greatest opportunity for black economic development lies in those cities with black mayors. But even great black mayors are not miracle workers. They have to have the support of the federal government in tackling the complex problems they face. The leaders of this country have turned their backs on the cities and, in particular, on the African Americans in them.

How can this country progress when it ignores a part of the population that has contributed so much? I don't want to appear to justify crime and hooliganism or graffiti on buildings, but when people have nothing to lose, when they know they have no skills to acquire meaningful work, the alternatives don't really matter. Young people in the inner cities have not been prepared for productive lives, so they choose destructive lives.

To fix a community, you need first to build its economic health and its educational system and the desire of its people for a better life. There was a story on *60 Minutes* several years ago in which they asked a resident of Cabrini Green in Chicago what she liked about the original *Cosby Show*. The young woman, who was a single mother, said that she and her family loved to see black people portrayed as successful and well educated and living in a nice house, even if it was only fantasy because "no black people really live that way." The woman didn't think that the lifestyle portrayed on the *Cosby Show* was attainable for her or her children or any African American. She enjoyed it but felt it had no more relevance to her life than *The Jetsons*.

Far too many young black people feel that if they can't be

Michael Jordan, they might as well settle for a life on the street. The idolization of celebrity is particularly detrimental in our community. It works against reality. Young people who think the only way to make money is through drugs or, fame will sooner or later end up in jail or in an early grave. To these people, all too often, the idea of starting their own business is as foreign as a career in nuclear physics. They've become lost because they can't see a way out for themselves.

How do you save a community full of such people? You can't simply go in and flood the area with police patrols or shut down all the known prostitutes or drug dealers. Unless the infrastructure is there, the crime and drugs and violence will creep back just as weeds will come back up through the cracks of a driveway that has not been properly repaired. Simply picking up the garbage won't make the rats go away.

Nearly three decades after the *Kerner Commission Report* described two distinct Americas—one white and rich, one black and poor—after millions have been spent without much progress, the question remains: How can we restore our inner cities and our black communities?

Recently I toured a neighborhood inhabited largely by low-income whites. The difference between this neighborhood and similar ones inhabited by low-income blacks is that most of the white residents had jobs. They may have been low-paying, menial jobs, but they were jobs that gave structure to their lives.

Famed black sociologist William Julius Wilson, now at Harvard University, has noted in his widely hailed studies of the inner-city neighborhoods in Chicago that the key economic force behind the decline of those neighborhoods was the loss of jobs in the industrial sector. Black workers were disproportionately concentrated in those jobs in the mid-20th century because it was one of the few areas open to them, and with the decline of industry, they were the biggest losers. As Wilson points out, there is a big difference between the working poor and the unemployed poor.

To fix a city, you need to provide a foundation of jobs and a tax base of businesses and factories. I had some experience in this while working with Kennedy on a project to revive my old neighborhood in Brooklyn. We took a block-by-block approach and did a lot of work, but in the end, it was a failed effort because the infrastructure was not there. Today I believe that the real key is for government and private enterprise to work together with neighborhood churches to rebuild the total infrastructure.

Churches? Yes. The racists who have been torching our churches obviously understand the importance of them, and so should we all. The black church is the largest and most powerful organization we have. Black churches collectively deposit $10 billion a year in white-owned banks and savings institutions, which in most cases refuse to make loans to blacks. Black churches have always served as the center of black neighborhoods. Now we must harness their power to lead both spiritually and economically. They have the best interests of the entire area at heart, and they have the power to move people to action.

African Americans have a heritage of great cooperation and mutual assistance, but that tradition has crumbled under pressure from within and without our racial community. We must shoulder our share of the blame and all of the responsibility for restoring that tradition in our neighborhoods and communities. No one cares more about doing it than those who have to live with it.

We need to increase our service to our own communities. The better you do, the more you should give, but you don't have to give money alone, you can give your time and your talent and skill and energy to community groups, literacy programs, mentoring programs and other beneficial organizations that build resources within the black community. Saving the black urban community is vital, even for those who have succeeded in moving out of the reach of street gangs, black-on-black violence and drugs. You may have moved to safer ground, but you cannot escape the stigma those scourges place on all African Americans of every economic and social class.

It is true that blacks are not the primary importers of drugs into black communities. We are not the ones who harvest the marijuana or the cocaine. We are not the pilots who fly it in. Nor are we the manufacturers of guns. But far too many of us are the end users. That is the reality. Our communities pay the cost in lost lives and lost quality of life. Just as we bear the brunt of drugs, crime and violence, we must take our part of the responsibility for clearing them out of our streets and out of our lives.

Blacks in business must take a leadership role in joining civic groups devoted to rebuilding neighborhoods, in helping young people escape the dead end of crime and drugs, in placing political and economic pressure on government leaders and forcing them to direct their resources where they are most needed in the African American community.

7. Rebuilding the Family Structure

As I noted earlier, my father was a stern and difficult man, but his presence in the household and his demands on us gave structure to our family. He may have been somewhat remote and overly strict, but he set well-defined boundaries for his children. My father has been gone a long time. I still remember his strictness, but the moments of kindness and expressed caring stand out with even greater clarity.

His partner, my mother, filled in the voids back in my childhood with her loving ways and her advocacy. They were a team, for better or worse, and they were there for us. Barbara and I have worked hard at building a cohesive and loving family because we believe that for African Americans facing an often hostile world, it is particularly vital to have a solid family foundation. There probably is no such thing as a perfect family. Each one is dysfunctional in one way or another, because none of us is perfect. But the mutual support and shared goals of a mother and father are vital to the development of children into contributing members of society.

The most recent census figures show that 30 percent of all homes in the country with children are headed by a single parent. But the figure is 65 percent for African American homes. It is no coincidence that black children are nearly three times as likely to be poor as whites. The dissolution of the traditional family—mother, father and children under one roof—is a tragedy for all of America. For black folks, it has been a disaster.

The black family was ripped apart by slavery but healed itself by extending out into the community to the often unrelated uncles, aunts and cousins that are part of black tradition. Families healed after slavery faded, and the family structure sustained us for long periods when we had little else. We need to return to traditional family values—not the kind that right-wing Republicans espouse, but those built on love, mutual respect and community. Even non-traditional families in which one parent is missing from the household can have such values. In fact, many do. We need to aspire again to be the best role models for our own children. And we need to understand the importance of solid family relationships in the development of our children.

8. Refocusing on Education

Most African Americans know the mantra: education, education, education. But today, that can be a death chant. Our schools are dangerous places. Almost three million crimes occur on or near school property every year. About half of violent crime involving teens occurs in school buildings, on school property or on nearby streets. Every day, 135,000 guns are taken into schools. It is little wonder that juvenile homicides are expected to skyrocket from 2,555 in 1990 to 8,000 by the year 2000.

In a recent *Black Enterprise* poll, 70 percent of respondents said they believe public school teachers have failed to provide quality education and learning skills to black children. More than half believed public schools have gotten worse for black children over the previous five years. When you look at the figures I began with, it's not hard to understand why. Most of the teachers are simply trying to get out alive. Teaching has assumed a secondary role, if it ranks that high in their priorities.

It is vital, I believe, that black teachers in particular have a greater sense of responsibility for the black children in their classrooms. My mother always felt that she could talk to the black teachers in my school, that they understood the importance of eliminating all distractions and giving us the tools and knowledge that we needed to compete.

My generation was really the first to have access to higher education in any numbers. We had the promise of education drummed into our heads. The numbers today would seem to bear that out, according to Edward Irons, who is a retired member of the *Black Enterprise* Board of Economists. He cites a 1992 study by the U.S. Department of Education: Compared with the poorest 20 percent of the U.S. population, the wealthiest 20 percent has a two-to-one chance of finishing high school, while the middle-income group is one and a half times more likely to finish high school. That is, 80 percent of high-income families will finish high school, while only 40 percent of low-income families will finish.

It's clear that while education is a function of economics, white males—whether educated or not—still hold and wield economic power in this country. High school graduates get jobs at a higher rate and make more money than nongraduates. But black graduates still earn less than white graduates do. In fact, some white high school graduates make more money than some black college graduates. But while education has rewarded blacks less than it has whites, blacks must still pursue it in order to be in the game.

I heard the mantra of education, education, education from the first day I prepared to head out for school dressed in knickers and knee socks. There was no other way to get ahead but through school. And the emphasis my parents put on education didn't stop when they sent me out the door. My mother followed me in the door whenever she felt it was necessary. She demanded that I get the best teachers, the best equipment, the best extra classes, the best of everything she could squeeze out of the system to benefit her children. We need to be as vigilant and as demanding of our schools as my mother. We cannot afford to give up on our schools, because that means we are giving up on our children and our hope for the future.

I have spent a good part of my avocational time working at improving education. In addition to my continuing support of my alma mater, Morgan State University, and serving on the board of trustees for Howard University, I have also worked with the New America Schools Development Corporation, a private and public alliance to uplift our schools. We are not entirely responsible for the condition of our school systems. Local, state and federal government has played a role in crippling our schools, and now it must play a role in reviving them. But we need to take the initiative and show government how to do it and why they must do it, because our children are falling behind in the classrooms and dying in the streets.

Be concerned. Be involved. Be unafraid to challenge the system. And most important, be unafraid to challenge your children. Or your neighbor's children. Take them to the library. Get them involved in reading programs, science programs, mathematics clubs. It is particularly vital that you help them find access to computers. Their future success clearly depends on it.

The technological revolution is comparable to the industrial revolution, and it will not wait for the disadvantaged or disenfranchised to catch up. The Internet and the emergence of information and knowledge as the driving forces in the business community have changed the rules of economic survival. If blacks don't embrace technology, all past economic progress and any hope for future growth will be crippled severely.

Many African Americans have recognized this and become part of the technology revolution, some in a big way. But more need to be if we are to ensure our economic empowerment into the next century. We must get on-line now. Advanced technologies are present in practically every part of our lives today, from voice mail to electronic banking, and the influence on our lives will only increase as time passes.

Traditionally, the opportunities for blacks have been much more limited than for whites. Now, faced with downsizing and cutbacks in education and affirmative action, technology offers us—and our children—a chance to stay in the game.

African Americans, who make up 10 percent of the labor force, are only 3 percent of scientists and engineers in this country. There are several reasons for this, but essentially the problem is that black children are not encouraged to develop interests in these areas soon enough, and that lack of exposure early on is extremely difficult to make up for later.

Open the world of learning to your children so that they understand that there are far better opportunities for them in education than in the streets. Make sure your children understand that you expect them to go to school each day, get their homework done and respect their teachers. Make them understand the consequences of failing to stay in school. Make them understand that black children and adults have to strive to be the best. We cannot survive by coasting. Whites often can. White people may be able to wander off the path, do drugs, carouse, defy authority and still be allowed to succeed in their careers. Blacks are not given that much latitude.

9. Maintaining Our Physical and Spiritual Health

I am into my sixth decade on this earth. I know because my knees tell me every morning, and I make it a point to assure them that I understand we are in this together, but that we need to keep each other going. So, at least four times a week, I take my knees and the rest of my body through a vigorous workout. I don't always feel like it, but I do it. You have to make time to work on your health and fitness. I know of very few successful men and women who are not physically active and attentive to their health.

For you and me this is not a matter of vanity. African Americans continue to top the statistics in high blood pressure, heart disease, diabetes, numerous types of cancer including breast cancer and colon cancer, AIDS and other illnesses related to poor lifestyle choices. I know that these statistics are due in large part also to the fact that many African Americans have difficulty getting good health care, but it is true also that far too may of us are killing ourselves by smoking, drinking, abusing drugs and practicing unsafe sex. If we are not healthy, we cannot be productive and provide for our families. Poor health impairs our ability to meet any of the other challenges. If you don't take responsibility for your health, you cannot take responsibility for any other aspect of your life. At least once a year, go in for a full physical examination so that nothing sneaks up on you and takes you away from your loved ones.

I believe that our health problems are at least partially rooted in the decline of spirituality and moral responsibility in our community. Again, whites are no better in this regard, but they can live that way and survive and stay on top. We cannot. We cannot compete in business or in any other aspect of this society if we are not physically and spiritually fit. Our faith historically has carried us through many trials and tribulations. One of our greatest challenges today is to renew our faith in ourselves as individuals and as a people. Unity is the key, working together for the common good, never forgetting to reach back, look down, extend a hand and then look for another to grasp and pull up.

10. Building Black Wealth

This is where our ultimate survival lies as a people. Without money, we have no leverage. Without leverage, we have no power. Without power, we won't matter. We will never matter. Not as individuals, not as a group. No one will listen. No one will care. Nothing will improve.

Money makes people listen. When you have it, then you have something others want and need. When you don't, you become invisible. Your needs become irrelevant. Your success, or lack of it, is your problem. How can we build wealth when we have so many obstacles to opportunity? If you pay attention to the challenges we've talked about, it will be difficult to deny you opportunity. If you read and follow the advice in this book, you will make your own opportunities in spite of the nuisances, hatred and ignorance you encounter.

Build wealth first by looking within. Start a business. Invest in the black community with your time and money. Patronize other black-owned businesses. Hire black people to work for you. Form alliances and partnerships with other black businesspeople. Network with each other for your mutual benefit. Reduce your debt. Increase your savings. Put money into assets that have long-term value, such as homes and continuing education.

We have $400 billion in combined annual income. That is wealth, and it can be power, but it is just paper if we don't leverage it for the good of the entire African American community. We have to get the maximum out of that money, as consumers and as a race of people. Each and every purchase, investment, or donation should be directed at leveraging it for the betterment of black America. Like it or not, in this society it's always about money and the leverage of economic power for the greatest power—the freedom to live as you want to live.

Well, there it is. Can you succeed in business without being white? The answer is a resounding YES! I hope I have helped you feel confident that you can. Will opportunities be handed to you? Probably not. Will money be easy to find? Clearly not. Will the color of your skin present problems? Absolutely. Will you have to work twice as hard? Undoubtedly. Will you be expected to stand in harm's way so that others can find the path? Yes. Yes. Yes.

There is one point that I want to make before I send you off into the world. While all too often you will face discrimination and ignorance because of your race, you will undoubtedly find, as I have, that there are good people of all races who understand that if we are all to thrive, we must learn to get along. Those are the people who will make the journey worthwhile for you. Hold onto those friends, as I have.

I have repeatedly noted that you and I cannot afford to rely on anyone else to help us, but the fact is that at nearly every point in my life, I have found people—of all races—willing to step up and lend assistance when they believed that the cause was just and my goals were worthy. I have had, and continue to have, white partners in business and in public service positions, and I believe that in every instance we both learn something about the value of cooperation and we benefit from the experience.

Whether you're looking for a mortgage, applying for a job or trying to grow or start a business, you cannot succeed by having the same exclusionary racial attitudes that so often hinder us in our business endeavors.

Never turn away someone who can be of assistance to you purely because of race. Your mission is far too important for that.

I have not promised that your journey will be easy. In fact I guarantee that it will be challenging. You too will come home bruised and battered, but if nothing else, I have shown you in these pages that the rewards are equal to the challenges. If you apply the lessons and advice I have offered here, I believe that you too can play this game and that you will succeed, not only in business but in life.